FOCUSED PSYCHOTHERAPY

A Casebook of Brief, Intermittent Psychotherapy Throughout the Life Cycle

FOCUSED PSYCHOTHERAPY

A Casebook of Brief, Intermittent Psychotherapy Throughout the Life Cycle

Nick Cummings, Ph.D., Sc.D.
and
Mike Sayama, Ph.D.

BRUNNER/MAZEL, *Publishers* • New York

Library of Congress Cataloging-in-Publication Data

Cummings, Nicholas A.
   Focused psychotherapy : a casebook of brief, intermittent
psychotherapy throughout the life cycle / Nick Cummings and Mike
Sayama.
      p.   cm.
   Includes bibliographical references and index.
   ISBN 0-87630-789-6
   1. Strategic therapy.   2. Brief psychotherapy.   I. Sayama, Mike
K.   II. Title.
   [DNLM: 1. Psychotherapy, Brief.   2. Psychotherapy, Brief—case
studies.   WM420.5.P5 C971f 1995]
RC489.S76C85   1995
616.89′14—dc20
DNLM/DLC
for Library of Congress   95-19865
                                                               CIP

Published by
BRUNNER/MAZEL, INC.
19 Union Square West
New York, New York 10003

Manufactured in the United States of America

10   9   8   7   6   5   4   3   2   1

ABOUT THE AUTHORS

DR. NICK CUMMINGS is a former president of the American Psychological Association and the founder of the four campuses of the California School of Professional Psychology, the nation's first professional school in psychology. He is the founding CEO of American Biodyne, now MedCo Behavioral Care Systems. He launched the National Council of Schools of Professional Psychology as well as the American Managed Behavioral Care Association. He is the founder of the National Academies of Practice in Washington, D.C., representing the 100 most distinguished practitioners in each of dentistry, medicine, nursing, optometry, osteopathic medicine, podiatric medicine, psychology, and social work. He served for 12 years as NAP's president. He wrote and implemented the first comprehensive psychotherapy insurance benefit at the Kaiser Permanente HMO in the 1950s, and he has been the seminal investigator in medical cost offset research that demonstrates savings in medical/surgical costs through psychological interventions. He practiced psychotherapy in San Francisco for 40 years and is currently president of the Foundation for Behavioral Health. Dr. Cummings obtained his bachelor's degree from the University of California (Berkeley), his master's degree from the Claremont Graduate School, and his Ph.D. in clinical psychology from Adelphi University. He holds three honorary doctorates for his innovations and has received the highest honors the profession can bestow, including the APA's award for Distinguished Contributions to Applied Psychology. He is the author of over 300 scientific articles, book chapters, and books.

DR. MIKE SAYAMA graduated from Yale University summa cum laude and is a native of Hawaii who received his Ph.D. in Clinical Psychology from the University of Michigan. Since then he has been in private practice and a staff psychologist with the Biodyne Institute Medicaid Research Project and the Veteran's Administration. Currently he is the Area Director of Hawaii Biodyne, a part of MedCo Behavioral Care Corporation. He has trained and worked with Dr. Nick Cummings for over ten years. Dr. Sayama has trained for 20 years in Zen and the martial arts, and has been ordained as a Zen Priest by Tenshin Tanouye, Archbishop of Chozen-ji, International Zen Dojo.

CONTENTS

ACKNOWLEDGMENTS

The authors acknowledge with gratitude the contributions of the scores of Kaiser Permanente psychiatrists, psychologists, and social workers who for 25 years, directly and indirectly, were participants in the research that developed the model of brief, intermittent psychotherapy throughout the life cycle.

Following that quarter-century were the pioneering psychologists in Hawaii who implemented the nation's first managed mental health-care delivery system through the joint auspices of the State of Hawaii and the federal Health Care Financing Administration (HCFA).

The authors have borrowed liberally from the brilliance of Erik H. Erikson's developmental model, which extended our understanding of the life cycle not only beyond the critical years of early childhood, but throughout the adolescent, adult, and elderly years.

The reader will recognize the genius of Milton Erickson's strategic therapy throughout this volume.

Introduction

As psychotherapists we must hold sacred what we might call the patient's bill of rights: **The patient is entitled to relief from pain, anxiety, and depression in the shortest time possible and with the least intrusive intervention.** To achieve this mission we must hone our clinical skills so that we can focus the dynamic process we call psychotherapy.

Our contract with the patient should be: **I shall never abandon you as long as you need me, and I shall never ask you to do anything until you're ready. In return for this, you'll be joining me in a partnership to make me obsolete as soon as possible.**

Focused Psychotherapy attempts to operationalize this mission and contract in the current context of healthcare reform. The book suggests a practical model of "brief, intermittent psychotherapy throughout the life cycle." The concept of brief, intermittent psychotherapy was first presented formally in the Cummings and VandenBos article on "The General Practice of Psychology" in 1979, but it had its beginnings at the Kaiser Permanente HMO in the 1950s when Cummings became chief psychologist in Northern California. Subsequently it was formally described as "Brief, Intermittent Psychotherapy Throughout the Life Cycle" and described in two publications by that name (Cummings, 1990, 1991b).

This was long before the advent of managed care, when psychotherapy was not even a benefit covered by most insurance plans. Today, the inability of the economy to sustain increasing budget deficits in government entitlement programs, benefit limitations, and managed care requirements create a socioeconomic context in which Focused Psychotherapy offers an approach that is financially viable but not clinically superficial. The lives of our patients can be transformed

1

profoundly by brief intermittent psychotherapy at times when developmental challenges or the stressors of life overwhelm patients' defenses and impair their capacity to adapt and grow. The following case of Kevin, the "Cafeteria Addict," illustrates brief intermittent psychotherapy. It is a case that spans more than two decades. Cummings wrote:

> In 1967, I was confronted with a young man of 28 whom we shall call Kevin. He arrived in my waiting room with no appointment, as a "drop in." Kevin was in a state of severe drug withdrawal and looked very disheveled. When I first saw him, I wondered how schizophrenic he might be. I had no history or prior knowledge of him.
>
> In the first session, I learned that Kevin had graduated from the University of Wisconsin with a degree in elementary school teaching. On Wednesday of his first week of teaching on his first job, he had been unable to cope and had run out of the classroom. Without stopping at his parents' home, where he lived, he had hitchhiked to San Francisco from Indianapolis. He arrived with just what he had on his back and in his pockets. He was introduced to drugs and within three weeks had become what I would term a "cafeteria addict," that is, one who will ingest anything put before him or her and be "high" all the time, yet still claim not to be addicted to anything. Detoxification is a problem with such addicts. While the withdrawal syndrome is predictable in users of heroin, barbiturates, cocaine, alcohol, or anxiolytics, it is extremely risky in a cafeteria addict; and it is difficult to plan appropriate intervention because not even the patient is aware of what has been ingested within the last 48 hours.
>
> At the University of Wisconsin, Kevin appeared to have been a very isolated young man. He had never had a date. His social life consisted mainly of returning to his parents' house on weekends and going to skid row with a couple of bottles of cheap wine where he could get the alcoholics intoxicated and then perform fellatio on them. To all intents and purposes, Kevin at this time could have been considered either schizophrenic or certainly borderline ambulatory schizophrenic.
>
> It was apparent that Kevin did not want to overcome his addiction, but simply wanted to be made to feel better. He was

startled when I refused him a second appointment, stressing his total lack of motivation to go clean. He became desperate when I explained that he would have to commit to staying clear of drugs for six months in order for therapy to be effective.

After some pleading on Kevin's part, I promised him a second appointment if he could refrain from drug-taking for 72 hours, a goal I considered to be well within the realm of possibility and one that would demonstrate some serious intent on his part. In the 70th hour, Kevin called and requested an appointment. I denied it, suspecting that he might not be able to hold out for the last two hours. Kevin reacted angrily, accusing me of being "crazy," but did, in fact, keep his promise and called again when the agreed-upon time period had expired.

At that second appointment, I began to prepare him to enter a 20-session group addiction program. He required six individual sessions before he entered group.

While brief therapy ranges from one to 20 sessions, the sessions can be spaced at intermittent intervals. Kevin was seen three days after the first session and as the need arose thereafter, until he was ready to enter our drug therapy program. Like those of most other patients in our brief therapy program, Kevin's sessions were spaced according to his clinical needs.

After Kevin graduated from the group addiction program, he stayed free of drugs and went back to work. His first job was relief work at the post office, his second was driving a cab, and his third was as an eligibility intake worker in the county hospital.

In 1968, Kevin came back to see me. Over the intervening year, he had married, and his wife, Amy, was pregnant. Kevin told me that even though therapy had helped him a great deal, he felt that his self-image was too low to allow him to think of himself as a father to his forthcoming child. In therapy, Kevin had established that his self-esteem had risen enough so that he was able to get married and maintain a happy married relationship. After four sessions, he felt comfortable about the impending birth.

Kevin was not seen in 1969. By 1970, not only was he the proud father of a son now a little over two years old, but Amy was pregnant again. They were in the process of buying their first house and Kevin needed to borrow money from his father-in-law, whom he hated, as a down payment for the house. In three sessions, I helped Kevin to raise his self-esteem to the point where he bought the house. He also settled his antagonism toward his father-in-law and they became very good friends over the next two or three years.

In 1971, Kevin returned for one session concerning a marital problem. He was harboring much anger toward Amy, which was being expressed through premature ejaculation. The symptom cleared. A few months later in 1971, Kevin called to say that as a result of the one session regarding his premature ejaculation, he wanted to go into couples' therapy. I referred him to one of my colleagues at our center, who saw Kevin and Amy for six marital sessions. During this time, Kevin resolved his overidentification with his first son. He had been convinced that his first son was going to turn out to be a "creep" like himself.

In 1972, Kevin returned once more, this time very anxious about the fact that he was about to take a civil service examination to become a probation officer. He had been hired as a temporary probation officer for the county and had completed six months of probation work, but he would lose his job if he did not pass the examination. He clearly was suffering from test anxiety, and Kevin and I decided that he would enter biofeedback training. After 12 sessions of biofeedback training, Kevin passed the civil service examination in the top eight and became a permanent probation officer for the county. In 1973, Kevin was not seen at all, although his wife, Amy, was seen by another therapist for four sessions.

In 1974, Kevin and Amy bought their first duplex. Kevin returned to therapy because he felt very nervous about buying their first rental property and was not sure if he was "good enough" to be a landlord. It took five sessions to resolve this issue. Kevin and Amy did buy the duplex, the first of four that they now own.

In 1975, Kevin came to see me in a homosexual panic. He came to the office unannounced and waited, shaking, for about three-and-one-half hours until I was able to see him upon completion of my scheduled appointments. He told the following story. One of his apartments was rented to a tall, handsome man toward whom Kevin had become very sexually attracted. One day, Kevin was there to collect the rent, and some abortive fondling occurred under the pretext that Kevin was to have a sexual experience with this man and waive the rent. But Kevin was overcome by panic, and before he did anything else, he jumped into his car, drove to my office, and ensconced himself in the waiting room. In five sessions, Kevin resolved his homosexual panic.

I did not see Kevin again until 1977. When I asked what the problem was that brought him in, he replied that he had just come in for a checkup. We talked for a session and I told him to call when he felt the need. In 1978, Kevin returned to boast that after two sons he was proud to be the father of a baby girl.

In 1979, I saw Kevin's older son, who was having a school problem. I also saw the younger son twice and Kevin three times. I did not see Kevin at all in 1980. In 1981, he visited me three times in regard to his potential promotion to supervisor in the probation office. He had become, in the estimation of his employers, the number one probation officer in the county. By that point, he was being assigned all of the difficult and interesting cases. Kevin was worried about becoming a "paper pusher" who sat at a desk; he wanted to do real fieldwork. At the end of three sessions, Kevin felt able to make his decision, and decided to become a supervisor.

In 1983, Kevin had two sessions. He had been offered a top federal Department of Justice job and did not know if he wanted to accept it. Again, after some discussion, he took responsibility for making his own decision and appears to be thoroughly enjoying the assignment that he eventually accepted.

In both 1987 and 1988, Kevin came in for single sessions. Both of his sons have since graduated from high school and college, and Kevin himself is enjoying retirement and being a grandfather. He was last seen in 1992 as he was contemplating retirement.

Kevin and his family were seen over a period of some 25 years, during which there were individual sessions with Kevin, his wife, and his two sons. There were a number of forms of intervention—drug therapy, couples' therapy, biofeedback, and emergency sessions. Over this period, a total of 93 sessions occurred for all family members. If Kevin had been seen in continuous long-term therapy for five years, would the outcome have been better? It certainly would have involved more than 93 sessions. But would it have produced the contented and happy marital, occupational, and life adjustment that Kevin made with the help of this brief, intermittent psychotherapy throughout the life cycle? Doubtlessly, I shall see Kevin again, as I shall Amy. If the family is like other families I have worked with over the past 25 or 30 years, the chances are that one day I will see not only Kevin's children, but perhaps even his grandchildren.

As "Kevin" illustrates, Focused Psychotherapy advocates a model of practice in which the psychotherapist is the psychological family practitioner. Just as in the general practice of medicine, treatment episodes are terminated, but the therapeutic relationship is maintained with the expectation that at times of great stress or developmental transitions, patients may again need treatment.

In this model of brief, intermittent psychotherapy, psychological change is considered inevitable and growth as ongoing and necessary throughout the life cycle. The goal of Focused Psychotherapy is to release the patient from situations that thwart the natural process of growth. Ideally, psychotherapy is brief and intermittent throughout the life cycle at times when old defenses no longer suffice and the patient is most receptive to change.

"Brief, Intermittent Psychotherapy Throughout the Life Cycle" and "Onion and Garlic Psychodynamics" are two of the major divisions in this book. The first presents an approach to psychotherapy; in the second, the application of this approach to various diagnostic categories is illustrated with cases. Because of its importance, a third major division discusses the treatment of suicidal patients.

In this approach to psychotherapy, anxiety is considered the fundamental psychological problem. When our defenses have been breached, we experience anxiety. We feel threatened and regress to prototypical ways of responding to the stress. These ways are strategies that were once "successful" responses to trauma early in life and, therefore, are imprinted deeply in us. As responses to the current life problem or developmental task, however, these strategies are maladaptive. Their ineffectiveness increases the anxiety, which, ironically, increases the regression and the resistance to change. In the first part of the book the metapsychological assumptions of this approach, techniques to utilize resistance in the service of healing and growth, and a way of structuring the treatment episode are described.

The second half of the book, "Onion and Garlic Psychodynamics," presents a diagnostic schema that differentiates between patients who suffer (Onion) and those who cause others to suffer (Garlic), as well as between patients who can be helped through insight (Analyzable) and patients who cannot (Nonanalyzable). Fourteen diagnostic categories are charted along these two dimensions. While they are for the most part consistent with the categories of DSM-IV, there are differences because disorders, in this volume, are grouped according to psychodynamics and treatment implications rather than descriptively according to symptomatology. We estimate that these 14 categories account for most of the cases seen in general practice. The psychodynamics and therapeutic strategy for each diagnostic category is articulated and illustrated with cases.

As will be seen, in order to fulfill the "patient's bill of rights," the therapist must hit the ground running, guard against therapeutic drift, and employ creative interventions that have evolved from honing one's skills. It is imperative that the patient be made a partner in his or her own treatment; above all else, it is the homework assigned that convinces the patient of the true nature of this patient-therapist joint endeavor.

Masterful psychotherapy is part science and part art. There is no substitute for the wisdom gained through years of practice and life experiences or for the intuition that allows the therapist to enter into unconscious realities hidden from the patient himself or herself. We harbor no delusions of revealing "the model" of psychotherapy. We hope simply that *Focused Psychotherapy* will be a whetstone against which psychotherapists will sharpen their own diagnostic categories and interventions.

Part I

BRIEF, INTERMITTENT PSYCHOTHERAPY THROUGHOUT THE LIFE CYCLE

1
The Developmental View

Growth is the striving of all living organisms, and psychological growth is unique to human beings. Who we are and what we can become are not limited physically. After youth, our bodies begin to decline, but psychologically we are just beginning our maturity.

Psychological growth requires achieving a deeper and broader identity through overcoming developmental crises throughout life. These crises arise out of developmental tasks such as entering school, the advent of adulthood, marriage, parenthood, divorce, midlife changes, adapting to old age, and facing death. A more mature identity is both the result and the means of fulfilling these developmental tasks.

We choose according to a natural drive to grow, to experience deeper and higher pleasure, but when we experience anxiety that we cannot face, our choice is more a reaction, a regression to earlier, more primitive defenses. This reaction is the repetition compulsion, which keeps patients reenacting behavior that was once successful but now perpetuates the vicious circle of their suffering. We react when the stress of life is truly unmanageable or when the present, because of its close association to the past, pokes at our unhealed trauma.

Growth, Anxiety, and the Repetition Compulsion

We encounter all manner of problems in addressing life: problems with our health, our finances, our jobs, our relationships. But from a psychological perspective, the fundamental problem is anxiety. Developmental crises entail changes in many spheres of life, and if the person cannot face and overcome the anxiety inherent in the magnitude of these changes, he or she will not be able to grow. Instead there will be a repetition of the original response to the first trauma, that is, to the first experience of life-threatening anxiety in childhood.

If an individual has not developed adaptive ways of coping because of recurring childhood trauma, he or she will experience anxiety even in the course of facing the stressors of daily life. Anxiety leads to regression and the repetition of a neurotic pattern of feeling, thought, and behavior over and over.

Simple conditioning theory would suggest that behavior that is not reinforced is naturally extinguished; but patients persist in repeating behavior without reward or, at times, even despite punishment. They persist because at the core of the behavior is their first successful response to trauma, and when more adaptive ways of coping are overwhelmed by anxiety, they reflexively repeat the early response.

B. F. Skinner determined that behavior learned at critical developmental windows was difficult to extinguish. Extrapolating Skinner to the clinical phenomenon of the repetition compulsion, we suggest that the first successful response to trauma becomes the modus operandi for life. The learning curve is instantaneous and the extinction curve is zero. The following examples illustrate.

A baby can learn panic attacks as a modus operandi in the following way. On her way home a mother remembers that she needs a quart of milk and a loaf of bread. Baby is asleep in a bassinet in the back seat of the car. That baby is in a very critical time of life. Mother pulls up to the convenience store and thinks, "Well, the baby's asleep. I don't want to awaken the baby. I'll only be a minute." To be safe she locks the car and goes into the store. It takes longer than she anticipated. Meanwhile the baby wakes up and starts to cry. The baby feels abandoned. Well-meaning passersby can't get in the car to comfort the baby, so they rap on the window, make gestures, and say "Kitchy, coo. Baby, everything's all right."

The baby sees these strange faces and goes into a severe panic attack, at which time the mother shows up and takes the baby in her arms. The baby has learned: Anytime you're abandoned, have a panic attack! This will bring back mother. Despite its never working again, throughout that person's life, he or she is absolutely wedded to that response because it happened at that critical time.

Mother gets sick and goes to the hospital during a critical age of the infant. She's away several days. The infant gets increasingly depressed: refuses to eat, sleeps all day, cries all night, and refuses comfort. The baby becomes severely clinically depressed. At the height of the depression, mother comes home from the hospital. The infant learns that the solution is, "Have a depression!" Thereafter, that patient, during every trauma, whether it's divorce, whether it's childbirth, or whether it's loss of a job, will react with depression, even though it's never rewarded again.

Eradicating that first successful response to trauma that happened at the critical age of the infant is impossible. If this is the goal, therapy will be interminable. The more realistic goal is to enlarge the patient's repertoire of responses to frustration and anxiety so that he or she does not reflexively fall back on the response that was successful in infancy.

While the first successful response to trauma is imprinted on everyone, not all people need psychotherapy because children growing up in a normal, healthy environment will develop many other adaptive alternatives in the course of living. The child brought up in a family that continues to induce trauma does not have the opportunity to develop other responses. Consider the child whose mother went to the hospital. If, a year later, mother and father divorce and, a year after that, the mother remarries and the stepfather sexually abuses the child a year later, the child never has an opportunity to develop any alternatives. Depression then becomes the modus operandi for life. So trauma must occur at a critical age and the subsequent environment and developmental history must be such that acquiring a greater repertoire of responses was precluded by behavior that solidified maladaptive patterns.

There is another dynamic that drives the repetition compulsion. Not only anxiety but the striving for growth compels us to repeat scenarios or scripts that are symbolic equivalents of early trauma upon which we are fixated. This repetition is an attempt to achieve mastery. To the extent that our energies are fixated on early trauma, they are not available for growth. Therefore, we are compelled to repeat the experience of the original traumatic experience in order to free our energies to grow.

Life presents innumerable possibilities to us. It is in this realm of possibility that we live and through our choices influence the situations that become reality for us. Each choice can either create new possibilities and lead to growth or impoverish the richness of life and lead to regression.

This realm of possibility functions similarly to the blank screen of psychoanalysis, upon which the patient projects patterns from the past that require resolution. Our passage through life may be compared to that of a ball flowing down a stream. To the extent that we are rounded and free of fixations, the movement of life together with our adaptive capacity allows us to free ourselves when we become stuck on problems. If, however, the present too closely resembles past traumatic situations the patient has not resolved, that patient will repeat an inadequate, fixated response. Psychotherapy may then be needed by the patient to acquire an adaptive response and free himself or herself to face the flow of the possibilities of life anew.

The interplay between stress, regression, and growth may be illustrated as follows:

Studies (as summarized by Kissin, Platz, & Su, 1970; Miller & Hester, 1987) reveal that a woman whose father was alcoholic has greater than 20 times the chance of marrying an alcoholic. Odds such as this cannot be explained by chance alone, as examination of her past and present behavior reveals. As a small child, she was frequently both observer and victim of her father's excessive drinking. As she became old enough to plead with her father to quit drinking, her father became genuinely touched and responded, "Because you love Daddy so much, I will stop drinking." Indeed, the father remained abstinent for a week or two, a very long time in the memory of a little girl. When he resumed drinking she recalled father's words and concluded that it was because she had not loved him enough. This initiated (1) the imprinting of a successful behavior (loving Daddy results in his not drinking) and (2) the guilt of having let father down by not loving him enough, along with the determination to master the situation through marriage(s). By so doing, this woman spends her life without developing additional responses to spousal alcoholism. Furthermore, stressful situations that have nothing to do with this cycle often cause a retreat into the pattern. For example, such a woman who is suffering extreme stress on the job may nag her husband into drinking so that she can retreat into the familiarity of the "if I love him enough, he will quit drinking" scenario. This pattern, as stressful as it may be, is familiar and thus less anxiety-provoking than the situation at work for which she has not even the slightest clue as to how it might be resolved.

For many women caught in this vortex, an extreme event or series of stressful events may spark a sudden growth, with a consequent breaking of the cycle. These may include the need to protect battered children from a drunken spouse, crass sexual infidelity, or the attention and affection of another person. Ignited here is the instantaneous growth response of exasperation: I've had enough! For other such women, however, psychotherapy is the vehicle through which growth occurs.

Obvious growth in the spouse of an alcoholic is mastery by acknowledging that "I am not the cause of the drinking," and that "My attempts to take responsibility actually result in the enabling of his drinking." From this will follow a reduction of anxiety, a forfeiture of neurotic guilt, and a subsequent discovery of alternative behaviors that are more successful. Fixation and regression, which have fueled the repetition compulsion, have given way to new vistas of growth.

Focusing Consciousness

In psychotherapy the therapist focuses his or her consciousness into the present moment in order to enter the patient's reality. The patient experiences a reality distorted by early emotional trauma, mistaken assumptions, and maladaptive behavioral circles. By entering this reality and utilizing their own knowledge of human personality and behavior, therapists can intervene in a variety of ways to help individuals free themselves from unnecessary suffering. The interventions may vary according to theoretical schools and the interaction of the personalities involved, yet still be effective. The most creative interventions, however, utilize the patient's resistance to change in the service of growth. They unlock the vicious circles of feeling, thought, and behavior that keep the person responding to present reality with immature strategies formed at earlier stages in life.

Psychotherapists can focus their consciousness upon the therapeutic encounter to the extent that they are free from unresolved trauma. In order to enter the patient's reality, the therapist must be able to let go of defenses. In this process, emotionally charged material will have the chance to surface. To the extent that the consciousness of the psychotherapist is occupied with defensive processes to escape the anxiety of experiencing repressed material, he or she will not be able to see the patient clearly. Conversely, if the therapist can be fully present with the patient, he or she can intuitively understand the salient dynamics of the patient's problem and formulate a treatment plan to fulfill the promise of relief in the shortest time possible and with the least intrusive intervention.

We suggest that the effectiveness of the psychotherapist is directly related to his or her maturity as a human being. This seems inescapable in the field of psychotherapy since the emotions and associations of the therapist are crucial to assessing and treating the patient.

2

Managed Care and Brief, Intermittent Psychotherapy Throughout the Life Cycle

Brief, intermittent psychotherapy throughout the life cycle now has over three decades of clinical experience and empirical research. It was developed long before the current cost-containment climate and is not a response to the need to bring down mental health-care expenditures. Yet, it is a natural response to managed care, and one that is in direct contrast to the new, popular utilization review and usual case management. It lacks the artificiality inherent in benefit designs that directly apply session limits, or indirectly discourage number of sessions by use of implied formulas.

Contrary to such designs, brief, intermittent psychotherapy throughout the life cycle is based on four simple premises: (1) Skilled brief psychotherapy is not only therapeutically effective, but also cost effective in that it brings rapid resolution to patient problems; (2) effective psychotherapy is focused, using different parameters and interventions for each specific psychological condition; (3) patients receive the amount of therapy needed, with most responding effectively to brief therapy, while some conditions will require long-term therapy or continuous therapy for life; (4) therapy is not terminated, but interrupted, and patients are encouraged to return if in future life stages or traumas another episode of therapy would be helpful. Each of these premises will be discussed in detail, but first it would be useful to explore the ramifications of managed care and why this therapeutic model is ideal in a managed care setting.

17

Why Managed Care: A Historical Perspective

Most psychotherapists view managed care as a recent phenomenon, mainly because the changes in healthcare delivery did not begin to impact on their practices until a few years ago. A more accurate beginning would be in the mid-1970s when the U.S. Congress and the Nixon Administration enacted and implemented the federal Health Maintenance Organization (HMO) legislation. Prior to that time, there were a number of HMOs, principally on the West Coast and in Minnesota. The giant Kaiser Permanente Health System in California had more enrollees than all the other HMOs combined and became the prototype for its successors: capitation (prospective reimbursement), physicians being owners of their system, and staff-model health-care delivery rather than network delivery.

Capitation is defined as the business practice in health care of paying the providers of services a negotiated rate for each individual enrollee. It differs from fee-for-service, defined as an after-the-fact reimbursement for services rendered, in that it is paid in advance for services that the providers have contracted to deliver. Also called "prospective reimbursement," the provider agrees to be contractually responsible for the care of the enrollees, also called members, of the insuring health plan. This negotiated rate, known in the industry simply as the "pmpm" (per member, per month), is critical. If set too low, the provider group will become insolvent; if set too high it ceases to be competitive.

The American Medical Association, which vigorously opposed capitated medicine while championing fee-for-service, lobbied the state legislatures and succeeded in having laws enacted that made the formation of HMOs difficult, if not impossible, in most states. The federal law rendered all of this crippling state legislation irrelevant inasmuch as federally chartered HMOs were made exempt from most state statutes. During the next decade, HMOs proliferated and prospered, invading new territory heretofore denied them.

The federal government continued to regard HMOs as far more cost effective than traditional fee-for-service health care, and augmented its enabling legislation with start-up grants and subsidies. Then, almost 10 years following the HMO legislation, the federal government stunned the entire health field by enacting at literally the eleventh hour before adjournment the legislation known as DRGs (Diagnosis Related Groups). Henceforth, hospitals would be reimbursed for Medicare and Medicaid patients on the basis of a schedule of days permitted for each of several hundred diagnoses. Gone were cost-plus-fifteen percent payments. If the hospital was able to limit or even reduce the number of hospital days, it made a profit. On the other hand, if it exceeded the allotted number of prescribed days, it lost money. The hospitals yelled "foul," but the DRGs were not capriciously determined. Years of HMO experience had demonstrated that fee-for-service hospitals were far less efficient, doubtlessly reflecting a financial incentive to prolong hospitalization. HMOs, with significantly less inpatient days per episode, revealed as good a morbidity rate as traditional hospitals, if not better.

By enacting the DRG legislation, the federal government not only ushered in the era of managed care, but inadvertently launched the full-scale industrialization of health care. After 200 years as a cottage industry, health care began a rapid industrialization, with the blessing of those who pay the bills: the employers. Decades of laws forbidding the corporate practice of medicine or the proprietary ownership of hospitals, clinics, and health systems were either ignored or repealed. At first, the AMA vigorously opposed this industrialization, only to suffer agonizing defeats. Today, only five percent of physicians do not derive a significant portion of their income from managed care.

The American Psychiatric Association (APA) at first actively opposed managed care, but then, seeing the inevitable, accommodated to the industrialized system, and has assured the preeminence of psychiatry within it. On the other hand, the American Psychological Association (APA) deluded itself into believing it could be a David confronting Goliath. Persisting in its strenuous opposition, the APA has rendered itself irrelevant and is being cut out of the decision-making process within the industry.

The Rodham Clinton healthcare proposal, which suffered humiliating defeat, had as its centerpiece managed care, which it called "managed competition." It was not that aspect of the proposal that was rejected by the American people, but the scepter of bigger government taking over health care. The American people have also let it be known that they want health-care reform, and the recent election almost guarantees that the industrialization of health care will continue to flourish and that the future solutions will be market-oriented.

The experience of the past 10 years has demonst care has slowed the inflationary spiral of health care cerns" of practitioners.

Practitioners tend to overlook the fact that psycho dom been without benefit restrictions. Most policie ment to 20 sessions, while a few liberal policies perm as 50 each year. As the demand for psychotherapy inc third-party payers adopted the 20-session limit. Years late design gave way to managed care (utilization review and ca ment), practitioners argued that this was unnecessary bec cases went only 20 sessions or less, overlooking the fact tha artificially created by insurers' benefit design. The fact is, restrictions, practitioners tend to see a patient as long as a pa willing to come in (Bloom, 1991) and without addressing the ph enon known as "therapeutic drift."

Another fact overlooked by practitioners is that by the mid-1 most insurors were dropping mental health benefits from their p cies. Rising medical and surgical costs had been tethered throu managed care, and the inflationary spiral in health care was bein driven by mental health and chemical dependency treatment (MH CD). Hospitals had already experienced 50 to 60 percent reductions in bed occupancies for medicine and surgery. Noting that no DRGs or other managed care existed in MH/CD, they rapidly converted their beds to these services and engaged in extensive television advertising aimed at promoting these services. Costs for MH/CD services increased several hundred percent, prompting many insurers to discontinue these benefits. Managed MH/CD entered the scene, growing rapidly because of success in reducing costs, especially those attributed to hospitalization. By demonstrating that MH/CD costs could be brought under control, managed care saved these benefits from extinction, a historical fact practitioners would prefer to forget in their antagonism toward any restrictions on practice.

The Birth of HMO Therapy

The development of HMO therapy, which was brief, intermittent psychotherapy throughout the life cycle, has been detailed elsewhere

(Cummings, 1991b; Cummings & VandenBos, 1981) and will only be summarized here. It led to the design and implementation of the nation's first large-scale comprehensive prepaid psychotherapy benefit in the late 1950s. Previous to that time, the consensus in the insurance industry was that psychotherapy should continue to be excluded as a benefit.

Early after its inception in the mid-1940s, the Kaiser Permanente HMO in Northern California discovered that 60 percent of physician visits were by patients who had no physical disease. The relationship between emotional stress and physical symptoms was not clearly understood at the time, and these patients were labelled "hypochondriacs." In time, the HMO physicians were persuaded to use a less pejorative term, and the designation "somatizer" was substituted to refer to persons who were displacing emotional problems into physical symptoms. Dr. Sidney Garfield, the founder of the Permanente Medical Group and the Kaiser Health Plan, called for a psychological (not psychiatric) system to address these emotional problems. Although a physician himself, Garfield felt strongly that the psychiatrist, who is first a physician, would only reinforce the patient's determined belief that the symptoms reflected physical disease. A series of studies at Kaiser Permanente had already shown that repeated visits to the physician with more and more laboratory tests intended to reassure the patient only reinforced the patient's erroneous belief. Finding the explanation in psychological conditioning and reinforcement research for why reassurance had the opposite effect, Garfield decided the somaticizer should be triaged into a psychological system.

Several years after this system had been established, Cummings and his colleagues launched a series of outcome experiments (Cummings & Follette, 1968; Cummings, Kahn, & Sparkman, 1965; Follette & Cummings, 1967). They hypothesized that if the patient's emotional distress had been addressed, the patient should reduce medical utilization, an indication that the somatic symptoms had disappeared. During the decade following the first of these publications, there were 28 replications of the original experiments in a variety of settings, all yielding positive results (Jones & Vischi, 1979). The reduction of medical utilization following psychological intervention is known as the "medical cost offset" phenomenon, which now comprises a large body of research, with studies numbering well over a hundred.

The Effect of Psychotherapy on Medical Utilization

In the first of a series of investigations into the relationship between psychological services and medical utilization in a prepaid health-care plan setting, Follette and Cummings (1967) compared the number and type of medical services sought before and after the intervention of psychotherapy for a large group of randomly selected patients. The outpatient and inpatient medical utilization by these patients for the year immediately before their initial interview in the Kaiser Permanente Department of Psychotherapy, as well as for the five years following that intervention, was studied for three groups of psychotherapy patients (one interview only, brief therapy with a mean of 6.2 interviews, and long-term therapy with a mean of 33.9 interviews) and a "control" group of matched patients who demonstrated similar criteria of distress but were not, in the six years under study, seen in psychotherapy.

The findings indicated that (1) persons in emotional distress were significantly higher users of both inpatient facilities (hospitalization) and outpatient medical facilities than the health plan average; (2) there were significant declines in medical utilization by those emotionally distressed individuals who received psychotherapy, compared to that of the "control" group of matched patients; (3) these declines remained constant during the five years following the termination of psychotherapy; (4) the most significant declines occurred in the second year after the initial interview, and those patients receiving one session only or brief psychotherapy (two to eight sessions) did not require additional psychotherapy to maintain the lower level of medical utilization for five years; and (5) patients seen two years or more in continuous psychotherapy demonstrated no overall decline in total outpatient utilization (inasmuch as psychotherapy visits tended to supplant medical visits). However, even for this group of long-term therapy patients, there was a significant decline in inpatient utilization (hospitalization), from an initial rate several times that of the health plan average to a level comparable to that of the general adult health plan population. Thus, even long-term therapy is cost-effective in reducing medical utilization if it is applied only to those patients who need and should receive long-term therapy.

In another study, Cummings and Follette sought to answer, in an eighth-year telephone follow-up, whether the results described previously were a therapeutic effect, were the consequences of extraneous factors, or were a deleterious effect (Cummings & Follette, 1976). It was hypothesized that, if better understanding of the problem had ocurred in the psychotherapeutic sessions, the patient would recall the actual problem rather than the presenting symptom and would have lost the presenting symptom and coped more effectively with the real problem. The results suggest that the reduction in medical utilization was the consequence of resolving the emotional distress that was being reflected in the symptoms and in the doctor's visits. The modal patient in this eighth-year follow-up may be described as follows: She or he denied ever having consulted a physician for the symptoms for which the referral was originally made. Rather, the actual problem discussed with the psychotherapist was recalled as the reason for the psychotherapy visit, and although the problem had been resolved, this resolution was attributed to the patient's own efforts and no credit was given the psychotherapist. These results confirm that the reduction in medical utilization reflected a diminution in the emotional distress that had been expressed in symptoms presented to the physician.

Length of Treatment

Although they demonstrated in this study that savings in medical services do offset the cost of providing psychotherapy, Cummings and Follette (1976) insisted that the services provided must also be therapeutic in that they reduce the patient's emotional distress. Both the cost savings and the therapeutic effectiveness demonstrated in the Kaiser Permanente studies were attributed by the authors to the therapists' expectations that emotional distress could be alleviated by brief, active psychotherapy. Such therapy, as Malan (1963, 1976) pointed out, involves the analysis of transference and resistance and the uncovering of unconscious conflicts, and has all the characteristics of long-term therapy, except length. Given this orientation, the Kaiser Permanente studies found over a five-year period that 84.6 percent of the patients seen in psychotherapy chose to come for 15 sessions or fewer (with a mean of 8.6). These studies did not regard these patients as "dropouts" from treatment. Rather, it was found on follow-up that they had achieved a satisfactory state of emotional well-being that had continued into the eighth year after the termination of therapy. Another 10.1 percent of the patients were in moderate-term therapy with a mean of 19.2 sessions, a figure that would probably be regarded as short-term in many traditional clinics. Finally, 5.3 percent of the patients were found to be "interminable," in that, once they had begun psychotherapy, they had continued, seemingly with no indication of termination.

The "Interminable" Patient

In another study, Cummings (1977) addressed the problem of the "interminable" patient, for whom treatment is neither cost-effective nor therapeutically effective. The concept that some persons are so emotionally crippled that they may have to be maintained for many years or for life was not satisfactory, for if five percent of all patients entering psychotherapy are "interminable," within a few years a program will be hampered by a monolithic caseload, a possibility that has become a fact in many public clinics where psychotherapy is offered at nominal or no cost.

It was originally hypothesized that these "interminable" patients required more intensive intervention, and the frequency of psychotherapy visits was doubled for one experimental group, tripled for another experimental group, and held constant for the control group. Surprisingly, the cost-therapeutic effectiveness ratios deteriorated in direct proportion to the increased intensity; that is, medical utilization increased and the patients manifested greater emotional distress. It was only by reversing the process and seeing these patients at spaced intervals of once every two or three months that the desired cost-therapeutic effect was obtained. These results are surprising in that they are contrary to traditionally held notions that more therapy is better; but they demonstrate the need for ongoing research, program evaluation, and innovation if psychotherapy is going to be made available to everyone as needed.

Cost Savings

The Kaiser Permanente findings regarding the offsetting of medical-cost savings by the provision of psychological services were quickly replicated by others (Goldberg, Krantz, & Locke, 1970; Rosen & Wiens, 1979). In fact, such findings have been replicated in over 20 widely varied healthcare delivery systems within a decade (Jones & Vischi, 1979). Even in the most methodologically rigorous review of the literature on the relationship between the provision of psychotherapy and medical utilization (Mumford, Schlesinger, & Glass, 1978) the "best estimate" of cost savings is seen to range between 9 percent and 24 percent, with the cost savings increasing as the interventions are tailored to the effective treatment of stress.

In summarizing the 20 years of Kaiser Permanente experience, Cummings and VandenBos (1981) concluded that not only is outcomes research useful in programmatic planning, but no comprehensive health plan can afford to be without an effective psychotherapy benefit. The Kaiser Health Plan went from regarding psychotherapy as an exclusion, to becoming the first large-scale health plan to include psychotherapy as an integral part of its benefit structure. In fact, the absence of a psychotherapy benefit leaves the patient little alternative but to translate stress into physical symptoms that will command the attention of a physician. Even the presence of a copayment for psychotherapy when none exists for medical care will incline the patient toward somaticizing.

Developing Focused Interventions by Use of Medical Cost Offset Research

Brief, intermittent psychotherapy throughout the life cycle has been subjected to an unprecedented 35 years of outcomes research. So that practitioners can appreciate how the medical cost offset phenomenon was employed in the development of focused interventions and continues to be used to refine the interventions, a case study of the development of one treatment protocol is given, that for Borderline Personality, which is included in the Appendix.

It is not atypical for practitioners to narrowly practice as they were trained, resisting change and evolution. This is more problematic in psychotherapy than in medical practice because psychotherapy has developed few specific treatments for specific conditions. If a practitioner was trained as a Freudian, the couch therapy is applied whether the problem is marital, occupational, or chemical dependency. Should the therapist be a behaviorist, densensitization and behavioral modification become the primary interventions, whatever the condition treated. It is logical to assume that certain conditions will more likely respond to certain types of interventions, while being resistant to others. Discovering these specifics would suggest that psychotherapy could be much more effective and efficient.

Cummings and his colleagues at Kaiser Permanente intuitively observed that certain conditions seemed to respond better to dynamically oriented therapy, others to behavior therapy, and still others to systems approaches. And within the school of therapy, some conditions were more effectively treated in individual therapy, others in group therapy, and still others in psychoeducational programs. They tentatively accepted the premise that all schools and modalities had truth, but none had all-encompassing truth. The optimal specific could well be an admixture of several approaches, and they set about to test this hypothesis through outcomes research utilizing medical offset as the criterion of efficacy. Since in society persons under stress somaticize their stress, a greater reduction of medical utilization in an aggregate group receiving one type of psychotherapy intervention over another aggregate group receiving a different intervention would be a measure of the effectiveness of the intervention.

The cost-therapeutic effectiveness ratio, also known as the efficiency-effectiveness ratio, was derived by dividing the average (mean) medical utilization for the entire group for the year prior to the intervention by the average (mean) medical utilization plus average (mean) psychotherapy visits for that same group in the year after the intervention:

$$r = \frac{\text{Mean (medical utilization year before)}}{\text{Mean (medical utilization year after)} + \text{Mean (psychotherapy sessions)}}$$

Differentially weighting by cost the various kinds of medical utilization, such as giving an outpatient visit a value of 1 and a day of hospitalization a value of 10, only complicated our computations and neither added precision nor altered outcome. But weighting individual therapy, group therapy, and psychoeducational programs did add precision. The formula adopted was based on psychotherapist time to accomplish a unit. Thus, individual therapy (1 therapist with 1 patient for 45 minutes) received a value of 1, while group therapy (1 therapist with 8 patients for 90 minutes) received a value of .25, and a psychoeducational group (1 therapist with 12 patients for 90 minutes) was given a value of .08. To clarify further, 10 sessions of individual therapy equals 10, the same number of group therapy sessions equals 2.5, and 10 sessions of psychoeducational programming yield less than 1. Emergency department visits were weighted 2, which means that 10 emergency department visits had a total value of 20.

To illustrate from actual research, a group of 83 borderline personality disorder patients were placed in individual psychotherapy, with the result that medical utilization declined slightly, but at an enormous expenditure of both individual sessions and emergency room visits:

$$r = \frac{163}{141 + 68} = .8$$

The ratio is low, indicating the interventions were neither therapeutically efficient (reduction in medical utilization) nor cost-efficient (number of mental health units). The staff over time created a focused set of interventions within individual therapy with some improvement in cost efficiency but little impact on therapeutic effectiveness with another group of 73 borderline personality patients:

$$r = \frac{167}{148 + 51} = .7$$

The overall effectiveness-efficiency ratio actually declined. With another population of 76 patients suffering from borderline personality disorder, a great deal of care and effort was expended in designing a 20-session group therapy, augmented with 10 sessions of individual therapy, and then with monthly follow-up sessions. Emergency department visits were virtually eliminated and the ratio rose dramatically:

$$r = \frac{166}{27 + 31} = 2.8$$

Learning a great deal from this group of patients, we sharpened the group therapy to 15 group therapy sessions, followed by 10 psychoeducational sessions, and with subsequent monthly follow-up individual sessions. This yielded a ratio and a program that were adopted as both effective and efficient:

$$r = \frac{171}{11 + 12} = 7.4$$

The research team continued to experiment with honing the program even further, but the work with borderline personality disorder, a category of resistant and highly acting-out patients, never achieved the ideal ratio of 9.0 or higher, which became the goal or standard. In this way, using medical offset, there were designed 68 focused, targeted interventions for 68 psychological/psychiatric conditions that became the methodology in what was termed brief, intermittent psychotherapy throughout the life cycle, an approach that concentrates on solving the problem in the "here and now" while also giving the patient a greater repertoire of responses to stress. These findings were the backbone of the clinical training and service delivery early at Kaiser Permanente and later at American Biodyne (Cummings, 1991a), as well as in the eight-year, longitudinal Hawaii Project with federal employees and Medicaid recipients (Pallak, Cummings, Dörken, & Henke, 1994).

Impact of Industrialization on Practice

All goods and services follow the laws of supply and demand: Increased demand over the available supply causes prices to escalate, whereas a glut of supply over demand results in prices falling. The glaring exception has been health care. An overproduction of practitioners should cause fees to drop; instead, the greater the number of healthcare practitioners, the higher have been the fees. This is because the practitioner controlled both the supply and the demand sides. It is the doctor who decides what is to be done, how and when it will be done, and in the case of psychotherapy, how long it will take. All this is rapidly changing, because those who pay the bills (principally the employers) are taking the economic supply/demand control away from the doctor. As intrusive and arbitrary as managed care can be, when the practitioners had the control there was no incentive within their ranks to reduce costs by increasing efficiency and effectiveness. Health-care costs escalated to 2½ times the inflation rate of the general economy, with mental health and chemical dependency treatment driving the costs disproportionate to their perceived importance to society (Cummings, 1995a).

It has not been difficult to predict the course of the industrialization of healthcare delivery. As in all the industrial revolutions that preceded this one, there are six characteristics that provide insights for practitioners of psychotherapy (Cummings, 1995a).

(1) Those who make the goods and provide the services (in our case, psychotherapy) lose control of the production and distribution of their own goods and services. The control passes to business interests.

(2) Because industrialization thrives on cheap labor, the master's-level psychotherapists will largely displace the present reliance on doctoral-level practitioners. Psychiatry and psychology have failed to prove that possession of a doctorate, be it M.D., Ph.D., or Psy.D., will accord the patient a better outcome. Most managed care companies (MCOs) and HMOs regard doctoral-level practitioners as overtrained and overqualified to spend most of their time performing psychotherapy. But in addition, all practitioners have and will continue to experience a reduction in revenue resulting from the lower fees "negotiated" as part of belonging to an MCO network.

(3) Efficiency and effectiveness increase under industrialization, with a consequent reduction in the numbers of practitioners required. For example, 38 HMOs the size and efficiency of Kaiser-Permanente can treat 250 million Americans with only 290,000 physicians, half the present number, and with only 5 percent of the gross national product (GNP) instead of the current 14 percent. It was predicted

several years ago (Cummings, 1988b) that industrialization will eventually reduce the number of psychotherapists needed to one-half the present number.

(4) Under industrialization, quality at first suffers, and then reaches a new higher level as the industry grows out of its infancy. Practitioners are seeing this wide disparity in quality and will soon begin to see a stabilization.

(5) The increased efficiency of industrialization makes possible distribution to the masses. As an illustration, no one would insist that Levitz furniture is of the quality of Chippendale, but the general population would not have adequate furniture without industrialization. Our health-care system will eventually have to be universal in its delivery. This is why every major health-care reform proposal, in the recent past, as well as in the future, will have "managed competition" as its centerpiece. To put it simply, everyone will have shoes, but there will be no Gucci loafers.

(6) Finally, there takes place a consolidation where successful companies buy the unsuccessful ones. This prediction, made years ago (Cummings, 1986), is exceeding all expectations in both intensity and timing. As predicted, the majority of health care in America may be in the hands of 12 to 18 "mega-meds" by the year 2000.

The Stampede Into Group Practices

Recognizing that solo practice is rapidly becoming an endangered species (Cummings, 1986; Cummings & Dörken, 1986; Dörken & Cummings, 1991), psychologists are forming multimodal group practices all over the nation at an astounding rate. The first prediction that new delivery systems were on the way was by Dörken (1974). Within a decade, Dörken's prophetic warning was becoming true, and Cummings was publishing "Blueprints" on how these new systems could become *practitioner*-driven rather than business-driven (Cummings & Fernandez, 1985; Cummings, 1986). In many instances, managed care companies have helped psychologists in their networks to identify exceptionally skilled colleagues and have encouraged their banding together and facilitated their transition from solo to group practices. The principles of the general practice of psychology

(Cummings & VandenBos, 1979) are receiving new and intensive interest, and the lines of demarcation among the various schools of psychology are blurring in favor of psychotherapy integration (Cummings, 1992). Among those practitioners so engaged, there is a new vitality, whereas for those who desperately cling to solo practice or who have waited too long and find the networks closed to new applicants, there is a growing fear and depression.

Focused Psychotherapy and Managed Care

The four primary delivery principles of brief, intermittent psychotherapy are clinically based and accord cost containment without having to resort to such business-driven initiatives as session limits, co-payments, deductibles, and first-dollar amounts. Without initially being in response to the need for cost containment, it is, nonetheless, complementary to managed care. Furthermore, it restores to the practitioner a sense of autonomy in a now clinically driven system. It is important to examine how each of these principles satisfies economic requirements through clinical expertise.

(1) Skilled brief psychotherapy is not only therapeutically effective, but also cost-effective in that it brings rapid resolution to patient problems. It is the obligation of psychotherapists to so hone their skills as to be able to bring relief to a patient's distress in the shortest time possible. The patient's resistance to therapy is not an excuse for the therapist's inefficiency, for all patients cling to the inadequate solutions practitioners call neuroses, personality disorders, or psychoses.

The psychotherapist must hit the ground running, with the very first session being therapeutic. The concept that one must devote the first session to merely taking a history is nonsense. Ideally a therapeutic contract is established in the first session, but this is not always possible. First, the therapist must determine what brings the patient in today (*operational diagnosis*) and what the unconscious motivation (*implicit contract*) and resistance are as opposed to the conscious but erroneous, explicit contract. When these are known, a treatment plan is made for every patient. Lack of a treatment plan renders the therapist akin to an airplane pilot without a flight plan. It prolongs the therapy and encourages therapeutic drift.

The therapist must do something novel in the first session. By doing something unexpected in the initial session, the therapist will cut through the expectations of the "trained" patient and will create instead an expectation that problems are to be immediately addressed.

(2) Effective psychotherapy is focused, using different paramters and interventions for each specific psychological condition. Traditionally, each school of psychotherapy dictated within its own theoretical structure a similar and identifiable approach to all psychological conditions. Focused psychotherapy demands that a therapist be aware that each psychological condition requires different entry points, strategies, and expectations. Awareness of these reduces the number of sessions necessary and minimizes the number of therapeutic failures.

From the first session and by therapeutic contract, the patient is made a partner in the treatment. This partnership is underscored by homework that is given at the end of the first session and each session thereafter. The homework is meaningful and individually tailored to each patient. There is no cookbook of homework assignments. Meaningful homework facilitates speedy recovery and minimizes resistance.

(3) The patient receives the amount of therapy needed by the patient, with most responding to brief therapy, while some conditions will require long-term therapy, while still others will require continuous therapy for life. Given therapists who are skilled in brief, intermittent therapy, years of longitudinal research has consistently demonstrated that 85 percent of the patients seen choose to come in for 15 sessions or less (with a mean of 8.6), 10 percent will need longer term psychotherapy with occasionally over 100 sessions (but with a mean of 17.2), while 5 percent will be seen for the remainder of their lives (Cummings, 1977). These "interminable" patients can be followed through specially designed programs that accord increased periods between sessions, with eventually twice a year being effective. The important point is that episodic length is determined by inherent need in the patient, rather than by any inefficiency and ineffectiveness of the therapist. The economic point remains that if 85 percent of patients respond to an average of 8 or 9 sessions, a health-care plan can afford to finance the 15 percent of patients who need long-term treatment.

By making the patient a partner in the therapy, the therapist assumes the role of a catalyst. Since the patient is essentially responsible for progress, negative transference is appreciably reduced.

(4) Therapy is not terminated, but interrupted, and the patient is encouraged to return if in future life stages or traumas another episode of therapy would be helpful. Traditionally, therapy was continued until both patient and therapist were reasonably assured the patient was "cured." It was as if both patient and therapist were accorded only one chance, a standard imposed upon no other form of health care. In medicine, a patient is treated, for example, for pneumonia only for as long as treatment is needed to relieve the infectious process. If the patient returns two years later with a broken leg, the initial treatment for pneumonia is not deemed a failure. But in traditional psychotherapy, an additional episode of treatment casts a negative aspersion on the initial episode. In focused psychotherapy, the treatment addresses the presenting problem, and although in the process there is a generalized ability to address subsequent problems, there is no supposition that life will not produce a future problem that will necessitate treatment.

Research has revealed that many patients continue therapy as "insurance" against a relapse (Cummings, 1977). They fear offending the therapist by quitting before they are formally released, jeopardizing their ability to return to that therapist should this be warranted at some future time. Knowing that one may return as needed empowers the patient to respond to the self-knowledge that the problem has been resolved. Finally, years of experience have demonstrated that patients who return build quickly on their previous therapy, and only one session or just a few sessions are necessary to resolve the new problem.

Essential Paradigm Shifts

In order to succeed in the current health-care climate, most psychotherapists will have to increase their proficiency in brief psychotherapy with additional training. But even more importantly, to be a part of the new emerging group practices there will be required a pervasive shift in values from the traditional approach, which is referred to as the *dyadic model*, to the time-effective approaches, which are referred to here as the *catalyst model*. Borrowing liberally from the training experiences of Bennett (1994) and Budman and Gurman (1988), and incorporating these with the authors' own retraining of hundreds of psychotherapists over five years, there emerge seven essential shifts in values (Cummings, 1995b).

Paradigm Shift 1

Dyadic model: Few clients are seen, but for lengthy courses of treatment, usually individually.

Catalyst model: Many clients are seen, for brief episodes of treatment, very often in nontraditional modes.

Outcomes research has already begun to demonstrate that many psychological conditions do better in brief episodes of problem-solving therapy (Cummings, 1994). Other examples are group programs designed to teach and facilitate independent living among the chronically mentally ill that maximize effectiveness, whereas continuous individual psychotherapy for these clients is only minimally impactful. Many therapists have found that it is much harder work to see a large volume of patients in brief episodes than to treat a few patients several times a week continuously for several years.

Paradigm Shift 2

Dyadic model: Treatment is continuous, often weekly or even more frequently.

Catalyst model: Treatment is brief and intermittent throughout the life cycle.

Brief, intermittent therapy throughout the life cycle has now been empirically studied for more than 30 years of follow-up (Cummings, 1992) and has been shown to be more efficient and effective than keeping the patient in treatment beyond the resolution of the life problem presented.

Paradigm Shift 3

Dyadic model: The therapist is the vehicle for change, and emphasis is on treating psychopathology. The aim is a "cure" in some form.

Catalyst model: The therapist is merely a catalyst for the client to change, and the emphasis is on restoring the inevitable drive to growth that has gone awry.

This is decidedly a developmental model that regards growth as the striving of every living organism. The therapist acts as a catalyst so that the client resumes the growth cycle that was temporarily derailed. It broadens the client's repertoire of responses to conflict, stress, or anxiety beyond the typical mode acquired in childhood. The client may, in future years and under exceptional stress, temporarily resort to the old mode, but it is surprising how little intervention is needed to resume growth in these intermittent contacts.

Paradigm Shift 4

Dyadic model: The therapy is the most important event in the client's life, and it is within the treatment span that the client changes.
Catalyst model: The therapy is an artificial situation like an operating room, and significant changes occur and keep occurring long after therapy has been interrupted.

This is especially difficult for therapists who need the narcissistic supplies accorded by grateful clients. Their long-term clients, whose dependency has been fostered, are grateful. In the newer model, the client recalls the experience as something that was accomplished by himself or herself.

Paradigm Shift 5

Dyadic model: Therapy continues until healing occurs and the client is terminated as "cured" to some degree.
Catalyst model: Therapy is yeast for growth outside therapy and formal treatment is only interrupted. The client has recourse to therapy as needed throughout the life cycle.

The client does not remain in treatment, as many do, for insurance against the fear the problem of symptom will recur. Termination anxiety is diminished or eliminated inasmuch as treatment is only interrupted and the client is encouraged to return as needed.

Paradigm Shift 6

Dyadic model: Individual and group pschotherapy in the office are the main modalities by which healing takes place.
Catalyst model: Every healing resource in the community is mobilized, often as a better approach than office practice.

Rather than disdaining support groups or self-help programs, the practitioner cooperates with and offers consultation to these resources.

Paradigm Shift 7

Dyadic model: Fee-for-service is the economic base for practice; the therapist must constantly fight against limitations on benefits.
Catalyst model: Prospective reimbursement, or capitation, free the therapist to provide whatever psychological services are needed by the client.

House calls, imperative with house-bound agoraphobics and desirable with the chronic mentally ill, as two examples, become standard. Prevention programs that include such things as stress management, assertiveness groups, healthy lifestyle programs, parenting groups, and vocational and marital counseling can be provided, whereas they would not be covered in fee-for-service insurance reimbursement.

What Does the Future Portend?

The industrialization of health care is progressing so rapidly that demonstrable changes seem to occur on almost a monthly basis. Practitioners have lost control over their own practice and become increasingly confused and insecure regarding the future. Yet there are discernable trends upon which educated guesses concerning the next decade can be formulated (Cummings, 1995a).

(1) By the year 2000, behavioral health carve-outs will disappear. The primary reason specialized behavioral health-care companies emerged in the first place is that the health insurers did not know how to control these costs. Now that the technology is available to

everyone, carving out behavioral health is unnecessary and behavioral health will become an integral part of comprehensive health care.

Recently, there has been an acceleration in the acquisition of managed behavioral health care by large, comprehensive health systems. Today, only a few small managed behavioral care companies remain independent and free-standing. Now that the "giants" have been acquired, it is anticipated that these minor companies will also become part of large, comprehensive health-care systems. The rapid movement toward the 12 to 18 "mega-meds" that will dominate American health care by the turn of the century is clearly discernable.

(2) Medical cost offset will become the most regarded outcomes research. The managed behavioral healthcare companies have succeeded in ringing out most of the fat in M/CD treatment, and there now remains the much greater savings to be accomplished by eliminating stress-related costs in medicine and surgery. A recent survey has shown that employers overwhelmingly believe that psychological intervention can significantly impact on medical and surgical costs by addressing effectively the large group of patients who somaticize stress and emotional disorders (Oss, 1993). Now that managed behavioral health care is becoming an integral part of comprehensive health care, the industry is able to conduct medical/surgical cost-offset research which was not possible under the carve-out systems.

(3) Community consortia will emerge and dictate the market. These groups will be dominated by the buyers who will insist not only on cost savings, but also on extent and quality of services. They will include broad representation from the community and will have the ability to monitor the delivery of services.

The consortia, which have already emerged in several major cities, will resemble the purchasing alliances proposed in the Rodham Clinton health-care reform proposal, but they will not have the force of law along with controversial government sanctions. Rather, they will constitute a market-oriented response with the power of economic force. The providers will have to demonstrate effectiveness through empirical research, not marketing clichés. The negative financial consequences will be severe for those providers who either oppose these consortia or are unable to demonstrate quality (Neer, 1994).

(4) Managed health care as it exists today will disappear. Practitioner special interest lobbying will succeed in the enactment in most states of so-called "any willing provider legislation." This will

curtail the MCOs' ability to choose for their networks the practitioners they would prefer and will force them to accelerate the step that is already in motion. This does not mean the diminution of managed care, but rather the next phase in the evolution of the industrialization. The MCOs will contract with exclusive provider organizations (EPOs) and thus circumvent the restrictive legislation. By the end of this century, there will be only two forms of health-care delivery systems: HMOs, which are essentially complex EPOs, and the new EPOs, which for lack of a better term can be called "community accountable health-care networks" (described below). Both will be capitated, managed health care.

(5) The Community Accountable Health-care Network (CAHN) is a name preferred by Neer (1994), but it should be expected that other names may emerge as the concept is implemented over the next several years. A few such groups have already emerged and have grown rapidly as MCOs continue to contract with them to provide capitated, comprehensive health services.

The driving force of these groups is the "practitioner equity model," a system of participant ownership first enunciated a half-century ago by Sidney Garfield, the founder of the Kaiser-Permanente health systems and the architect of what was to become the modern HMO: "What makes a cutting-edge health system work is dedicated doctors who believe in the concept and are participant owners" (personal communication, May 1959). At the present time, not all of the emerging exclusive provider organizations have participant ownership, but the ones that succeed in the future will very likely manifest this format.

Ownership by the providers does not mean that the community accountable health-care network will be a democracy. The landscape was cluttered in the 1980s with the failures of physician-owned managed care. These physicians structured their organizations so that everyone had a voice, overlooking the propensity of providers to obsess any issue to oblivion. Participant ownership requires strong management, with a strict limitation on the providers' ability to meddle in administration.

Prospective reimbursement (capitation) will be the only method of payment, and skill in pricing the capitated rate is one of the keys to success. Priced too low, the delivery will fail. On the other hand, pricing it too high makes the delivery system noncompetitive. This will be a new era in pricing, eliminating "low-balling" practices prevalent at the present time. "Low-balling" is merely underpricing one's competitors with the intent of making up the loss by skimping on the delivery of contracted services. The community oversight will closely monitor the extent and quality of what is actually delivered.

(6) The hospital will no longer be the centerpiece of America's healthcare delivery system. Historically, the acute care hospitals and their medical staffs have played a pivotal role. In the future, this will change dramatically with the acute care hospitals becoming equal partners in the accountable healthcare networks. Already, we are witnessing one of the largest proprietary hospital corporations in the country developing all-purpose health-care networks.

(7) There will be a downsizing in the number of psychotherapists, as well as of M/CD practitioners in general. There is an oversupply of specialists, and psychotherapists must realistically regard themselves as part of that oversupply. Market forces will operate so that the accountable networks will be able to deeply discount the disproportionately high incomes of specialists. Psychotherapists have not been among the ranks of high-income specialists, but they can expect an erosion of present incomes. There are just too many master's-level therapists available at much lower costs. The exceptions will be those psychologists who are supervisors and principal researchers, as well as, of course, those gifted psychologists who attain senior management positions. And as master's-level therapists perform most of the psychotherapy, they will be doing so from empirically derived treatment protocols. The best protocol is directly applicable to about one-third of the patients suffering from the psychological condition addressed by that protocol. The other two-thirds will require supervision by the doctoral-level psychologist.

The prediction of 50 percent attrition of psychotherapists has an exception for doctoral-level psychology, but only if professional psychologists obtain the privilege to prescribe psychotropic medication. If that enabling legislation is enacted, doctoral-level psychologists will experience only 25 percent attrition. The other 25 percent will be an additional attrition among psychiatrists, for just as managed care companies now are unwilling to pay for the doctoral-level psychotherapist, they will be unwilling to pay the higher cost for a psychiatrist when a cheaper psychologist can also prescribe medication.

The primary value of the doctoral-level psychologist will not be in routine psychotherapy. Supervising subdoctoral therapists will be important, but even more important will be the role professional psychologists can play in the behavioral health system that the buyers will insist be a part of every community-accountable health-care network. This role will also include the ability to design and execute outcomes research, of which the pivotal investigations will involve medical cost offset. These will be integral to the success of the accountable network, but the number of doctoral-level professional psychologists in existence today will far exceed the future demand.

The health-care systems at the turn of the century must be able to demonstrate efficiency, effectiveness, and quality above that offered by their competitors. At the present time, there seems to be an inability on the part of managed care companies to do this convincingly. Similarly, practitioners will have difficulty in demonstrating in fee-for-service solo practice that they have an incentive to maximize efficiency and effectiveness.

3
Psychojudo

The Japanese martial art of Judo can serve as an apt metaphor for psychotherapeutic intervention. The patients before us are in conflict with themselves. They cling to the neurotic modus operandi that has served seemingly well in the past, and yet this past salvation traps them in the present suffering. The capacity to resolve developmental tasks and the ordinary problems of life has been impaired by a fixated response. This conflict is played out in the therapeutic encounter. The more directly the therapist attempts to wrest clients from their maladaptive patterns, the more the clients are likely to resist. Instead of fighting against the resistance, psychojudo suggests using the resistance and converting it into momentum for change. The following description of Judo by its founder Kano Jigoro is instructive.

What then does this "gentleness" or "giving way" really mean?...Let us say that the strength of a man standing in front of me is represented by ten units, whereas my strength, less than his, is represented by seven units. Now, if he pushed me with all his force I would surely be pushed back or thrown, even if I used all my strength against him. But if instead of opposing him I were to give way to his strength by withdrawing my body just as he pushed, taking care at the same time to keep my balance, then he would naturally lean forward and thus lose his balance. In this new position he may become so weak, not in his actual physical strength, but because of his awkward position, as to have his strength represented for the moment by only three units instead of his normal ten. But meanwhile, I, by keeping my balance, retain my full strength, as originally represented by seven units, and I can defeat my opponent by using

41

only half of my strength, that is, half of my seven units, or three and one-half, against his three. This leaves one-half of my strength available for any (other) purpose. If I had greater strength than my opponent I could of course push him back. But even if I wished to, and had the power to do so, it would still be better (more efficient) for me to give way, because by so doing I should have greatly saved my energy and exhausted my opponents.

Kano Jigoro (1860–1938)
The Founder of Modern Judo
(Drager, 1974, 116–117).

The patient is entitled to his or her resistance. The therapist, struggling to help the patient, has difficulty seeing resistance as anything but the enemy. However, the patient sees giving up the resistance as leading to the abyss. Psychotherapists must appreciate the patient's desperation as expressed by the old Spanish proverb that says, "Death rather than change," and never strong-arm the resistance. Flow with the patient's resistance and turn it into momentum for change and growth. For example:

A woman is living with a man who could aptly be called "der Stunken." She works from 8 to 5, supports both of them, comes home, cooks dinner, and cleans house while der Stunken lies on the couch all day, blowing grass, and pretending to write poetry. It's a common syndrome. This woman comes in and says, "I'm tired of this."

Her therapist says, "Do you want to get out of the relationship?"

She says, "I can't stand it any longer."

So the therapist accepts the explicit contract and begins to work on helping this woman leave der Stunken. The more the therapist tries to help her leave der Stunken, the more she digs in because the therapist has overlooked this woman's low self-esteem. In the back of her mind, this woman feels that this is the only person she's worthy of, and her fantasy is that she can make him better. She dislikes herself so much that the only alternative she sees to der Stunken is the abyss of eternal loneliness. The therapist missed the implicit contract, which is what she says to herself. This woman is saying, "Help me become more loveable so that he'll get a job and we'll have a nice relationship." She isn't coming in to leave him.

If you listen to the patient's unconscious dialogue with your third ear and can come up with not only the patient's context but the patient's own words, you'll be amazed how fast therapy can move. To understand the implicit contract is to appreciate that the patient is like an ocean liner. It may take 10 miles to turn an ocean liner around. It must use the momentum of the original direction before it can turn 180 degrees. Thus, the therapist can utilize resistance in the service of growth. When I began seeing this woman, I said to her what she's been saying to herself, "Next week I want you to go out and do three things that you've never done before to make this man love you. I am not convinced that you have done everything possible to make this man love you."

She came in the following week, told me what she had done, but it hadn't worked. Der Stunken is still lying around all day smoking grass. I told her: "I'm still not convinced that you've done everything that you can do to make him love you. I want you to go out next week and do three other things that you've never done before to make him love you." I've never had a woman who went beyond three sessions with this homework who didn't come in and announce that she'd left der Stunken.

Her self-esteem has improved because she realized through this process that it's not she, it's he, that's the jerk. She's also learned experientially the futility of changing der Stunken. Now, therapy can begin to develop her skills and make her an independent person, and she will then sop it up like a sponge because she's not fighting you with one hand.

The following cases illustrate the principle of psychojudo. They have in common the strategy of designing a treatment plan around the resistance: utilizing the resistance in the service of growth when possible, deflecting it if not, or overwhelming it when no other alternative is available. Without identifying the resistance that precludes the natural process of change, the therapist cannot understand the conflicting motivations of the patient and find the therapeutic leverage to assist the patient in changing.

After each case is narrated, a legend of pertinent information is provided as a summary to the case. This legend includes the psychological mechanism demonstrated by the patient, as well as the psychological diagnosis. The operational diagnosis, implicit contract, and personality type will not have meaning to the reader until those sections are covered later in this volume. They are provided prior to their description so that at a later time the reader can refer back to each case. Finally, the legend will list the homework given and the therapeutic technique employed.

Do Something Novel in the First Session

Doing something novel and unpredictable in the first session cuts through the expectations of the "trained patient" and creates a mental set that problems will immediately be addressed. Although for some patients the experience of someone truly listening is itself novel, psychotherapists tend to rely too much on this intervention. Doing something novel catapults the patient into treatment in spite of the resistance. This technique is particularly effective with jaded and covertly cynical patients, such as those with personality disorders.

Case Illustration: Amazing Grace

Grace was referred by a colleague who, after seeing her for three years, felt such hostility toward her that he disqualified himself from treating her. He warned me that Grace, a "schizoholic," would generally alternate among three behaviors: She would appear drunk at one session, urinate in the chair in the next session, and, finally, do some semblance of therapeutic work in the third. One never knew which of the sessions would be the urination session. To protect himself from the consequences, he put the kind of rubber sheet used in a baby's crib over the therapy chair. All attempts to stop this erratic behavior resulted in Grace's falling to the floor, stopping breathing, turning blue and becoming cyanotic, at which point the therapist was obliged to call the paramedics to resuscitate her, literally saving her life.

With this in mind, I decided to assume certain educated risks and became an authority on cyanosis during the next couple of weeks. When Grace arrived for her appointment, even though forewarned as to her appearance, no one could be prepared. She was beyond slovenly. It was as if Grace had turned ugliness into her own peculiar art form. After all, what kind of person would urinate through her own clothing on purpose?

At the first therapy session, I warned Grace that urinating in the chair would end our therapeutic relationship. I did this on the grounds that it would be deleterious to continue treating a patient who was behaving in a most regressed, antitherapeutic fashion and to impotently expect change in the face of extreme opposition. Grace's reaction to my warning was to clear her throat and spit on the carpet. When I asked her to clean it up, she countered that I had not told her she could not spit on the carpet.

I explained that there were many unacceptable kinds of behavior, as she was quite aware, and that I had no intention of warning her about every one of them. Any recurrences of such incidents would result in our terminating therapy.

Grace stared at me without saying a word for several minutes before falling to the floor. She stopped breathing, and began to turn blue, which is a symptom of cyanosis. Instead of calling the paramedics, I did what I had prepared and planned to do and went to my desk to retrieve my camera. I discovered, much to my dismay, that the camera was empty. While I searched frantically for the film, I talked excitedly to Grace, encouraging her to keep up the performance so it could be recorded for medical history. Every once in a while, Grace would open one eye and stare at me in total disbelief.

Finally, when I got the camera loaded and began to take pictures, my flash did not work. Before I could get the flash attachment functional with a new battery, Grace was back in her chair, apparently ready to begin a more constructive relationship. I saw Grace four times before going to the next step in her therapy.

Grace's behavior frequently brought her to San Francisco's various hospital emergency rooms, and her cyanotic attacks had often been repeated there. After my fourth session with Grace, I obtained her permission to have my telephone number at the emergency rooms, with instructions that I should be called if her behavior became troublesome. As expected, Grace did subsequently become cyanotic during an emergency room intervention, and I was summoned to deal with her. This first time, the fact of my physical presence was enough to cause her to stop the behavior. Subsequently, a brief exchange by telephone sufficed. Within three weeks, Grace had stopped the behavior completely.

Real therapy could now begin. Grace was born an unwanted child to a mother who reminded her every day of her childhood that her arrival had ruined her life. The little girl's response was to become the "awful" child she was accused of being. She worked at being ugly and obnoxious. As an adult, her ultimate self-deprecation and contempt for the world was to urinate in the chair of any authority figure.

The case of Grace illustrates how the "primary patient" can sometimes be the therapist. The primary patient was very obviously the psychiatrist who referred Grace; the emergency room staff who dealt with her "cyanosis" were the secondary patients. After a further 18 sessions, Grace and I terminated. During this time, she had changed her appearance from that of a bag lady to that of a self-respecting human being, had begun to groom herself, and had stopped drinking. Although she was still schizophrenic, she was no longer a schizoholic who felt compelled to go through life getting attention by exhibiting antisocial behaviors.

It may be that other interventions may have had a therapeutic effect on Grace, but it is doubtful that anything but a very novel approach could have so rapidly cut through the stonewall resistance of this thoroughly "trained" patient. Grace's regression into infancy was profound. She was willing to sink into any depth of self-deprecation to prove her mother, the therapist, and the world unworthy and unloving. She was a prime candidate for psychojudo, and the reader will recognize several other techniques, which will now be discussed.

LEGEND

Psychological Mechanism:	Withdrawal and Denial
Diagnosis:	Schizophrenic Alcoholic
Operational Diagnosis:	Original therapist abandoning her
Implicit Contract:	I shall continue to run my own therapy

Personality Type:	Garlic
Homework:	No urination in treatment
Therapeutic Techniques:	Doing the unexpected (novel)
	Preventing regression to
	infantilism
	Encouraging (reward)
	abstinence

Prescribing the Resistance

Prescribing the resistance can also fulfill the goal of doing something novel. By directing the patient to continue behavior that seems antitherapeutic, the therapist surprises the patient's defenses, engages the patient in a positive working relationship, and forces oppositional patients to adopt the position of the therapist.

Such was the case of Patricia, who had thwarted all attempts to treat her son. Not until later was it discovered that her stonewalling the current therapist was only the latest in a series of such behaviors. Prescribing the resistance is particularly useful in patients who otherwise prevent treatment from ever occurring unless their demands are met by the therapist. On the other hand, strong-arming her resistance would guarantee therapeutic failure. By prescribing the resistance, the therapist also joined the resistance and slowly, as if one were turning around an ocean liner rather than making the abrupt turn capable of a motorcycle, this resistance was transformed into a valid treatment procedure.

Case Illustration: Patricia, the Overprotective Co-Therapist

A social worker had arranged with her patient's mother to allow the visiting psychologist to sit in on their next session. This is how Patricia and the identified patient, her son Billy, were seen jointly by the therapist and the visiting psychologist.

Billy, age 10, was referred by a beleaguered school system that was unable to cope with the boy's attacks on other students, his abusiveness toward his teachers, and his truancy. The center had interviewed the mother and the son and, in keeping with good practice, had asked the mother to enter therapy for herself while Billy was being seen by the child therapist. She flatly refused to enter treatment or for Billy to be seen unless she was in the room. Her position was that Billy was the patient, and she knew more about him than anyone else. The center stood firm, and essentially denied treatment. The school was up in arms and demanded something be done by the center. It was at this point that Patricia agreed to be seen with Billy by the visiting psychologist and the social worker.

Just before going into the joint session, the visiting psychologist was handed a 40-page, nicely bound and indexed case history of Billy. It was written by Patricia, who was an R.N. with several years of pediatric nursing experience. It was a remarkable document that professionally identified all of the variables in Billy's case. The boy had never known his father, who disappeared shortly after Billy was born. Patricia suffered a postpartum psychosis, and Billy was in foster homes for the first three years of his life. Once Patricia recovered, she returned to nursing while Billy was cared for by a series of day care centers or reluctant relatives. At the present time, he is what is known as a "latch-key kid." During the time between the end of school and the return of his mother from work, he is on his own. But there are many days Billy does not show up at school at all. There was an abusive and alcoholic stepfather who was in and out of the home, as Patricia seemed to always take him back. All of the information was there, presented by Patricia without any defensiveness.

In contrast to her written material, Patricia's behavior was very defensive. Once in the social worker's office, and before sitting down, she demanded that certain conditions be understood. "Billy is the patient, not me, and no one sees Billy without me." She stated flatly that if the visiting psychologist did not agree with those conditions, she and Billy were leaving immediately. It was obvious to everyone except Patricia that she felt so guilty and responsible for Billy's difficulties that she had plunged into extreme defensiveness and denial. This resistance could not be strong-armed. It was time to do something novel and unexpected.

The visiting psychologist responded unequivocally that Billy was the patient. Not only would he not be seen without her, he insisted that Patricia join in a treatment plan as the social worker's co-therapist. "I just had the opportunity to read this brilliantly presented case history. You really understand Billy's problems better than any of us can, and I ask that you consider coming on board as his co-therapist." Patricia was pleased, but stunned. She had so prepared herself for a battle and for walking out that she was speechless for several minutes. During that time, the psychologist continued to extol the accuracy and professionalism of the document she had written. The social worker, who had not anticipated this approach, was also stunned. When she recovered, she not only was cooperative, she acknowledged that she would welcome Patricia as her co-therapist.

It was now necessary to work out the details. Recovered from her surprise, Patricia enthusiastically entered into the plans. The social worker would be in charge of the case and Patricia, as co-therapist, would be a resource and the person who would implement at home what would be discovered in therapy. Because Patricia would be the co-therapist, she would not be able to use any of Billy's time on her own tensions and problems. This would contaminate the role of co-therapist. Patricia expressed her concern: What if she needed help at some point? The psychologist replied, "You'll just have to tough it through, unless you have a better idea."

After some silence, Patricia asked why she could not be seeing someone else separately. The psychologist pondered the question, and then agreed that would work, but only if Patricia made certain it did not in any way contaminate her function as co-therapist. While seeing her own therapist, she must clearly be the patient, not Billy. She agreed this would be of paramount importance.

The arrangement proceeded better than the best expectations. In her role as patient, Patricia learned she was a guilty, ineffectual, and overly protective mother. As the co-therapist who implemented insights from therapy, she became an engaged, effective parent. She stuck by her decision to separate from the stepfather and allowed Billy to return to the Cub Scouts. She had defensively pulled him out of there when the adult leader spoke with her about Billy's problems. The real reason had been that Billy had begun to relate positively to this man as a sorely needed male surrogate.

Billy steadily improved. After a number of sessions, the therapist and co-therapist agreed that Billy could profit from seeing a male therapist. Patricia insisted that Billy be transferred to a male social worker "and both of us women bow out." Patricia ended her careers as co-therapist and overprotector.

LEGEND

Psychological Mechanism:	Overidentification; Perfectionism
Diagnosis:	Postpartum Psychosis in Remission
Operational Diagnosis:	Okay, I'll see your boss.
Implicit Contract:	My treatment plan or none
Personality Type:	Garlic
Homework:	Be therapist's co-therapist for Billy
Therapeutic Technique:	Prescribing the resistance

Humoring the Resistance

While generally useful in establishing rapport and disarming the resistance, humor is especially effective with borderline patients. The more a patient plays psychological games, the more likely that person will enjoy therapeutic, or constructive, humor. How outrageous the therapist can be is established by the degree to which the patient behaves outrageously. The constructive humor will be understood just below the surface of the patient's consciousness, just as the patient realizes in the very accessible preconscious level when he or she is "pulling someone's leg." This process is clearly illustrated in the case of Mona.

It cannot be overemphasized that the therapist not only can, but must be, as outrageous as the patient in the kind of case where humoring the resistance is the treatment of choice. Listen carefully to the patient and adjust the therapeutic response accordingly. If the therapist is too reserved, the intervention will fall flat. If the therapist exceeds the patient's intensity, anger will result. In either situation, over- or underplaying the humor, the patient will quit therapy. Mona not only responded to the appropriate level of humoring her resistance, she was relieved of the highly eroticized lesbian transference, which was preventing treatment. Humoring the resistance is the apparent successful point of entry for this "woman scorned."

Case Illustration: Mona—Lay That Pistol Down

A petite social worker originally from Turkey was entangled with a woman about 6′2″ who was threatening to kill her with a gun. This patient had a history of assault, and she had a pistol. You can imagine the therapist's countertransference at this point. So she asked the senior author to see the patient.

We went into the office and in the introduction I extended my hand to this woman who was wearing aviator dark glasses. She said, "I don't shake hands."

I said, "You're very wise. Do you know how many germs are transmitted by people shaking hands? And I feel particularly infectious today. You're very wise."

She looked at me, and I motioned her to sit down, so she went across the room to the chair that was farthest away from me. We sat down with the social worker next to me and the patient way over there.

We sat there and looked at each other till she finally said, "Aren't you going to say something?"

I said, "I can't."

She said, "Why can't you?!"

"I can't see your eyes. I never talk to people if I can't see their eyes. Because I talk to people's eyes."

"Oh," she said, "What do you mean?"

"Well, if you take off your glasses we can talk."

She took off her glasses. Though she rejected shaking hands, we've made enough rapport for this. Now that she had taken off her glasses, we talked. It became apparent to me that this woman was very much in love with the therapist. She was a borderline woman whose homosexuality was getting in her way. She had erotic transference toward the social worker. I said, "You know, I want you to name three things you like about your therapist and three things you don't like about her. And you can do it in whatever order you want, but I want three of one and three of the other."

She said, "Fine, let me do what I like first. She listens to me. She's always there for me, and she helps me."

"I would give that therapist an A, can't do any better than that. Three things you don't like?"

She struggled and struggled. She couldn't think of anything. I began to realize how profoundly in love this person was with the therapist. I said. "You've got to give me three."

She said, "I can't."

I said, "You've got to give me three."

She said, "Okay. She's dark complected. She was born in Turkey, and she's short."

I said, "I won't accept any of those three."

She said, "Why not?"

I said, "Because she can't help those. She can't change her complexion. She can't change her birthplace and she can't suddenly stretch herself to six feet tall. I can't accept those. I want you to name three things that you don't like about her that she can change."

This was a useful intervention in that the patient, in her eroticized transference, was ambivalent. She wanted to make the therapist look bad only because she sensed her love was rejected. Basically, she liked the way the therapist looked. So she struggled and finally she said, "I can only think of one."

I said, "What's that?"

She said, "She wears baggy pants." The therapist had on a skirt that day, but apparently she would frequently wear those Middle Eastern pants that kind of bloom out. I said, "Okay, thank you. Now, have you noticed that the more you like your therapist the more you want to kill her?"

She said, "You know that?"

I said, "Yeah, it's very obvious. When you feel like killing her, can you leave the room for ten minutes and walk down the hall?"

She said, "Can I do that?"

I said, "Yes. That's a rule."

She said, "What is she going to do?"

I said, "She's going to quit wearing baggy pants."

"Fine, it's a deal."

"Fine, in order to do this you have to give up your pistol." She agreed to give up her pistol.

Pretty near the end of the session, she said. "Dr. Cummings?"

I said, "Yeah?"

"This Biodyne stuff, does it really work?"

When a patient asks that, you know something's happened, something's connected. So I looked at her and said, "Do you want the truth?"

She said, "Yeah."

I said, "It's a scam!"

She said, "Why do you do it?

I said, "Very simple. It's a great living and I give a livelihood to all these therapists and you know, this center is just one of scores of centers we've got in 39 states. We give a lot of jobs to a lot of therapists."

She said, "Can I join the scam?"

"Of course. We have to have some people pretending to be therapists, and we have to have people pretending to be patients."

She said, "How do I do that?"

I said, "Very simply. To join the scam, you're going to be a patient now. You have to keep every appointment. You can't call after hours. You can't threaten your therapist, and you can't show up at emergency rooms."

She said, "I can do that." She continued her treatment and became a model patient. At the end of every session she said, "This scam is really something. You know, sometimes I really think I'm a patient." Thinking of therapy as a scam gave this patient just enough distance to work on herself without feeling overwhelmingly vulnerable, and the rules of being a model patient gave her parameters that propped up her ego.

LEGEND

Psychological Mechanism:	Projective Identification, Splitting
Diagnosis:	Borderline Personality Disorder
Operational Diagnosis:	I love her
Implicit Contract:	If I cannot have her, I'll kill her
Personality Type:	Garlic
Homework:	Pretend to be a patient so as to join the scam
Therapeutic Technique:	Humoring the resistance

Mobilizing Rage in the Service of Health

Rage is a more galvanizing emotion than love. Love may ultimately be the stronger emotion, but love takes longer. Rage is immediate and can be utilized to empower change in a patient. Frieda Fromm-Reichman called this "the mobilization of rage in the service of health." Most psychotherapists do not lack compassion, but have difficulty coping with the tough love that is inherent in mobilizing rage in the services of health.

Just as one would not trust a surgeon who fears the sight of blood, why trust a therapist who cannot stand the sight of "psychic blood" when an intervention that might be termed psychological surgery is in the best interest of the patient. Mobilization of rage in the interest of health is a powerful technique in the hands of a compassionate therapist. It is deadly in the hands of a noncompassionate therapist. Similarly, the surgeon's scalpel in the wrong hands would be inappropriate, sadistic, or fatal.

The case of Elaine justified the use of this technique in that the therapist who had never seen her had to (1) keep her on the phone long enough to learn the salient facts and quickly establish a therapeutic bond, and (2) prevent her from committing suicide. She was going to kill herself because she was in a rage at her regular therapist. She saw him as abandoning her when she most needed him. By mobilizing that rage in the service of the patient's health, the therapist was able to save her life by taking the added step of paradoxical intention.

Case Illustration: Elaine—Death by Drowning

In a busy practice, one is frequently called upon to handle emergencies on the telephone. These are usually difficult cases made even more difficult by the absence of visual cues. Often, these cases are suicidal. The practitioner should bear in mind that beneath all of the determination to destroy oneself there is a part of the patient that wants to be talked out of it. Otherwise, the patient would not have telephoned. But conventional interventions often replicate everything that has been said to the patient by relatives, friends, and lovers. Such talk has already been discounted, so it is not effective. When all else fails, the appropriate mobilization of rage in the interest of health is very effective.

In this case, shortly after the center in Hawaii opened one morning, Elaine telephoned asking for her therapist who was out of town and unavailable, but would be back day after tomorrow. She informed the receptionist this was too late. She had promised her therapist she would not commit suicide until she talked with him. She believed that she had fulfilled that promise by calling, and would now proceed to kill herself. This, of course, had been a poorly constructed non-suicide pact. The therapist should have obtained believable assurance that the patient would not attempt suicide until patient and therapist had their next scheduled session. The agreement must also be within the ability of the patient and in accordance with the dictum that a patient is not asked to do what he/she is not able to do.

Elaine agreed to talk with the therapist's supervisor, who was visiting from the mainland. This psychologist took the position that to really fulfill her promise that she had to talk to her therapist before she committed suicide, she had the obligation to talk to his surrogate. She agreed. In the meantime, the receptionist had given the psychologist Elaine's psychological chart. Unfortunately, the writing was illegible, so the psychologist would have to obtain the pertinent information from the patient herself.

He began by asking Elaine why she planned to kill herself. She replied that the building she and her three children were living in had been condemned and she was being forced to move. The four of them had been living in one room, with a shared bath and toilet down the hall. They slept, ate, and lived in this one room that had been home for two years. With the deadline for leaving the condemned building rapidly approaching, Elaine had found a three-room apartment with its own bath and toilet. She and her daughter could have their own room separate from the two boys, but the welfare office could not give her the extra money required for the higher rent. She had decided that her three children could be taken care of better by the state than by her. "As orphans they will get the things I can't give them."

The psychologist expressed admiration for Elaine's dedication to her children, and lamented that the loss of such a good mother would be a tragedy. Had she considered other ways of helping her children short of having to kill herself? She recounted six things she had thought of doing, and one by one she discounted each as ineffective. The psychologist agreed with her that, sadly, she was right: committing suicide would be the best assurance her children would be properly cared for. Again he expressed admiration for her dedication as a mother.

Then Elaine was asked to relay more about herself. She was born and grew up in Puerto Rico and moved to Hawaii for better opportunity. It was also ascertained that she had been married twice, and each of the three children had a different father. She had not married the father of the third child. In her conversation, the patient sounded both childish and hysterical.

The psychologist asked how she planned to commit suicide. She said she was going to ingest the contents of a bottle of Valium and then walk into the surf and drown. This form of suicide is frequent where the ocean is warm, but rare in colder climates. She had decided that at 11:00 that morning, when the children would be with a friend, she would walk out into the ocean. She could not state how much Valium she had, so the psychologist asked her to count the pills. She did so, and reported there were 27. Then she was asked to look on the label and report whether they were 1, 3, or 5 mg. She responded they were each 1 mg. The therapist then advised her she did not have enough Valium. "You have just enough so you will be rescued but not drown, and end up alive and probably disfigured for life." (This latter was stated authoritatively for, already having determined the patient's hysterical personality, the therapist was connecting with that part of a hysteric that would rather be dead than disfigured.) The patient owed it to her children to do this right and he recommended at least 100 mg and certainly never less than 75. She wondered where she could obtain the additional Valium and the psychologist pointed out she had already demonstrated she could get small amounts from each of several physicians. She might not be able to obtain the additional medication by 11:00 A.M., but it was certainly doable by the end of the day.

The patient was silent. The psychologist interrupted the silence by saying he had noticed that she was scheduled to see her therapist at 2:00 P.M. day after tomorrow. He wanted her permission to cancel that appointment as she would be dead anyway. "The center has three patients waiting for a cancellation. If you do not cancel, the hour will go to waste and a needy patient will be deprived." There followed a long silence, after which the patient said she did not want to cancel the appointment unless she acquired the requisite amount of Valium. If she obtained the extra pills, she would call and cancel.

The patient did not cancel. As the psychologist expected, she kept her appointment with her therapist two days later. But before entering the office, she stuck her head through the doorway and asked the receptionist, "Has that awful Dr. Cummings gone back to the mainland?" Assured that he had, she entered the center. But every week before entering the waiting room she would ask if Dr. Cummings was still on the mainland. She also never again threatened suicide. Rage had been mobilized in the interest of her health.

LEGEND

Psychological Mechanism:	Repression and Displacement
Diagnosis:	Hysterical Personality Disorder
Operational Diagnosis:	Welfare Dept. denied me
Implicit Contract:	Perpetuate my dependence
Personality Type:	Onion
Homework:	Get enough Valium
Therapeutic Techniques:	Mobilization of rage
	Prescribing the symptom through paradoxical intention

In contrast to Mona, Elaine was in a rage at a therapist who not only was present for her, but was also knocking himself out to successfully treat her. Again, rage at the therapist was making the patient suicidal. The therapist must remember that the greater the intensity of the rage, the greater the energy that can be mobilized in the service of saving the patient's life. In the following case, the senior author purposely allowed himself to be scapegoated by the patient in the interest of restoring the primary therapist's credibility.

Case Illustration: Linda, the Infatuated

A 22-year-old overweight woman who was on welfare consulted the therapist for weight control. Treatment proceeded well. Linda lost a significant amount of weight and had enrolled in a community college course in practical nursing. She showed promise of soon being a thin, self-supporting, and self-respecting young woman

Her history revealed turmoil. Her mother had committed suicide and the father, inexplicably blaming Linda, had not spoken to her in several years. The patient responded with depression, obesity, failure in school, and an inability to support herself without welfare. Although she came in for weight control, her depression became the focus of the therapy. Amazingly, the depression lifted rapidly and Linda manifested the aforementioned behavioral changes.

Suddenly, Linda regressed back into depression. She regained her weight and began to fail in her nursing course. She was on academic probation and she actively declared that suicide was the only solution. She had amassed a large cache of prescription drugs which she would use to overdose and kill herself. So critical were her threats that the therapist appropriately got her to surrender her pills while therapy continued for 30 days. She insisted on the contract that at the end of 30 days if she wanted her pills back the psychologist would return them. He agreed.

At the end of the 30 days, Linda was even more depressed and she demanded her pills back. She would not enter into a therapeutic contract to not commit suicide before her next visit, and her therapist was properly concerned. He refused to return her pills. The therapeutic relationship had come to a standstill. The psychologist called his supervisor, who at the time was the senior author. The therapist realized the therapeutic breach and was painfully aware that an angry, determined patient could find other ways to kill herself if she were denied her cache of pills. As Linda was still in the office, she agreed to speak with Dr. Cummings.

Patient and supervisor talked for about 20 minutes. The patient reiterated her decision to commit suicide, especially now that her therapist had "lied" to her. She responded to the supervisor's request that she give herself one more week, at which time the supervisor would be visiting the center and could meet with her to attempt to resolve her angry complaint against the therapist. If the circumstances warranted, her therapist would be properly chastised. She eagerly agreed, and seemed to look forward to her "day in court."

The following week, it took less than 15 minutes to ascertain that Linda was totally infatuated with her therapist, who was a young and eligible psychologist. He made up for the father who rejected her and he could be the lover she never had and always wanted. Her therapist had been blind to her many signs of infatuation, and she interpreted this as rejection. Her suicide would be that of a woman scorned.

The visiting supervisor confided that he was convinced that she would kill herself, and apologized for his colleague who had broken his therapeutic contract with her. He said he would be returning her pills and he wanted to be notified as soon as she had committed suicide. He would then fire her therapist for incompetence. Linda was shocked and began to extol the virtues of the therapist. She said she had tried several therapists before, but no one understood her until now. The supervisor scoffed at this and interjected that he was not able to prevent a simple suicide and, therefore, indeed he was incompetent. She began to plead for him, even bursting into tears. The supervisor brushed her entreaties aside and added that he was not going to wait until several more of his patients killed themselves before he got rid of this incompetent. Finally, distraught and desperate, Linda promised she would not commit suicide and would continue in her therapy if only the therapist was not fired. The supervisor grudgingly agreed, but voiced his skepticism that she could be helped.

Linda continued with her therapist, who now made analysis and resolution of her eroticized transference the first therapeutic priority. With this new emphasis in treatment, Linda was able to settle into a realistic transference and recapture her previous progress.

LEGEND

Psychological Mechanism:	Repression and Introjection
Diagnosis:	Depressed Hysteric
Operational Diagnosis:	You have rejected me
Implicit Contract:	Help me by loving me
Personality Type:	Onion
Homework:	Destroy therapist's career
Therapeutic Technique:	Mobilization of rage

Since the dynamic of reactive depression is anger turned inward to an introject of the hated object, mobilizing rage can be particularly useful in expelling the introject, as in the cases of John and Lenore presented in the discussion of Depression in the Onion and Garlic Dynamics in Chapter 5.

Denying Treatment

For somebody who is determined to be there for nontherapeutic reasons, the most therapeutic thing you can do is deny treatment. Often, when you deny treatment to somebody who is not there for any legitimate reason, he/she will return later legitimately. One such patient remarked, "Well, there was one message that came through. If I'm here to bullshit you, I may as well not come in at all."

Denying treatment is especially effective when engaging an addict who is in denial. This technique in the context of Exclusion Therapy has been previously presented in several papers (Cummings, 1969, 1970, 1979)

The case of Kevin presented at the beginning of this volume is illustrative of the technique of denying treatment to increase the patient's motivation. When one employs this approach, it is important that the therapist verbalize what the patient is secretly saying to him or herself. By becoming the resistance, the therapist forces the patient to take the role of the therapist.

The case of Glenda illustrates the appropriate usefulness of denying treatment. What made this approach the treatment of choice was that overriding Glenda's arrogance and manipulativeness was the underlying figure of a terrified little girl who had been orphaned by the untimely deaths of two irresponsible, substance-abusing parents. Denying treatment to Glenda meant that the therapist was even more powerful than the grandmother he was willing to defy if necessary. Glenda's demeanor toward the therapist, once he denied treatment, was to grab him as if he were a lifeline. Without this clinging, desperate transference, the denial of treatment would have accorded her the excuse to leave and never return. On the other hand, to have even temporarily and only slightly accepted any of Glenda's manipulativeness in the interest of establishing rapport would have relegated the therapist to the category of irresponsibility she reserved for her deceased parents.

Case Illustration: Glenda's Grandmother

Glenda's indolent life style in San Francisco was made possible by a regular monthly check from her wealthy grandmother in New Jersey. This 20-year-old woman was ostensibly attending nursing school, but actually she was not doing much of anything as she dabbled in San Francisco's drug culture and pretended to paint. Her grandmother had grown suspicious and, checking with the nursing school, she learned that Glenda had not attended classes beyond the first week almost two years ago. Her grandmother was furious since she had received regular letters from Glenda describing her nursing classes and indicating how well she was doing. She consulted a psychologist in New Jersey who advised her to make the monthly checks contingent upon the granddaughter's being in psychotherapy. The psychologist also recommended Nick Cummings in San Francisco.

The patient breezed in on the first therapy session as one who is used to getting her own way. She was confident that she could talk her way out of anything, and immediately initiated an ingratiating manner designed to draw the psychologist into a plot to appease her grandmother. The psychotherapist sidestepped this thrust and sought to learn as much as he could about Glenda. It was a tale of a sordid life style made possible by too much money in the hands of parents who lacked stability. Her mother had been married and divorced seven times. Her father had died of a combination of cocaine and alcohol when Glenda was 11. The patient was deposited in a series of expensive boarding schools from New England to Switzerland, and managed to get thrown out of several of them. Three years ago, her mother was killed in a head-on collision while driving at 90 miles an hour. Her blood alcohol level was .21 according to the autopsy. The grandmother, long ago having realized the destructive effect money had on her daughter (Glenda's mother), had arranged to take charge of the family fortune. Glenda inherited nothing until her grandmother died, so she was completely dependent on the very generous checks, which were to keep her more than comfortable while she was ostensibly attending nursing school.

Succinctly, Glenda was a spoiled brat. But at 20 she was also a lonely, frightened, abandoned little girl who had not one clue as to how she might conduct an adult life. It was with this latter that the psychologist connected. The patient latched onto the therapist in her needy, frightened fashion, but it was evident in her cynical smugness that she had conned the therapist and was about to manipulate him. So she was stunned when she was told the psychologist would not see her because she had no intention of giving up drugs and entering school.

"You have to see me. If you don't, Grandmother will be furious." The psychologist replied, "I am a psychotherapist, not a baby-sitter hired by your grandmother." There followed a series of rationalizations in which Glenda escalated her volubility, all of which were deflected by the psychologist. Little by little, the patient began to talk as if she were the therapist, culminating with her sobbing, "I don't want to die like my drug-ridden father and my drunken mother." By the end of the first session, Glenda entered treatment subject to a series of conditions as part of the therapeutic contract. Her $6,500 monthly allowance was cut to $2,500 and she would also have to pay for her therapy sessions out of that. She would refrain from all mind-altering substances. She would resume school at the beginning of the next semester, which was to be in three weeks, and she would succeed in school. Any violation of the therapeutic contract would result in the suspension of both her therapy and her allowance. If her grandmother did not agree, the therapist would not see the patient.

An amazed grandmother eagerly agreed, but was properly skeptical. The patient entered an incredibly turbulent treatment. She alternately soaked up like a sponge the parenting of which she had been deprived and heaped upon the therapist all of the hostility intended for her parents who had betrayed her. She was seen for more than two years, illustrating that our goal is not brief therapy, but effective and efficient therapy. If the latter two are present, the length will take care of itself.

LEGEND

Psychological Mechanism:	Denial, Splitting, Projective Identification
Diagnosis:	Narcissistic Personality
Operational Diagnosis:	Grandmother about to stop my allowance

Implicit Contract:	Join me in fooling Grandmother
Personality Type:	Garlic
Homework:	Abstinence; resume school; reduce allowance
Therapeutic Technique:	Denying treatment

Joining the Delusion

Frieda Fromm-Reichman was a remarkable therapist in the days before major tranquilizers. She used to wear this beat up white coat because all good doctors in those days wore white coats, with the pockets stuffed with candy. She used to go around giving schizophrenics candy. She taught that delusions occupy time and space, and there's room for only one person. So if the therapist gets into it, the patient has to get out of it. She would find a patient playing with his or her feces after defecating in the middle of the floor. She would put on rubber gloves and get down on the floor and play with the patient's feces. The patient would stop. She was a very, very warm person. She used to say that there's no such thing as a hopeless patient; there are only hopeless techniques, and we have to discover new techniques.

Once the patient had allowed her into his or her psychological space because she had joined in smearing feces, he or she was open to what the therapist might say. Dr. Fromm-Reichman would give the patient a candy bar and say, "I'll be back tomorrow with another candy bar. But you must let me know what you prefer, feces or candy. If you are not playing with your feces, I'll know you prefer candy." Time and time again, using smearing feces with the patient as her passport into the patient's psychological space, she made effective contact with deeply regressed schizophrenics when everyone else had failed.

The case of delusional Sam illustrates the point that Fromm-Reichman (1950) made over and over again: Just because a patient is seemingly attentive to the therapist does not mean the therapist has been accepted one iota. With schizophrenics, the therapist has no influence until that patient lets the therapist into his or her life space. The patient does not accord this unless the therapist has demonstrated eligibiilty, as defined by the patient, to be let in. With Sam, calling the police would have completely alienated him from the present therapist and probably subsequent therapists as well. On the other hand, the therapist's effectively joining Sam's delusion was the entrée into the patient's personal world. Once the therapist was let in, then the patient had to vacate it, inasmuch as a delusion seems to occupy psychological space in which there is room for only one person. The patient abandoned his delusion, but only after he had learned to trust and rely upon the therapist, a process that began only after the therapist joined the delusion.

Case Illustration: Sam—LSD for the City Reservoir

A very concerned psychologist consulted the senior author by telephone. He had just seen a patient for the second time who threatened to dump several pounds of LSD into the city reservoir. He had been making LSD in his home laboratory for months and had now accumulated this large quantity. When a certain combination of lights, sounds, colors, and numbers came together in the universe in a prescribed order, it would be the signal for him to back his pick-up truck to the city reservoir and throw in the LSD. The patient, though psychotic, had an advanced degree in chemistry and could talk scientifically far beyond the comprehension of the therapist.

The therapist had diagnosed the patient as paranoid schizophrenic, and he was not certain that the cache of LSD was not also a part of the delusional system and did not exist. But if it did exist, he did not wish to take the chance that the city's water supply would be poisoned. Interestingly, during the 1960s and 1970s, it was an often expressed fantasy of hippie patients that through the city reservoir an entire population would simultaneously "flip out on acid."

The therapist wanted to call in the police, which would destroy any potential therapeutic relationship. The senior author assured him over the telephone that LSD, being an acid, would be quickly diluted and neutralized in the water. It would require an enormous amount of any kind of acid to have a significant effect on such a large supply of water, a fact the patient as a chemist would know well were it not for his delusion.

A treatment plan was devised in which the therapist would join the delusion. Since the therapist could make no sense of the system in which lights, sounds, colors, and numbers would come together in the universe, the entry point was obvious. The patient, over the next several sessions, would teach this "coming together in the universe" to the therapist so both of them would recognize the signal when it occurred. The therapist agreed, but still feared the consequences of a poisoned city water supply. He called a friend who was a chemistry professor for the accuracy of the information he had been given in the telephone consultation and was completely reassured.

Over the next several weeks, the therapist listened intently as the patient used all kinds of didactic means to teach him the "system," as the anticipated coming together in the universe came to be called. During this time, the therapist was also providing a refuge from a world with which the patient no longer could cope. After eight sessions, the therapist still did not understand the "system," but he telephoned the senior author to tell him the patient had completely abandoned the delusion and they were discussing the real issues of independent living outside the hospital and within the limitations of his schizophrenia.

LEGEND

Psychological Mechanism:	Withdrawal, Delusion, Projection
Diagnosis:	Schizophrenia, Paranoid
Operational Diagnosis:	Decompensation of thought disorder
Implicit Contract:	I am not crazy or impotent
Personality Type:	Garlic
Homework:	Teach therapist the codes
Therapeutic Techniques:	Humor the resistance Enter the delusion

In joining a delusion, the therapist also has to effectively humor the resistance. This was true in the case of Sam, and is even better illustrated in the case of Dennis. This latter case also underscores the importance, in joining the delusion, of never stating an untruth. A paranoid patient is overly sensitive to hearing a lie, and the therapist must tailor his or her responses to something that the therapist can personally believe. Declaring to a paranoid, "I believe you," will result in the patient's fleeing from intended therapy. Note in the case of Dennis how the therapist retained his integrity without contradicting the patient's belief. The ultimate rapport was the result of the therapist's refusal to be told, for his own safety, the content of the delusion.

Case Illustration: Dennis, The CIA's Menace

A smiling, friendly, 31-year-old single man consulted the psychologist on referral from his dentist. In spite of Dennis' affability, there seemed something guarded in his demeanor. He volunteered, "My dentist thinks I'm crazy because I want him to remove all my teeth." The patient went on to state that even though the dentist cannot find anything wrong with his teeth, they do give him a great deal of trouble. "He says if you say I am not crazy, he will go ahead. Do you thing I'm crazy?" Every psychotherapist recognizes that such a question is not just rhetorical. It is a key question, the answer to which is critical as to whether the patient develops any trust. A perfunctory negative response or some kind of reassurance will be seen as mechanical and raise a warning flag to the paranoid patient. Most often, the best approach is to follow the cues presented by the patient, both in content and behavior.

Duplicating the patient's affability, the therapist responded, "I had an uncle who had all of his teeth removed and he was crazy. But I knew why he was crazy, and it had nothing to do with his teeth. Why should I think you are crazy?" The patient relaxed somewhat as he laughed along with the therapist. Then, without responding to the question, he talked of his background. The patient had graduated from a prestigious university with a degree in engineering. After college he married a woman he had occasionally dated, but the marriage lasted only eight months. He confided that she had left because she found the patient to be boring. His father, also an engineer, died of a heart attack three years ago. His widowed mother lived alone in the family home in the Midwest. A sister, two years older than Dennis, had committed suicide by jumping off a building about three years ago. After graduation from college and again until about three years ago, Dennis worked in a defense plant in a highly classified position.

Abruptly, Dennis asked the therapist if he believed a tooth could act as a radio receiver. The therapist responded genuinely that he had heard that certain fillings could behave like a crystal set, but he was not an expert on the subject. He added, "You're the engineer and you would know better than I. Other than that I've heard of the possibility, I would defer to you." The patient reflected for a minute or two, seemed satisfied, and proceeded to tell his story.

In his employment in the defense plant with a super-secret project, he began to discover certain irregularities. He reported these to his supervisor, and shortly thereafter he began to be singled out for discrimination. At first, he was denied a well-deserved promotion. Then he was transferred to a relatively menial job since his supervisor continued to rate his performance as unsatisfactory. Finally, a little over two years ago, he was discharged. With his firing, his security clearance was revoked. He had not worked since, living on modest savings and a small inheritance from his father.

Then the patient fell silent for about two or three minutes, during which time he stared intently at the psychologist. He broke the silence abruptly, "What would you say if I told you I discovered a classified document which would have international repercussions if revealed, and might even lead to World War III, and that's why they're after me?" The therapist replied, "I would not want anyone after me, so please don't tell me the secret." This was the right answer. It enabled the patient to tell the rest of his story.

This man had an elaborate delusion, and as in all such psychotic cases, doubting the authenticity of the patient's belief is tantamount to strong-arming the resistance in a neurotic or personality disordered patient. It is imperative that the therapist show no skepticism. On the other hand, the paranoid patient's hypersensitivity to insincerity will detect any posturing on the part of the therapist. It will be noted that the therapist's responses to critical questions not only did not challenge the patient's beliefs, but also were limited statements he could genuinely defend. They had been carefully selected to fulfill both criteria. The decisive response was the therapist's declaration that he did not wish to know the international secret. This is convincing to a paranoid, whereas any attempt to imply "I believe you" would be rejected.

Dennis became very intense as he recounted a sequence of events beginning over three years ago in which "they" attempted to intimidate him so as to curtail his pursuing the irregularities he had discovered. He believed his father did not die of natural causes, but was murdered by the CIA with a drug that would simulate a heart attack. He also believed that his sister was pushed out of an 18-story window. The reason they did not murder him was because the CIA, finding itself under constant congressional scrutiny for overstepping its authority in the past, could not risk another scandal. It developed the strategy of driving him insane. They sent constant threatening messages through the bridgework in his teeth and they followed him 24 hours a day to prevent his passing on the international secret. Once he was declared insane and was committed to a mental hospital, he could talk about the international secret and no one would believe him. It was an effective strategy. The patient feared it was succeeding.

This is a brilliant delusion devised by an intelligent man to account for his gradual decompensation into psychosis. The delusion was restitutive. It enabled the patient to cling to some explanation of reality, and therefore must not be attacked. But this delusion could also cause the patient to turn against the therapist. One error and the therapist would become one of "them." Therapy requires that the therapist join the patient in the delusion in a therapeutic manner. Just because a psychotic talks about the delusion does not mean the therapist has been allowed into the patient's life space. It is only after the therapist has been permitted into that space that the patient's psychosis can be treated. The eventual outcome will be that, since all delusions occupy psychological space in which there is room for only one person, the patient abandons the delusion. This is how it worked with Dennis.

The psychologist stressed that he was not an expert in international intrigue, although he had been engaged in one covert operation in World War II and recognized many of the characteristics in what was ostensibly being done to Dennis. What, then, would be the goal of psychotherapy? Almost as if the therapist had put words in the patient's mouth, Dennis replied, "But you are an expert on mental illness. You could help to keep me from succumbing and becoming insane." The therapist indicated he would very much like to work with the patient in that regard, but the patient would have to promise that in the course of therapy he would never reveal the international secret. Even more reassured, the patient agreed and eagerly accepted the homework assigned to him.

The therapist asked whether the patient had noticed that the CIA frequently changed operatives, so whenever he looked back there was a different person following him. The patient replied in the affirmative, and was amazed that the therapist knew this. This was "standard operating procedure," designed to escape detection. The patient was to keep a precise log, describing each CIA agent, recording the exact time he (they were always males) began following and the exact time he was replaced. Then the patient would do the same with the second operative, and so on through the entire day and the entire week. The patient enthusiastically agreed.

The patient was a meticulous, scientifically trained engineer. He arrived the following week with an extensive log that was the epitome of precision. The therapist congratulated the patient on his work and expressed confidence that, with this kind of material, in time they would discover the CIA pattern and be able to neutralize its effects on the patient's emotional health. From the patient's log, they constructed color-coded charts that were taped to the wall. The patient was as pleased as the therapist. Dennis left, thanking the therapist, "I already feel more confident knowing there is someone on my side."

During the third session, while translating the log into color-coded charts to hang on the office wall, the therapist abruptly stopped. "Dennis, look at your description of this new man following you. Your excellent log has noted how well dressed he is in an expensive suit. That man is not CIA, he is FBI. The FBI agents are the best dressed operatives in the world. J. Edgar Hoover used to demand it. Not only is the CIA watching you, so is the FBI. You must have some international secret. Please, please! Do not ever reveal it to me." The patient was amazed and impressed.

By the fourth session, the psychologist's office began looking like a Pentagon war room. As more color-coded charts were being taped to the now fully covered wall, the therapist again abruptly noted a discrepancy. "Dennis, look at this guy who fell in behind you at 3:03 P.M. on Tuesday. He is neither CIA nor FBI. By your notes, he is short, stocky, and heavy-faced. This is KGB. That description fits every KGB agent in the world. You must have some secret. Even the Russians are watching you. I never want to be privy to that secret you hold." The patient nodded in amazement.

During the fifth session, while the therapist was at the height of his animation, the patient embarrassingly interrupted: "Nick, while you were discovering the KGB agent last week it occurred to me that this is all my imagination. I didn't want to say anything because you were having such a good time with it." The delusion had imploded. The psychological space could no longer contain the patient *and* the therapist, to say nothing about an ever-expanding premise. Now, psychotherapy in the regular sense could begin.

Over the next several sessions, Dennis talked about the impact on him of his father's fatal heart attack and his sister's suicide, which occurred the same year. It had always been difficult for him to face, much less express emotions. His engineer father was an undemonstrative man who created a sterile atmosphere more akin to a laboratory than to a home. His sister, who had just gone through a very emotional divorce, became even more depressed when the father died. Within months, she ended her life. The patient now recognized that he, too, had snapped, but his response was to slide gradually into the psychosis that began the year of his father's death. Many times, the patient thanked the therapist for not attacking his delusion the way other therapists had done. "I never went back after the one session with them." Then, in admiration, he added, "You should get an Oscar for that performance." The therapist had to confess to the patient, "Dennis, I had so put myself in your shoes that I no longer felt it as a performance." Dennis smiled, "I know. That's why I hated to stop you. No one had ever done that for me before."

LEGEND

Psychological Mechanism:	Withdrawal (delusions), Projection
Diagnosis:	Schizophrenia, Paranoid
Operational Diagnosis:	Decompensation of thought disorder
Implicit Contract:	Prove I am not going crazy
Personality Type:	Onion
Homework:	Keep careful log of spying
Therapeutic Technique:	Joining the delusion

Overwhelming the Resistance

In certain cases the resistance must be overwhelmed, but these are rare and severe cases. Overwhelming the resistance as a conscious, necessary strategy must not be confused with strong-arming the resistance in unplanned and unstrategic therapy. This was the case with Beth, the most severe case of rage depression that the senior author had encountered in over 40 years of practice. She required drastic therapeutic risks, which are not generally recommended. The case is presented to illustrate how the most profound determination to punish by slow, torturous suicide can respond to equally profound confrontation.

This case is not for the fainthearted or the inexperienced. But it does demonstrate three important points: (1) The same psychodynamics and therapeutic entry points prevail as in any other rage depression. The introject, which is the internalized rage, must be expelled. (2) Only the intensity of the patient's determination is different. In this case, the intensity is extreme. (3) For the treatment to be successful, the intensity of the therapeutic response must equal the intensity of the patient's resistance. In fact, the matching of intensity is a necessary condition, and the therapist must derive therapeutic cues and take direction from the intense patient's behavior. And perhaps this case illustrates that there are fewer hopeless cases than we believe and that some so-called hopeless cases may actually reflect the therapist's lack of experience and determination. In fulfilling the therapist's side of the therapeutic contract, it is our responsibility to continue to hone our skills until each of us is a master therapist.

Being older and wiser, the senior author would never undertake such a procedure again. In fact, immediately after initiating the therapeutic plan and throughout its implementation I (Nick) deeply regretted ever beginning the course of treatment. Unequivocally it is not something that should ever be done by any therapist. But it happened, and it is included here for one important reason: More than any case we have ever encountered, it demonstrates the power of psychotherapy in the hands of a patient-dedicated, skilled therapist. Whenever we might falter in implementing one of the many active, but certainly less dangerous techniques delineated in this volume, we think of Beth and all else becomes reasonable and doable by comparison.

Following the dramatic first phase of treatment, Beth and her therapist discussed at some length and at her initiation the dangers involved in challenging her to end her life. She confided that what actually saved her life was the realization that should she kill herself in the manner prescribed, the therapist's career would, at the least, be over, and at worst there would be a prison sentence. "That someone would take that chance for me forced me to really look at the hate and venom that was inside me." This was also a profound experience for the therapist, and since that time he has realized the greatest therapeutic ingredient is the therapist's courageous commitment to the patient. Traditional and wimpy do-gooders often just increase the patient's sick resolve. Even Beth, who was determined to eventuate her slow, painful death, could discern this.

Case Illustration: Beth—Death by Neurodermatitis

Beth was a woman in her mid-fifties who was referred by her son's therapist in a distant city. For five years she had suffered from a progressive, intractable, morbid neurodermatitis that if it continued to progress would eventually claim her life. Her distraught husband had taken her to every conceivable medical and psychiatric setting, but the neurodermatitis progressively got worse until her eyes were shut and her entire body was covered with giant hives. Only the soles of her feet remained free and she avoided pain by standing. Eventually, even the soles of her feet succumbed to the skin eruptions. The family was told that, eventually, Beth would develop these sores in her trachea and would choke herself to death. Her son was beside himself, and prevailed upon his therapist to call to make the referral.

The husband came in alone since Beth had not agreed to be seen. He asked if the psychologist wanted his wife's medical and psychiatric records and, upon receiving an affirmative reply, the next day delivered 11 file boxes of records. The events leading up to the illness were frankly presented by the husband, a nationally recognized economist whose almost ten-year affair with his secretary was discovered five years ago by his wife. Beth was enraged by the betrayal and vowed to punish her husband. An active woman all of her life, she quickly lapsed into depression and indolence. Soon the neurodermatitis appeared and rapidly grew worse. Her husband took her from physician to physician and from psychotherapist to psychotherapist, but all attempts to help her were thwarted by this angry woman.

After two weeks, Beth agreed to come in, an event that required considerable logistics. The husband had equipped a station wagon with a collapsible gurney upon which Beth was wheeled in by the husband and a male nurse. Beth lay upon thick pads of foam rubber and she was swathed in layers of cotton. Her eyes were closed, but she examined the therapist by prying one set of swollen eyelids open with her thumb and forefinger. Even through this small slit, one could see the contempt and defiance in Beth's eye. She had been hospitalized many times, both medically and psychiatrically, and she challenged the new therapist right off by asking, "And what do you think you can do that hasn't already been tried?"

There was not anything one could say that would make an impression on her. Beth frankly admitted her rage and her determination to die, but according to her own schedule and only when she was convinced her 63-year-old husband had been punished enough. She readily described herself as a witch, bitch, and monster. What if her 63-year-old husband, who had already suffered two heart attacks, should die first? She quietly responded, "That would be nice." Every inventive, innovative paradox, doublebind, and reframing that the therapist could conjure would receive the contemptuous response, "That's cute, but it won't work, Doctor." To the suggestion that she was also hurting her innocent adult son, she shrugged, "The Bible says the sins of the father are visited upon the third and fourth generation." The sores were engulfing Beth's mucous membranes and she was already wheezing. She let everyone know she would not accept the insertion of a tube into her trachea. She was determined to die. Her eight sessions with the psychologist were nothing more than a funeral dirge.

The therapist was baffled and spent a great deal of time reflecting on the case. He finally decided to fall back upon his war experiences when untried, high-risk heroics were applied as all else failed to save a life. A plan evolved in the psychologist's mind, but it was a drastic strategy that could be justified only by the fact that otherwise the patient would die. He explained the plan to the husband and son; in desperation, they agreed to proceed with it. They signed a legal consent, a document that was not worth anything under the circumstances, but it at least made husband, son, and psychologist feel somewhat better.

A search for a psychiatric hospital that would cooperate was not easy to find. Finally, a small facility agreed and Beth was hospitalized some distance from her home city. She was kept comfortable and medically stabilized, but in isolation. She was allowed no visitors, no therapeutic activities, and no television, radio, or reading material. Every Friday, she would have a bedside session with the psychologist, who would be her only mental health professional as well as her only visitor.

In the first such session, the psychologist spent 15 minutes explaining to Beth that he was going to put a cyanide capsule on her bedside table. It was real cyanide and had been taken from a high-ranking German prisoner in World War II and kept as a war souvenir. He would then leave the room for 15 minutes, during which time the patient had the option of ending it all. He then added that this might be a relief for all concerned, but he doubted that she had the courage. After all, she was too much of a coward to end her life quickly, which was why she had chosen the neurodermatitis. Then the psychologist left the room for 15 minutes.

Only his most intense war experiences could match the emotions of that quarter of an hour. He sweated clear through his suit as he experienced strong chest pains. At the appointed time, the therapist reentered the room, found Beth alive and defiant, and put the cyanide back in his pocket. He then spent 15 minutes telling Beth she was indeed a coward, and a fraud as well. He would be back next Friday when the procedure would be repeated. This ritual was repeated on four additional Fridays.

During the intervening days between the Fridays, the therapist slept poorly and ate little. He lost several pounds and experienced almost constant hyperidrosis and frequent chest pains. He questioned over and over the wisdom of what he was doing. He felt the constant terror that the next Friday would be *it*. But each time he reviewed the case he arrived at the same conclusion and was determined to press on. Those Friday 15-minute episodes outside Beth's hospital room never got easier. His suit would be as wet as if he had stood under a shower. Had the psychologist chosen to use a harmless capsule, claiming it was cyanide, Beth would have seen through the ruse.

The therapist's emotions left no doubt but that the game was real and deadly.

On the sixth Friday, the psychologist immediately noticed that one eye was open and the swelling on her face was down considerably. Beth no longer scowled defiantly, but rather berated the psychologist for what must be the worst therapeutic maneuver of all time. Therapy had begun: She was beginning to expel the introject. Thereafter, Beth was seen daily and in some of the stormiest sessions this psychologist had ever seen. As her anger rose in crescendo, her neurodermatitis subsided, leaving only the permanent scars and disfigurement that were to be her depression's legacy. Yes, she divorced her husband and she rebuilt her life in other directions. But at least she had a life to rebuild.

LEGEND

Psychological mechanism:	Introjection
Diagnosis:	Rage Depression (Major Depression)
Operational Diagnosis:	I'll see you for my son's sake
Implicit Contract:	You will fail to prevent my death
Personality Type:	Onion
Homework:	Commit suicide rapidly
Therapeutic Techniques:	Mobilization of rage
	Overwhelming the resistance

Psychojudo with a Family

The following case illustrates how the principle of psychojudo can be applied to family therapy. This dysfunctional family collectively had over 50 years of psychotherapy, with no end in sight. From the beginning, it was apparent to the therapist he would have to skillfully apply psychojudo. It was also important to employ interventions that were novel so these "trained" patients would not have a rehearsed response.

In applying psychojudo with a family, it must be kept in mind that the family is a system that supports the collective pathology. The identified patient is not necessarily the primary patient, but all will be patients to one extent or another. To complicate matters, along with the family system, each family member will have his or her individual reason for being there (operational diagnosis) and an equally individual expectation from therapy (implicit contract as opposed to the explicit contract). The therapist must determine each of these personalized responses, along with understanding the family's pathological system that binds all the players together. Finally, the therapist, who behaved seemingly in an outrageous fashion, derived his cues from the outrageousness of this dysfunctional family.

Case Illustration: Marlene and Her Schizophrenogenic Family

Marlene was 29 when she first came into treatment. She had her big "3-0," as she called it, during the family therapy series. It was Irene, the mother, who initially called for Marlene's appointment, but shortly thereafter there was another call from Marvin, the father. The family was thought to consist only of two other persons: Carol was Irene and Marvin's second daughter and Marlene's sister, and Robin was Marvin's second wife.

The choice of family therapy in this case may be surprising to some, but the reasons become apparent in the description of the case. In treating families it is important to utilize within the systems approach the same techniques and concepts that are useful in individual therapy.

Marlene had suffered four psychotic episodes for which she had been hospitalized. She had been diagnosed as suffering from bipolar disorder and had been on lithium carbonate for three years. Three of her four hospitalizations occurred while she was taking lithium. Carol had just graduated from high school and would begin college in the fall. Marvin was trained as a lawyer, but rather than practicing law he founded and managed a large and successful publishing company that specialized in legal books. Marvin and Irene were divorced when Marlene was 13 years old. Robin, whom he married shortly after his divorce, had been having a secret affair with Marvin for a number of years. This disclosure left Irene hurt and angry, and she pursued and obtained a substantial settlement that included regular monthly payments as a combination of alimony and child support.

It was not until Marlene was seen that it was learned there was a 33-year-old brother who had been committed over 25 years ago to a private institution, the bill for which was being paid by a trust fund created by Marvin. This brother, Dick, was diagnosed as autistic in his first year of life, and Irene and Marvin kept him at home until he was age six. With the beginning of school, it became apparent that Dick would require far greater therapeutic management than could be provided at home. Marlene was about three when Dick was institutionalized and did not remember the event that was so painful to both parents.

As stated, the first contact came from Irene, who attempted to make an appointment for her daughter. The psychologist advised her that Marlene would have to make her own appointment, which she did within an hour. Two days after Marlene's appointment had been scheduled, Marvin called, stating he had pertinent information and wanted to come in before his daughter had her appointment. The father was advised that Marlene would have to give her consent and within the context of what would take place in her appointment. Marvin seemed angry, but accepted it. After another two days the psychologist received a large manilla envelope from Irene. It was close to 60 typed pages of history, very professionally done since Irene was a master's level counselor. In this treatise, Irene noted that Robin was a psychiatric social worker. As the treating psychologist speculated about the number of unsolicited "co-therapists," he made the decision to explore family therapy if the session with Marlene seemed to warrant it.

Marlene arrived precisely on time for her appointment. She was a short, plain, 29-year-old who immediately announced that her occupation was that of a waitress. She then went on to explain with a paradoxical mixture of both defensiveness and defiance, "No one in my family wants me to be a waitress. They think its terrible." The psychologist replied, "So I've heard," and then he explained he had received a phone call from her father and the equivalent to the collected papers of Sigmund Freud from her mother. Marlene laughed and said, "Well, that's my family."

In the ensuing session, Marlene's subtle and most often well hidden thought disorder became apparent. She manifested many of the signs of pseudoneurotic schizophrenia. If, in fact, she had been misdiagnosed, it was no wonder the lithium regimen had not prevented her hospitalizations. As she talked, her isolation became clear. Her sole activity, outside work, was watching baseball games on television and reading about baseball. She was a walking encyclopedia of baseball statistics. This was the only real interest in her life. Work, on the other hand, gave her the illusion of having a family. The regular customers were assigned mythical roles as cousins, aunts, uncles, and even grandparents. The restaurant owner, sensing her limitations, benevolently protected her. Talking with Marlene during the first session was like talking to an eight-year-old. When asked about her parents, her life, her feelings, she would childishly and laconically answer, "Fine," or "Good," or "Okay."

The psychologist discussed with her the possibility of family therapy. She responded, "Do you really want to be in the same room with my family?" When asked if they were really that bad, she laughingly replied, "Yeah, yeah. We're pretty bad." She was asked to think about the possibility and told a decision would be postponed until the second session.

Marlene came in the following week and announced, "I haven't been able to think about anything but family therapy." Then she paradoxically began to talk about baseball. The therapist interrupted, "We were going to decide about family therapy." She replied, "Oh, yeah. I think that would be fine." The therapist did not just accept this, but asked on what basis she made her decision. She said cogently, "Well, I can't talk to my family because they won't listen to me. So if we get them all in the same room with you, maybe they will listen to me." Together, we called the family members and everyone readily agreed except Carol. Since she had just turned 18, she believed she had a choice to refuse. She was told she certainly had that right, but her presence might be helpful to Marlene. On that basis, she agreed to come in. Robin had expected to be excluded, as she was the stepmother. She was delighted to be included.

So, the cast of characters assembled. Irene turned out to be a very attractive, statuesque woman of 52 with long hair and penetrating blue eyes. She was one of these remarkable women who in her fifties looks as good as she did in her thirties. Marvin, on the other hand, was short like Marlene, and he came in with his legal brief case. Robin turned out to be a Southern belle, peroxide blond, flashy, articulate, and hysterical. Carol was the perfect child with straight A's through the city's premier academic high school.

Being institutionalized, Dick was never seen by the therapist. Irene and Marvin separately visited him no less than two or three times a month. Robin participated in the visits with Marvin and was very much a part of the family. As might be expected, there was considerable rivalry between Irene and Robin, a situation that Marvin seemed to encourage.

The session began with Irene distributing copies of her treatment plan. It was very well written, but Robin questioned its validity. She criticized it as being too rigid and insisted that what everyone should do is hug each other. She announced, "Love will overcome all adversity," and then she walked across the room and dramatically hugged the therapist's favorite plant, a beautiful 5-foot rubber tree. She broke it in three places. The tension between Irene and Robin was at a critical point.

Then Carol began to talk. As if she had reconsidered after witnessing strange behaviors that opened the first family session, she stated she had a right not to be there. The therapist reiterated that everyone's presence was voluntary and he would appreciate her participation. Marvin launched into a 10-minute speech justifying Carol's position and ending with a comprehensive definition of patients' rights. At this point, Carol decided to stay.

Irene again seized the floor, demanding that they get back to her treatment plan. The interplay between Irene and Robin was not what it seemed. Marvin cleverly set Irene and Robin against each other as he had evidently been doing for 17 years. It was apparent that Irene and Robin had much to like in each other and would have resolved their differences had not Marvin actively prevented it.

When they finally seemed to run down, they looked to the therapist to proceed. He talked baseball with Marlene. The reaction was instantaneous. Irene was furious, screaming, "What kind of treatment is this?" Marvin protested that he was paying for all this and he was not going to pay for talk about baseball. Robin attempted to be the peacemaker, but was drowned out by Irene who demanded to know why we had arrived at the end of the session without engaging her treatment plan. She accused the psychologist of incompetence, whereupon Robin defended him, saying, "I think Dr. Cummings is wonderful. We all need to hug each other." Then she caught a glimpse of the rubber tree, which was now a heap of rubble, and abruptly stopped talking.

The therapist took advantage of the pause and assigned homework. "Irene, your treatment plan is incomplete and lacking authenticity. Your assignment is to write a new treatment plan." He then instructed Marvin to write a brief about parliamentary procedures in therapy and be prepared to chair the meeting. Embarrassed, Marvin confessed, "I'm not really an authority on patients' rights." The therapist then asked, "How about divorce. Are you an authority on why you are paying such high alimony?" Irene became furious all over again.

At this moment Carol interjected, "What am I going to do? The therapist replied, "Well, I want you to tell us what you are doing to get ready for college and where you will be going to college." This was based on Irene's initial 60-page treatise, which revealed that Irene was determined that Carol would stay home, attending college via the subway, while Carol was just as adamant that she would go away to school.

Robin asked, "What do you want me to do?" The therapist quickly responded, "I want you to bring me a new rubber tree." By this time everyone except Marlene, who was enjoying seeing her family "out-kooked," thought the therapist was very strange. The identified patient was the only one who really understood what the therapist was doing.

Marlene asked, "What do you want me to do?" She was told her job would be to grade everyone on how well they did their respective homework. Marlene stood up smiling, as if having gotten the cue she was ending the session. She appeared to be much taller than her 5-foot stature.

During the ensuing week, both Marvin and Robin called the psychologist to ask what he was doing and what he hoped to accomplish. They were instructed to ask at the second session. Unless it was an emergency, the psychologist wanted everyone present whenever there was any communication whatsoever. They seemed annoyed, but resigned. Irene called, left a message, then called back to cancel it.

Marlene came in the next session looking absolutely smashing. She was totally different from the first session in which she looked drab, as if she had just been waiting on tables for eight hours. She was well dressed, well groomed. She brought a compilation of the batting averages of her favorite players because the therapist had confessed ignorance. She brought this in a chart and she was prepared to criticize everybody's homework.

It was learned at this point that Marlene and Marvin once had a very close relationship to the point where Irene used to complain about it and said, "I want to have another daughter and that one is going to be mine." So, she had Carol. It was part of the family understanding that Marlene would be Marvin's daughter and Carol would be Irene's daughter. Following the divorce, Irene had both children. With the beginning of adolescence Marlene showed no rebelliousness, but began to do poorly in school. She would daydream in school and disappear after recess or between class changes, only to be found later just wandering around the hall. She was constantly accused of playing hooky as she would just wander away in a kind of daze. As soon as Marlene was 18, she left home, got a job as a waitress, and did not speak to her mother until three years ago.

It was also learned at this time that her mother had been in psychotherapy for 22 years. Marvin was in orthodox psychoanalysis with a very well known psychoanalyst since the year before his divorce. So, that made 18 years. Robin was in treatment with about six people as she was one of the growth circuit people who are constantly pursuing therapy fads.

Marlene had been in treatment with four psychiatrists. After each psychotic break, the family changed her psychotherapist. Thus the current therapist was number five. One of the things he did immediately was to have a psychopharmacologist physician colleague change Marlene's medication. The physician put her on Melaril, discontinued the lithium, and started the appropriate blood tests.

Irene and Marvin said, "Of course we can continue our other therapy while we're being seen in family therapy here?" The therapist turned to Marlene, "Marlene, what do you think about that?" She said, "I think that's crazy." So he then replied, "Okay, you can't. You don't have to terminate your therapy, just interrupt it for a while. I'm only going to have a few sessions with you." Marvin said, "A few sessions?" He replied, "Yes," and turned to Marlene and said, "Do you think I could stand any more than that?" She said, "Of course you couldn't. Nobody could." Then he said, "I think that we can make the sacrifice for Marlene's family therapy here." It was so stated because they had each called and referred to it as "Marlene's family therapy." The therapist then concluded, "You can make that sacrifice and not see your shrinks for a few weeks." At this point, Robin made the biggest protest. She was not in therapy just weekly, she was in something everyday. Eventually they all agreed.

The therapist then turned to the homework and called upon Irene first. She had condensed her treatment plan to five pages. Marvin, on the other hand, had prepared an extensive legal brief that concluded that only the therapist could chair the meeting. "You are the doctor and you are responsible because you are the expert." Robin had brought in a gorgeous new rubber tree, complete with ceramic vase. The psychologist ignored it until Robin, unable to stand it any longer, asked, "Where do you want the new plant?" She was told she could put it anywhere. She replaced the old tree in the exact same spot and took the remains of the old tree out into the waiting room. Then she returned and stood admiring the new tree, but she made no attempt to hug it.

Marlene rated Robin's rubber plant an "A" and she flunked Irene and Marvin. As she failed them she said, "All my life my father only knows two ways to talk to me. Either as a lawyer or he talks baby talk." The therapist then said, "Marvin, we've seen the law side of you, now talk baby talk with Marlene." He was very embarrassed. Marlene started talking baby talk with him. Indeed, they had a language. They did talk baby talk. It was quite remarkable.

Irene was flunked by Marlene because she said, "My mother has always tried to be my psychologist and I resented it. This is why after I left home at 18 I never talked to her until my first hospitalization." It was during Marlene's psychoses that her mother was in her glory. She arranged the hospitalizations, and she chose the psychiatrist and every subsequent psychiatrist.

Why, after years of stabilized crazy behavior, did this family fall apart as represented by Marlene's four psychotic breaks? During those years, Irene made a monument of her divorce, vowing to never recover from it while making Marvin pay for his leaving her. Marvin responded by pitting Irene and Robin against each other as they both fought for Marvin's attention. So, what had changed? The answer to that would be the operational diagnosis. Carol had changed and, by so doing, she changed all the family dynamics.

Carol was about to leave home and Irene could not tolerate this. She had lost Dick to the institution. Marlene, who was Marvin's favorite, at least had been with her until age 18. Since that time, Marlene had refused to see or talk with her mother. If, indeed, she ever had Marlene, she definitely lost her when she left home at age 18. Now there was the threat she would lose Carol.

Two days before the third family session, Irene called the therapist's answering service late at night, stating it was an emergency as she had just killed someone. The therapist called her back and obtained the following story from Irene. "I was thinking this afternoon about my father's partner in business and I said, 'I wonder if that old goat is still alive?' And as I was going to bed and having my cup of hot chocolate and reading the newspaper, I saw on the obituary page that he had just died. I killed him."

It was now clear that Irene's own latent schizophrenia could decompensate and become overt. The therapist calmed her and then stated emphatically, "No, no, Irene, you didn't kill him. You can't kill people by thoughts and also I want you to read that obituary carefully. You will find out that he died yesterday and you only had the thought this afternoon." "Oh," she said. "Oh, okay." Then she settled down and we terminated the phone call.

At the next session, the whole family discussed where Carol was going to go to college. She had done her homework on time but the family had not gotten to it the previous week. Carol was very adamant about the fact that she was going to go away to college. She was not going to commute to college from home. Her mother brought up every possible objection. Her father had given her, for high school graduation, a compact car. Her mother was saying that if she ever had a wreck in a small car she'd be killed because it lacked the protection of size. And what are the ground rules going to be, what time will she have to be in the dormitory at night?

Well, it became very clear that this mother was having a very difficult time letting go of Carol. So, it was hypothesized that if we could settle Irene's empty nest syndrome, it would not only help Carol get to college, but Marlene would not have to continue having psychotic breaks. Mother seemed to be precipitating Marlene's active psychosis in a pathetic plea that if she could not have Carol, she would get Marlene back. At this time, everyone recalled Marlene's first break at age 13 to 14 in school. Irene came through for Marlene and helped her regain some semblance of stability. But Marlene intuitively realized that her future was that of being mother's dependent invalid, and she fled as soon as she could. Irene, on the other hand, was saying that if she lost Carol she would settle for a "crippled" Marlene. She would be Marlene's real therapist and, since she hired and fired the psychiatrists, she would thwart their helping Marlene.

All of this was openly discussed at the third family session. Marvin was amazed and said, "I do think you're right." Robin was quietly sympathetic as she silently and genuinely reached out to Irene.

Irene began to talk of her own mother's divorce and remarriage. Irene's father disappeared after her mother left him to marry the very wealthy stepfather. There was then a half-sister who was her mother's favorite. The mother died first, and when the wealthy stepfather died, all the money went to the half-sister. Irene got nothing and she saw this as the story of her life. She lost Marvin to Robin, Dick to the institution, and now Carol to her independence. She would at least have Marlene. She wept profusely. The family wept in empathy.

Irene's homework at this point was to find what she would do with her loneliness because Carol and Marlene, indeed, were going to stand on their own two feet. The therapist gently said, "I don't want your treatment plan for Marlene. I want your treatment plan for Irene."

The family came to the fourth session and by this time everybody had stopped being "kooky." They were being cooperative human beings. Robin and Irene had grown close. Robin was feeling empathic toward Irene, saying "I know how you feel. When Marvin and I got married, I immediately wanted to have a child and Marvin said no, that he already had three children and he didn't want any more. I felt alone and left out."

So, at this point everything focused on Irene's treatment plan for herself. It was quite remarkable. She agreed in her treatment plan that Carol should indeed go away to college, Marlene should indeed do what she wanted, and if it suited her to be a waitress, she should continue to be a waitress.

It was also evident that Marvin was the one who most objected to Marlene's being a waitress. Her mother was perfectly happy and realized it was Marvin who wanted her to go to college. He said, "When she was a little girl, I fantasized that she would become a lawyer." Within several weeks of termination, Marlene went out and got a waitress job, but she also enrolled in an A.A. program at the community college to become a paralegal.

With full family consent, the family therapy was terminated after the five sessions, and Irene began individual sessions with the psychologist.

LEGEND

Psychological Mechanism:	Withdrawal (delusions)
Diagnosis:	Schizo-affective Psychosis
Operational Diagnosis:	Empty Nest Syndrome
Implicit Contract:	Keep Marlene the identified patient
Personality Type:	Onion
Homework:	Extensive and varied by family members
Therapeutic Technique:	Psychojudo with a family

4
Structuring the Episode

In brief, intermittent psychotherapy it is expected that patients will have episodes of treatment throughout the life cycle. For each treatment episode the focused psychotherapist must answer four questions:

1. *Who's presenting?* The psychotherapist makes a differential diagnosis, which will inform him or her about the psychodynamics of the patient and the entry points to treatment.
2. *Why now?* The psychotherapist makes an operational diagnosis to determine the precipitating incident that brings the patient to seek psychotherapy at this particular time.
3. *What for?* The psychotherapist determines the implicit contract of the patient, which often differs from the stated, explicit request.
4. *How?* The psychotherapist formulates homework, a behavioral assignment that enables the patient to continue the process of change between sessions. Homework operationalizes the therapeutic contract.

Answering these questions will enable the therapist to structure effectively the episode of psychotherapy. The differential diagnosis may be stable over time, but personality is layered and different dynamics may be in play at different times. Clearly, "Why now," "What for," and "How" are questions that must be answered specific to the current episode. To a certain extent, these questions should be considered not only in each episode but also in each session of psychotherapy.

Who's Presenting?—The Differential Diagnosis

There are two broad categories that can usefully differentiate patients according to implications for treatment. Defense mechanisms can be divided into two kinds: onion and garlic. After eating onions, one suffers their aftertaste with each burp or swallow. On the other hand, after eating garlic, one no longer is aware of the garlic odor, but everyone around suffers the smell. Similarly, there are patients who suffer (onion) and patients who cause others to suffer (garlic). As a general therapeutic axiom: Always treat garlic before onion. Denial is at the core of garlic psychodynamics and cannot be broken by onion therapy, which is guilt reduction. Reducing guilt in a garlic patient is like pouring gasoline on a fire, but psychotherapists do it because training in psychotherapy has been mainly onion therapy. Garlic patients may feign guilt, but they are actually upset about the trouble they are in. When you reduce the anxiety in a garlic patient, they will lose their motivation for treatment and leave saying, "Goodbye, Doc, I didn't need you in the first place." With onion patients, it is legitimate to relieve some of their pain as soon as possible.

If you remember *garlic before onion*, you can reduce your therapeutic failures significantly. Because so many garlics have onion underneath, they will sense your vulnerability as a caring, empathic person and dangle onion in front of you. You must work through the garlic defenses before doing onion therapy.

In addition to the onion-garlic dimension, patients must be differentiated as to whether they are analyzable or not. Analyzable patients can benefit from uncovering therapy, understand through reasoning, and obtain change through insight into their behavior. Nonanalyzable patients deteriorate with uncovering therapy and learn by action and consequences rather than by reason or insight. The narcissistic and borderline personalities straddle the analyzable-nonanalyzable line because, while they share many similarities, they present very different therapeutic challenges. Both show low ego strength, low self-control, the tendency to perversions, addictions, and acting out. The narcissistic personality, however, has a pervasive sense of vulnerability so that at the point when they are ready to plunge the knife and destroy you as a therapist, they pull their arm back because they feel terrified of having to live without you. The borderline will go ahead and destroy you, hang your scalp on his/her belt, and go on to the next therapist. The narcissistic personality will eventually respond to insight. The borderline personality will deteriorate with uncovering therapy.

In the second half of this book, "Onion and Garlic Psychodynamics," 14 diagnostic categories are presented on a fourfold table created along these two dimensions. The objective of the differential diagnosis is to determine which diagnostic category most aptly fits the psychodynamics of the patient. This simple chart, however, belies the complexity of fully assessing the interplay of psychodynamics and life events that are impacting the patient's personality at any time. The following case of Marla illustrates this.

One of the most difficult therapeutic decisions is that of threatening the garlic while postponing treatment on the onion's guilt and suffering. The more onion the basic personality, the greater the therapist's difficulty. The epitome of onion is the all-suffering agoraphobic. For this reason, the 10 percent to 15 percent of agoraphobics who become addicted to either tranquilizers or alcohol as a way of surviving in the face of restricting phobias are almost always missed by the psychotherapist. Addictions are denial, thus, always garlic. It is as if the therapist cannot face the therapeutically painful task at hand. It is easier to overlook the garlic.

The case of Marla demonstrates the futility of treating the underlying onion before addressing the overlay of garlic, in this instance chemical dependency. This also illustrates the technique of being prepared to deny treatment if the patient is not willing to make a commitment to abstinence.

Case Illustration: Marla—Garlic over Onion

Such a case was that of Marla, a housebound agoraphobic who failed to make even the slightest gains in her desensitization program. In contrast to the people-pleasing compliance of the agoraphobic, Marla was belligerent and highly resistive, with scores of excuses why she had not done her homework. After over eight months of therapeutic standoff, her highly skilled psychologist, who specialized in phobias, referred Marla in total exasperation. The psychologist had completely missed the severe garlic overlay. The psychologist was blinded not only by the severe phobias, but also by the tragedy the patient had suffered.

Marla was a 33-year-old single woman who lived with her 35-year-old lover, Dave. She had created a unique and successful public accounting business serving small businesses, the majority of which could be characterized as mom-and-pop operations. Marla had a well-equipped van she would drive to her clients' places of business, where she would either work on their business books on the spot or take the more complicated work with her. Her agoraphobia threatened the loss of her highly successful practice.

The patient eagerly accepted the referral to the new psychologist and she spent the first part of the session complaining that her former psychologist had actually exacerbated her condition. Marla's phobias began 19 months earlier following a severe auto accident that necessitated two plastic surgeries to repair scars on her face. The initial phobia was the fear of driving, which became so intense that she could not service her clients. Dave, an insurance adjuster who had total control of his own schedule, literally saved Marla's bookkeeping practice by becoming her chauffeur. Recently, Dave had begun to protest, and was threatening to leave the relationship of four years.

Dave and Marla had set three different dates to be married, but each was postponed at Marla's insistence. This was the real reason why Dave was about to break off the relationship. At the present time, Marla made it clear she could not marry until she had recovered from her severe phobias, which had grown to the point that she could not leave the house without Dave. She resisted any insight into her ambivalence in her love life, and denied in advance that her phobias had anything to do with her not wanting to get married right now.

The greatest denial was reserved for her Valium and alcohol addictions. Marla's phobias began about four years ago when her relationship with Dave became serious. Shortly after the setting of the first marriage date, Marla began to experience panic attacks while driving. She was prescribed Valium by her physician and this enabled her to continue her itinerant bookkeeping business. On especially difficult days, she added alcohol to the Valium, and soon Marla was self-medicating herself to the point of nearly perpetual intoxication. The day of the auto accident, she had had considerable wine to drink on top of her Valium, a fact that Marla reluctantly admitted to her therapist only after several sessions and after she became totally abstinent. The matter of her alcohol/Valium blood level at the time of the accident had become a significant issue in her pending lawsuit against the driver who hit her.

From the first session, Marla's addiction was obvious to the psychologist. Her hands were tremulous, her eyes were bloodshot, her speech was slurred, and her patience was thin. Her behavior would become belligerent whenever her denial was threatened. Marla did not give up her alcohol and Valium without a fight. After explaining that treatment was futile as long as she relied on her addiction, abstinence was made a condition for continuing treatment. "All insight is soluble in alcohol" and, until she was "clean," therapy would continue to be the same waste of time the previous eight months had been with her first psychologist.

Once abstinent, Marla lost her garlic demeanor. She became timid, guilt-ridden, and self-effacing, but her treatment proceeded in earnest. She faced her fear of marriage, eagerly performed her homework, and had desensitized herself within two months. She accepted her responsibility to say either "Yes" or "No" to Dave regardless of the consequences, and in time she said "Yes." Dave and Marla are married. She remains sober and has learned to retreat and then desensitize herself whenever her phobias threaten her during difficult times in her life.

LEGEND

Psychological Mechanism:	Denial, Displacement
Diagnosis:	Agoraphobia, Alcohol Dependence
Operational Diagnosis:	Previous therapist gave up
Implicit Contract:	Don't treat my drinking
Personality Type:	Onion attempting to hide garlic
Therapeutic Techniques:	Addictive Therapy (abstinence) followed by Desensitization

Why Now?—The Operational Diagnosis

In addition to bonding, the ideal goal for the first session is to determine the operational diagnosis and the implicit contract. Without these two, the effectiveness of a treatment plan will be based on luck. The operational diagnosis tells you why the patient is coming in now instead of last week, last year, or next month. Patients respond in many different ways to the seemingly simple question, "What brings you in for treatment now?"

A patient may say, "I'm here because I drink too much, and I want to stop." Accepting that overlooks the fact that this patient has probably been drinking too much for years. So why is he seeking treatment now? Finding out that after 10 years of threatening, his wife finally kicked him out of the house gets you closer to the operational diagnosis.

The operational diagnosis assesses the motivation of the patient. By identifying the event precipitating the treatment episode, the therapist can more clearly understand the pain that leads the patient to seek psychotherapy at this particular time. In this example, the patient may not want to stop drinking. The pain is the impending loss of his marriage and the patient may want psychotherapy solely to patch things up with his wife. A treatment plan to achieve abstinence will be met with resistance unless the implicit contract of the patient is addressed and a therapeutic contract agreed to.

When it is difficult to determine the operational diagnosis, this simple question is often useful: "What were you thinking the precise moment you picked up the phone and called for an appointment? Don't tell me what you were thinking last week, last year. Tell me what you were thinking the moment you decided to pick up the phone." Many patients have thought of making an appointment many times before, but they never called. What was pushing them to go through with it this time?

The importance of the operational diagnosis is clear in the case below. The wrong operational diagnosis would have resulted in initiating bereavement counseling, with the strong possibility that the patient would have committed suicide.

Case Illustration: Arthur to Ashes

I was asked to sit in on an intake session with an elderly man who was in tears. He had been widowed about 11 months ago. The therapist immediately started bereavement counseling. I interrupted, saying, "Whoa. We don't have an operational diagnosis." I began interviewing the man and asked, "If your wife died 11 months ago, why are you coming in now?"

"Well," he said, "I have one more thing to do. I have to scatter my wife's ashes in the Atlantic." He had them in an urn. His wife had been cremated.

I asked, "You cremated your wife?"

He started crying, "Yes, I never should have done it."

I said, "Aren't you Jewish? Isn't that against your religion?"

He said, "Yes. I never should have done it. I never should have done it."

I kept probing. His wife had terminal cancer. She was in excruciating pain. They made a pact that he would poison her. He would have her cremated so in case anybody got suspicious, they wouldn't be able to detect the poison and have him stand trial for murder. They also agreed that within a year he would scatter her ashes into the Atlantic and then poison himself. I said, "When is the year?"

He said, "A week from Monday."

If we had continued bereavement counseling with this depressed man, he would be dead today. Do not assume just because somebody is widowed that bereavement is the issue. Listen for self-recrimination and loathing which signals depression. In bereavement, what you hear is longing: I keep looking for my husband. I keep looking for my wife. When I hear footsteps, I think my husband's coming home; he walked like that. Oh, I hear my wife's high heels coming. You're missing the person. If you have uncomplicated bereavement, do bereavement counseling. If you have depression mixed in with the bereavement, stop the bereavement counseling, treat the depression, and then at some point you can go back to the bereavement counseling.

I spoke very bluntly to him: "It's very obvious from everything you're feeling right now, that you really feel you did wrong in cremating your wife." He was an Orthodox Jewish man and felt guilty about the cremation. The poisoning, he felt, was compassionate and humanitarian. She apparently was in terrible pain. So I said to him: "Look, you say you did wrong. Now you're going to compound the wrong? By poisoning yourself and leaving instructions to be cremated and having your ashes scattered in the Atlantic? You're going to do two wrongs. Two wrongs make a right, huh?"

While we are talking like this, he is crying the whole time. He made a nonsuicide pact, we nullified the agreement with his wife. We went over it again and again as if I were his lawyer making a contract. God only knows why they made the pact for him to kill himself. They had been married 44 years. At the moment that they made the decision to use poison, he may have said, "I don't think I could live without you." She may have said, "Then why don't you join me?" Who knows? There were very intense emotions when they made that pact.

LEGEND

Psychological Mechanism:	Introjection covered by Denial
Diagnosis:	Rage depression primary to bereavement
Operational Diagnosis:	It is time to kill myself
Implicit Contract:	Do I deserve to die?
Personality Type:	Onion
Therapeutic Techniques:	Rewrite death contract

What for?—The Implicit Contract

The implicit contract, in contrast to the operational diagnosis, which tells you why the patient is coming in now, tells you what the patient is coming into treatment for. The implicit contract always bears the resistance. If the difference between the implicit contract and the explicit contract is too great, therapy will be sabotaged. Therapy might sometimes proceed well without having ferreted out the implicit contract, but it will take longer.

Returning to the example of the patient whose explicit contract is "Help me stop drinking," if the operational diagnosis is "My boss said that he'll fire me if I have liquor on my breath after lunch one more time," he really does not want to become abstinent. Even though the explicit contract is, "Help me quit drinking," the implicit contract might be, "Show me how not to drink during the day except on the weekends so that I can drink everyday after 5:00 and all weekend." Or if the patient is the kind of alcoholic who never makes it to work on Monday because he has been on a weekend binge, the implicit contract may be: "Show me how to stop early enough Sunday night so I can get to work on Monday morning." The implicit contract of the alcoholic whose wife threatened to kick him out might be, "Gee, maybe if I come into therapy, my wife will be impressed and take me back home, and I won't have to quit drinking." Each, however, will say, "Help me stop drinking." Most therapists accept the explicit contract at face value, even though it is the implicit contract that determines the course of treatment.

In every first session, every patient will throw out to us the implicit contract, although it may be as an aside. Our patients will tell us in an inadvertent way when we are most distracted, when we are most hooked into their content or most impressed with their psychological mindedness, their motivation, or their great empathy. We learned to do this as children. Junior breaks mother's favorite vase. He is afraid to tell mother, cleans it up, and throws it in the garbage can, thinking mother is not going to find out. He feels guilty, however. After three days, he can't stand it any longer as he fears, "She knows. She knows." So Junior waits until mother is on the phone talking to a friend and in the middle of a conversation, he tugs on her apron and says, "Mommy, I smashed your vase." Mother says, "Yes, I know, Junior. Go watch television." Mother never heard him. Junior says, "Whew, I told her. Now I don't have to feel guilty any more."

Let's take the example of a middle-aged spinster who looks up and makes an appointment with a handsome young male psychologist. In the course of the first session she says, "I'm glad you have a comfortable office because I'm going to be here a long time." It is said as an aside to the barrage of her explicit contract: She has a terrible principal who doesn't understand her or back up the classroom teachers, and her terrible students slash teachers' tires when they flunk. When the therapist is concentrating on this poor woman's life and the 10 more years of torture before she can retire, she slips in the remark about the comfortable office. By not responding to this, the therapist has made a contract for long-term therapy. The patient will conclude, "Well, I told him. Everything's okay. We all know why I'm here." The therapist has agreed not only to long-term therapy, but also to be nontherapeutic during this time. This young man didn't realize until a year and a half later that he was her weekly date in her otherwise dateless life. Nothing happens therapeutically because the patient is trying to get gratification rather than gain understanding or effect change in her life. The saddest part is that the therapist is not dealing with the real pain this woman has.

Suppose you elicit an implicit contract that you know is not therapeutic and cannot be accomplished. With most patients, the best approach is to outrightly discuss it with the patient.

For example, a man may come in and say, "I want to save my marriage. I've been very bad. I've not been fair to my wife. I've been having an affair for the last three years. I want to save my marriage. I know it's my fault. I don't need couples' therapy because it's all me. My wife is wonderful." About halfway through the session, he sighs and says, "I'm afraid, no matter what I do, we'll probably end up in divorce."

He just threw out the implicit contract. It is appropriate to ask him, "You know, I don't hear something right. If you've already decided to divorce your wife, why are you seeing me?" In the course of discussion, it turns out the operational diagnosis is that after three years of hearing him promise that he would leave his wife, his mistress will not take it any longer and has given him an ultimatum, "You either leave your wife or you can't see me any more." His unconscious fantasy is, "I will come into therapy. My mistress will be impressed. I will say to her, 'How can you rush me. Wait until I work this out in therapy.' If I can get into long-term therapy, I can have my wife and my mistress for another three years." Missing this, you have just made a contract to be nontherapeutic.

More succinctly stated, his implicit contract was, "Let me appease my mistress and my guilt so I can have both my wife and mistress as long as possible before getting a divorce." Unconsciously, he planned to use therapy to hold off his mistress for another three years. But, at some point, he would have to leave his wife to go with the mistress. Then he would want to be able to say to his family and friends, "I did everything in the world to save my marriage, including going into psychotherapy."

This must be discussed with him. "This is not a legitimate way to go. You have to make up your mind. Now if you want to come in to save your marriage, that's a legitimate thing to work on. If you want to come in to stall your mistress for three years, I'm sorry. I have too many patients who want to see me so I don't have time to play that game with you." Now, with this kind of man, an intellectually honest kind of person, nothing sociopathic about him, even though he is being manipulative, it will take hold. Unless we are dealing with the garlic patient, the implicit contract is just below the patient's awareness and he/she grabs it when it is presented. The more you can use the words the patient uses to talk to himself, the more effective it will be.

He responded, "My god, my god. You're right. I don't know what to do."

The therapist responded, "I don't know what you're going to do either, but I want you to take a week and think about it and come back next week and tell me what you want to come here for. This time I want you to really reach down into your kishkas and come up with the reason. I don't want any of this B.S."

He came in the next week and said, "I've wrestled all week where I want to be, and I've really decided that I want to stay with my wife and children. I want help in extricating from my mistress."

With other patients, the approach is to go with the resistance and bring it around, as in the case described earlier of the woman supporting a man who wouldn't work. With this kind of woman, if you sat down and discussed with her, "You're not able to leave this man right now because of your low self-esteem or poor interpersonal skills," the therapy would not have progressed as efficiently as if you just went with the resistance. She would have agreed, and after spending many weeks in skills training and raising her self-esteem by various means, she still would not have been able to leave her husband.

With more reasonable, open people who can learn from verbal insight, discussing the implicit contract with them might be the best way to go. With garlic patients, discussion is ineffective because they are in denial. They will look you right in the face and say, "No, Doctor. That isn't it at all." The woman in this case was a garlic enabler, and it was most effective to raise her self-esteem by allowing her to experience the futility of her implicit contract.

Resistance is real, but often it is not the main determiner of unduly protracting therapy. Very often, the therapist, having accepted the explicit contract at face value, is working toward a different goal than the patient. The patient always strives toward the implicit contract. There ensues a wrestling match between therapist and patient that unnecessarily prolongs psychotherapy.

How?—The Therapeutic Contract and Homework

The operational diagnosis and the implicit contract guide the therapist in formulating the therapeutic contract. In it's pure form, the contract says "I will never abandon you as long as you need me, and I will never ask you to do anything until you're ready. In return for this, you'll be joining me in a partnership to make me obsolete as soon as possible." The therapist must operationalize this agreement into a treatment plan with specific objectives and homework assignments to help the patient realize these objectives. Giving homework makes the patient realize that he or she is expected to be responsible for his or her own therapy. These assignments must be meaningful in light of the patient's motivations. They must also be designed to redirect rather than oppose the resistance.

Homework is at the heart of targeted, focused psychotherapy. It is the critical feature that convinces patients that they are truly partners in their own treatment. It should be given at every session, and never in a perfunctory or dispirited manner. Too often, overworked psychotherapists assign homework in a manner that telegraphs to the patient that the therapist does not really regard it as important. The therapist is seduced by the fascinating content of the patient's disclosures, forgetting that understanding is not measured by what the patient says, but by demonstrable changes in behavior and attitudes. Homework is intended to be the first line of behavioral change, opening the door to increasingly greater changes.

Homework must be inspired in its construction and assignment. It must fit the immediate therapeutic needs of the patient. No matter how cleverly contrived, if it does not respond to the moment in this individual patient, it will be of only limited value. Therefore, there is no cookbook of homework from which the therapist can choose items to assign. Homework must always be individually tailored.

The exercises usually found in self-help books are only generally useful. They have demonstrated value in psychoeducational groups, and even in some group therapies, but in individual psychotherapy the homework must reflect the therapist's understanding of the individual patient. As such, homework requires attention to several critical rules.

The homework must not violate the therapist's contract with the patient that he or she will not be asked to do something until able to do so. If the assignment is too hard, it will hinder the therapy. The patient will either feel hopeless or will resent the therapist's betrayal of the therapeutic promise. On the other hand, if the homework is too easy, the patient will lack a sense of accomplishment and will feel either unworthy or, again, hopeless.

The therapist cannot assign homework until both the implicit contract and the operational diagnosis have been determined. To do otherwise will most likely result in the assigned homework being in direct, but undetected, confrontation with the resistance. Accordingly, it will fail along with the therapy. The homework must go in the direction of the resistance, while at the same time having the propensity to diffuse it.

Some brief cases may help illustrate the foregoing principles of homework. The first (discussed in more detail on pages 42–43) is a patient for whom the homework was a paradoxical intention, designed not to strong-arm her resistance, but to address her implicit contract that her lover could be changed. Previously presented to illustrate "psychojudo," it is discussed here to demonstrate how this technique may be incorporated into homework.

Case Illustration: Paula's der Stunken

Paula, a restaurant server in her twenties, asked for help in leaving her abusive live-in male lover who had not worked in two years, and whom we shall call der Stunken. To have accepted this explicit contract, would have violated her implicit contract, which the therapist skillfully discerned. Paula was looking for ways to change the lover. The operational diagnosis (Why is she coming in now?) was the lover's sudden interest in another woman. The therapist assigned the homework that the patient do three things she had never done before that would cause her boyfriend to love her. When the following week she described what she had done to no avail, the therapist reassigned the same homework, stating: "I am still not convinced you have done *everything* possible to make him love you." This, of course, is what the patient unconsciously was saying to herself. After three weeks of this assignment, the patient came in and reported she had left der Stunken, stating for the first time that there was nothing that was going to cause him to change, as he would remain worthless. To her surprise, within 36 hours he moved in with another woman. The patient discovered that there is a shortage of der Stunkens, as there are so many unfortunate women with low self-esteem ready to be victimized.

LEGEND

Psychological Mechanism:	Displacement
Diagnosis:	Hysterical Personality
Operational Diagnosis:	I fear he is getting ready to leave me
Implicit Contract:	Help me change him through my love
Personality Type:	Onion
Homework:	Love him even more
Therapeutic Techniques:	Paradoxical intention

In the next case example the operational diagnosis and the implicit contract together expected that the therapist would somehow return the spouse and children without the patient having to change. By verbalizing the patient's implicit demands as if to have made these his own, the therapist forces the patient into the position of taking the therapist's role.

Case Illustration: Leonard the Lush

Leonard at 43 asked for help in quitting drinking. He had been an alcoholic for many years. His wife had taken the children and left him (operational diagnosis). In keeping with the fact that no addict really wants to quit, Leonard's implicit contract was: "Help me cut down enough to get my wife back. Also, take me back to the halcyon days when I could control my drinking." The therapist challenged the patient's motivation indirectly by suggesting he need not become abstinent. "You've been conning your wife for 15 years. What do you need to do to con her for another 15 years?" If done well, this challenge externalizes the patient's implicit contract, placing the patient in the unlikely role of speaking as the doctor: "No, I must quit. My health and my marriage are both in jeopardy. I can't just con her and myself anymore." This sets the patient up for the first homework, which is to prove to a skeptical therapist that he really wants to quit drinking. In Leonard's case, it was decided that seven days "cold turkey" would convince the therapist of his determination, and earn the patient a second appointment. The length of the period of abstinence must fit the rule of being something the patient can accomplish without its being too easy. Learning from the patient the length of his spontaneous abstinences, as all alcoholics occasionally put themselves "on the wagon," reveals the length of time for the homework. With some patients it can be two weeks, for others two days, and at times only half a day.

LEGEND

Psychological Mechanism:	Denial
Diagnosis:	Alcohol Addiction
Operational Diagnosis:	Wife has left me
Implicit Contract:	Help me get my wife back by just cutting down on drinking
Personality Type:	Garlic
Homework:	Abstinence
Therapeutic Technique:	Denying treatment

In addressing the implicit contract, it is important in assigning homework that the therapist always bear in mind the therapeutic contract, which states, "I will never ask you to do something until you are able. . . ." In the following example, the therapist skillfully tailored the homework to that which the patient could realistically accomplish, and then enforced it.

Case Illustration: Thelma's Therapist

Thelma was transferred from another therapist. A 28-year-old patient with a borderline personality, Thelma had been indulged by her therapist and allowed unlimited "emergency" phone calls. Her abuse of this ploy clearly had to be limited, and this would be her homework. But Thelma could not go from unlimited phone calls to none. A careful scrutiny with the patient of her phone calls revealed an average of three critical calls in a two-week period. Thelma, therefore, was limited to three calls per two weeks as part of her homework. She could save up unused allowable calls, giving her further incentive to wean herself away from the manipulative overdependency. Thelma used up her first three phone calls in the first week, and discovered that in keeping with their agreement the therapist did not respond to the next call.

LEGEND

Psychological Mechanism:	Projective Identification; Splitting
Diagnosis:	Borderline Personality Disorder
Operational Diagnosis:	Abandoned by previous therapist
Implicit Contract:	I shall continue to demand unlimited attention
Personality Type:	Garlic
Homework:	Limit emergencies
Therapeutic Technique:	Setting limits (boundaries)

Prescribing the symptom is often useful when the patient has converted anger into a psychophysiological symptom. In the following case of Arlo, he was manifesting his anger at his wife by denying her sexual satisfaction through his impotence. His operational diagnosis had to do with his realization that he was as deprived of satisfaction as was his spouse. His implicit contract had to do with wanting to continue punishing his wife while exempting himself from the deprivation. Many men resolve this dual need through premature ejaculation: The man has an orgasm immediately on entering, leaving the woman frustrated. The therapist sought to prevent the substitution of premature ejaculation for total lack of erection by a homework that mobilized the defiance toward the therapist and away from the spouse.

Case Illustration: Arlo and His Rhino

Arlo had suffered from performance anxiety all of his life, but at 38 he was now impotent every time he attempted sexual intimacy. Arlo's case, like the cases of most such patients, was reminiscent of the story of how to make gold out of dog feces. One places the dog feces in an old fashioned nut grinder. As one turns the crank, if one does not think of the word "rhinoceros" the feces will come out gold. In Arlo's case, the word "rhinoceros" was the phrase, "Will I get an erection this time?"

Of course the fearful thought would prevent the successful performance. Arlo was instructed to have sex without an erection, with the therapist stating that it was important that the patient find ways to be sexually intimate without an erection. He was strongly instructed that should an erection occur, he must suppress it. After several weeks of the symptom being prescribed, the patient found himself in defiance of the therapist's instructions, the therapist all the while decrying the noncompliance. It is imperative that a paradox of this type be maintained until the patient is ready to give up the symptom. To relax the instructions prematurely will result in the return of the symptom in even more entrenched form. In Arlo's case, this readiness occurred when the patient, himself, revealed the nature of the paradox. "I now know why you did this and I thank you."

LEGEND

Psychological Mechanism:	Intellectualization, Doing and Undoing
Diagnosis:	Obsessive Personality
Operational Diagnosis:	Impotence
Implicit Contract:	Help me be defiant without suffering
Personality Type:	Onion
Homework:	Be impotent
Therapeutic Technique:	Prescribing the symptom

In other cases, the therapy can be concluded without the patient and therapist articulating the nature of the paradoxical intention. This is not unusual in treatment with an adolescent who focuses on the action resulting from the homework and ignores the ideation. Such was the outcome with Jacob.

Case Illustration: Bringing Up Jacob's Parents

Jacob was an adolescent dragged in by his parents who complained he never performed his chores. In an individual session with Jacob, the patient insisted that his parents did not care about him, for when he did one chore it was not acknowledged. They continued to forbid his use of the family car and withheld other privileges. The therapist expressed interest in determining how far "out to lunch" his parents were. He suggested Jacob perform two chores the next week and see whether his parents noticed.

Jacob, of course, reported in the next session that his three (not two) performed chores were completely ignored by the parents. Increasingly over the next several weeks resulted in Jacob's doing all of the expected chores. The patient was smug in his parents' not acknowledging them, while at the same time the parents confided in the therapist that Jacob was a changed boy, but they were afraid to mention it because he might revert to his former obstinacy. Jacob's smugness included the fact that his out-to-lunch parents were now allowing his privileges, including liberal use of the family car.

LEGEND

Psychological Mechanism:	Denial
Diagnosis:	Adolescent Rebellion
Operational Diagnosis:	They took away the car
Implicit Contract:	Prove my parents are jerks
Personality Type:	Garlic
Homework:	Do chores as parent trap
Therapeutic Technique:	Humoring the resistance

From the illustrations, and from the more comprehensive case histories presented in this volume, it is apparent that appropriate homework facilitates the therapeutic process. If it is presented cleverly, it will be incorporated by the patient as compatible. Yet there are times when homework in certain overly obstinate patients must be enforced. Such was the case of Roland (Chapter 6) where confronting his mother was a prerequisite to therapeutic breakthrough, and that of Grace (Chapter 3) in whom there had to be a curtailing of an infantilization of such proportions that therapy was at a standstill.

Enforcing homework is also essential in treating the special circumstances presented with anorexics, who are among the most argumentive of our patients, and with bulimics, who are the most deceitful. Both of these eating disorders pose a threat to life: in anorexics from complications of near starvation, and in bulimics from possible cancer stemming from the constant regurgitation of stomach acids through the esophagus. Both are subject to severe metabolic distress, including electrolyte imbalances. There has been considerable professional and public hysteria regarding the death rate of these cases, with one set of irresponsible statistics estimating that in 1992 about 50,000 women died of anorexia. The Centers for Disease Control and Prevention asserts that for that year there were 17 known cases of mortality. So, even though the danger is considerably less than previously believed, therapeutic caution is still indicated in these life threatening cases and homework must be strictly enforced.

The case of Melanie, an anorexic, illustrates the importance of not losing sight of possible life-threatening consequences in enforcing homework. The failure to do her homework, which was the intake of one 1,000 calorie meal per day, would not lead to denying treatment, for that might well accelerate weight loss, but rather to hospitalization, which would result in forced feeding and thus save her life.

Case Illustration: Melanie—Anything but Hospitalization

The patient had been a high school cheerleader and a very pretty and popular adolescent until age 17 when she became anorexic. Her weight had dropped in a few months from 114 to 76, and her parents and the family's physician were alarmed. Hospitalization was contemplated, and Melanie agreed to come to see the psychologist as a last and desperate attempt to avoid hospitalization. The patient manifested the perfectionism, argumentativeness, and distorted body image that are typical in anorexia. She was meticulously and fashionably dressed and coiffured. Although emaciated, she complained that the fat hung from her arms and wrists and that she had to lose more weight.

The therapist used the leverage of hospitalization to assign the homework, all under a barrage of arguments from the patient. Finally an agreement was reached. The patient would have one 1,000 calorie meal per day, and her mother, who had been given materials sufficient to assess compliance, would record and document the amount of food intake. Failure to eat a 1,000 calorie meal each day would result in Melanie being hospitalized. The agreement, along with the nutritional charts and other materials given the mother, was signed and initialled on each page as is recommended with these argumentative patients. Also, a therapeutic plan that included individual therapy, group therapy for eating disorders, and family therapy was signed and initialled on each page. Protesting and arguing each step of the way, Melanie gained weight and emerged from the physiologic danger zone. Menstruation, which had stopped, resumed when she crossed the 100-pound mark.

LEGEND

Psychological Mechanism:	Displacement; Dissociation
Diagnosis:	Anorexia Nervosa
Operational Diagnosis:	They want to hospitalize me
Implicit Contract:	Help me avoid hospitalization
Personality Type:	Garlic covering onion
Homework:	1,000 calorie per day meal
Therapeutic Technique:	Enforce the homework

It is possible at times to assign homework that cleverly blocks the patient's implicit contract. In bulimia, the implicit contract is usually the requirement that therapy enable the patient to continue denying that she is purging. The denial has been jeopardized by health problems resulting from purging: severe electrolyte imbalances or the appearance of precancerous tissue in the esophagus because of the repeated passage of stomach acid. The homework assigned to Brenda was successful in attacking her denial.

Case Illustration: Bulimic Brenda

Brenda, a fashion model at age 18, kept her fashionable, required figure by purging. She would eat enormous amounts of food, and would induce vomiting or use laxatives, or both. She came to treatment because she had made herself physically ill. She was forced to forfeit several work assignments, and her modeling career was in jeopardy. She was accompanied by her mother, who had been aware for some time of Brenda's bulimic behavior, but had been convinced several times that she had stopped her purging, only to discover that Brenda had lied again. The bulimic patient herself is so into denial that she believes her own lies. As part of this denial, the bulimic will vomit in the toilet or sink with her eyes closed, and then quickly flush or wash the vomit so as not to have to confront it.

The therapist appropriately ascertained that Brenda was not yet ready to stop purging, so he made it clear she could continue to purge, but that she would have to vomit each time into a plastic bag. She was then to freeze the bag and its contents, and bring all the frozen bags to the next session. The patient was shocked and filled with revulsion, but was told that failure to comply would result in termination of her sick leave and a possible end of her modeling career. It was the signed sick leave that was protecting her contract. Of importance here is also the therapist's own revulsion, an understandable countertransference.

Brenda's purging stopped with one incident with the plastic bag. She could no longer maintain her denial as she froze and brought the bag and its contents to therapy. She could not face bringing the bag upstairs to the office, and she and the psychologist went to the parking lot where Brenda opened the car trunk and with intense emotion revealed the bag. Her mother, who was waiting in the car, shared her daughter's revulsion which, secretly, was rivaled by that of the therapist. Brenda never purged again. It has been found that this is a very successful technique, with the purging behavior abruptly abandoned with the first bagging, although some patients go to a second bagging.

LEGEND

Psychological Mechanism:	Denial of Addiction to Food
Diagnosis:	Bulimia
Operational Diagnosis:	Behavior making her physically ill
Implicit Contract:	Restore ability to purge
Personality Type:	Garlic
Homework:	Purge into bag and save it
Therapeutic Techniques:	Prescribing the symptom
	Enforcing the homework

Part II

ONION AND GARLIC PSYCHODYNAMICS

Whereas DSM-IV diagnoses are required for insurance reimbursement, the diagnostic schema presented in "Onion and Garlic Psychodynamics" is designed solely to assist the therapist in fulfilling the clinical mission of relieving the patient of pain, anxiety, and depression in the shortest time possible. In contrast to the descriptive symptomatology of DSM-IV, this schema differentiates diagnoses according to psychodynamics and treatment implications. It differentiates patients on the two dimensions of onion–garlic and analyzable–nonanalyzable. These dimensions result in a fourfold chart in which about 90 percent of cases can be classified according to 14 diagnostic categories. This Onion–Garlic chart is presented on page 111 (Cummings, 1993).

Each diagnostic category can be described in terms of the predominant defense mechanism with which the patient approaches life, and each has an entry point that will focus and facilitate treatment. All of the analyzable onion people show a generalized defense mechanism called repression, of which there are different types. Garlic patients always show the mechanism of denial. Patients below the line show the mechanism of withdrawal from reality because of the existence of a thought disorder.

In the following chapters, the dynamics and therapeutic entry point are presented for each diagnostic category and illustrated with a case.

The Onion–Garlic Chart

	Onion (Repression)	Garlic (Denial)

ANALYZABLE	Anxiety
	Phobias
	Depression
	Hysteria/
	conversion
	Obsessive-
	  compulsive
	  personality
		Addictions
		Personality styles
		Personality
		  disorders
		Impulse neuroses
		Hypomania
		Narcissistic
		  personality

		Borderline personality
	Onion (Withdrawal)	Garlic (Withdrawal)

NON-ANALYZABLE	Schizophrenias
	  controlled by
	  individual
	  suffering
		Schizophrenias
		  controlled by
		  attacking the
		  environment
		Impulse
		  Schizophrenia

5
Onion/Analyzable

Anxiety Disorders

Dynamics

Anxiety neurosis is distinguished by its lack of defense mechanisms. Without any defense mechanism to transform or deflect the anxiety, the person feels naked anxiety and may shake 24 hours a day.

Entry

All anxiety states on presentation are overwhelming and cry out only for immediate relief. The tension, apprehension, inability to concentrate, and tremulousness add up to the patient's feeling that he or she is about to jump out of his or her skin. Under these circumstances, attempts to engage the patient in psychotherapy are futile and even cruel. The necessary entry point is anxiolytic medication to calm this patient sufficiently so that he/she can tolerate psychotherapy. It is how that medication is dispensed that makes the difference in treatment. Unfortunately, in an age when nonpsychiatric physicians freely prescribe all kinds of tranquilizers, sedatives, and anxiolytics, too often these patients get medication and nothing else. Psychotherapy to develop relaxation skills and insight into their anxiety is definitely needed.

One word of caution should be interjected here. People with personality disorders, when they are in great difficulty with the police, with authorities, with the boss, or with their spouse, tend to develop situational anxiety not over what they have done or any unconscious material, but because they are now being made uncomfortable or are being deprived of something they want. Lowering the anxiety in someone with a personality disorder who is in trouble will merely make him/her comfortable enough to leave therapy. Instead, raising the anxiety in a personality disorder is the entry point to treatment. The psychotherapist must make the differential diagnosis between a neurotic free-floating anxiety or panic and the discomfort of a personality disorder that has gotten into trouble.

Anxiety states require different treatment approaches in accordance with whether the basic, underlying personality is onion or garlic. Unless the therapist is cognizant of this, psychotherapy may never really get underway. The cases below illustrate this important difference.

Case Illustration: Ethan and Donald

Ethan, age 48, was a civil servant working in a sewage treatment plant. He had been married for 24 years and had two grown children when his spouse informed him that she wanted a divorce. A conscientious, methodical man who had always put his family first, he quickly decompensated into an anxiety state. Change had always been difficult for Ethan, and disruption was impossible. He pleaded with his spouse to tell him what he had done wrong. Factually, she had no complaints other than his being just plain dull. She confessed that married life the past several years had been tolerable only because of her secret extramarital affair. It was only a matter of time when both children were out of the home that she would leave Ethan for the other man. These disclosures were devastating to Ethan and his anxiety was so great he could neither eat nor sleep.

The anxiety grew worse and soon the patient was not able to work. Before that had happened, his co-workers urged Ethan to see a doctor for a tranquilizer. He refused on religious grounds. Early in the marriage, and in response to his spouse's prodding, Ethan had espoused the Christian Science faith. Some time ago, the spouse drifted away from the church, but Ethan continued to be a devout member. To see a physician was a violation of his religion. Instead, he was seeing a Christian Science practitioner daily with no relief from his symptoms. Finally, he accepted the advice of friends that seeing a psychologist in an attempt to save his marriage was not a violation of the prohibition against receiving medical treatment.

At the time Ethan was first seen by the psychologist, he had been in this state for almost two weeks. He paced about the office constantly, pleading "Please help me." He was seen early in the morning and again in the early afternoon. The first two sessions were spent in listening and trying to help Ethan accept medication. Initially, he staunchly refused, but eventually he agreed to a prescription in exchange for the psychologist's asking the spouse to postpone filing for divorce for two months while Ethan continued in treatment.

With the anxiolytic medication and the postponement of the divorce, the anxiety diminished rapidly and Ethan returned to his usual methodical self. He entered psychotherapy, as would be predicted from his basic onion personality, and although the divorce proceeded to conclusion, Ethan was able to adjust to the loss. Several months after psychotherapy was concluded, he came in for two sessions in which he discussed his new love for a woman in the church who had admired him secretly for several years. It was only after Ethan's divorce that she let her feelings be known.

Donald was 47 when his third wife announced she could no longer forgive his marital infidelity and was filing for divorce. She was 15 years younger than Donald, and the marriage was only six years in duration at the time of the separation. Although Donald had two children with each of his two previous wives, all four children either were or had been living with their respective mothers. His present spouse had been married once before, but only briefly, and she had no children.

When Donald first received the news from his spouse, he threw a temper tantrum of such magnitude that the police were summoned. Finding himself blocked in his aggressive acting out, Donald lapsed into a severe anxiety state that, nonetheless, did not curtail his eloquent and manipulative pleas of contrition. In fact, his wife recanted and agreed to postpone the divorce if he sought treatment for his womanizing.

In the first session, Donald manifested the vulnerability of the narcissistic personality disorder. His anxiety, which was intense, revealed the fear that he would not be able to manage without his spouse. He further exemplified the narcissistic wound that such a personality disorder experiences when he is the one who is rejected. He paced about the office, making no attempt to hide his tremulousness and apprehension. He had tried medicating himself with alcohol, but his spouse put her foot down and threatened to leave immediately if he continued to drink.

Arrangements were made through his primary care physician for Donald to receive a 48-hour supply of anxiolytic medication. This would carry him to the second psychotherapy appointment. His family medical practitioner had experienced Donald's manipulativeness several times, and he was eager to work with the psychologist. Despite these precautions, Donald manipulated a seven-day supply of medication from the nurse in a manner that has never been entirely clear. Feeling much better and with the divorce on hold, Donald missed his second appointment. Within five days, Donald was pleading to return. He was out of medication, having taken more than the prescribed dosage, and his spouse had learned that he had failed to keep his second appointment with the psychologist. She was furious and was threatening once again to reinstate the divorce proceedings.

When Donald returned, he was seen with his spouse and limits were set and agreed upon. The patient would keep semiweekly appointments, and only enough medication would be provided to carry him between appointments. Unbeknownst to the patient, the dosage was purposely kept low so that it cut the edge off the anxiety, but did not completely eliminate it. Any attempts at self-medication would terminate therapy. Both patient and spouse agreed that she would be kept informed, and any breach of the rules would require her to proceed with the divorce.

To the extent that someone with a personality disorder was able, Donald settled into psychotherapy. It was his idea to quit his job as a travelling salesman, stating it provided too many temptations and opportunities for philandering. He obtained a position selling automobiles at a local dealership and was home every night. His sales talents and manipulative ability served him well on the new job, and the couple prospered as Donald became the star salesperson at the dealership. One might say one needs garlic to do the job of garlic. The medication had been discontinued as unnecessary for some time, but the spouse, with the insistence of the psychologist, kept up the heat.

Ironically, Donald's marriage was saved whereas Ethan's marriage could not be saved.

LEGEND

Ethan:

Psychological Mechanism:	None
Diagnosis:	Anxiety state
Operational Diagnosis:	Wife's divorce
Implicit Contract:	Get my wife back
Personality Type:	Onion
Homework:	Reexamine religious prohibition
Therapeutic Techniques:	Anxiolytic medication and insight therapy

Donald:

Psychological Mechanism:	None
Diagnosis:	Anxiety state
Operational Diagnosis	Wife's divorce
Implicit Contract:	Get my wife back
Personality Type:	Garlic
Homework:	No self-medication
Therapeutic Techniques:	Partial anxiolytic therapy Turn up heat

Phobic Disorders

Dynamics

The defense mechanism in phobias is displacement. Thoughts or feelings that are unacceptable are displaced onto an event, or a situation, or a geographical location. The unacceptable thought or feeling reflects an ambivalence the patient has regarding a significant person in his or her life. The ambivalence usually started in childhood with a parent or a sibling. It has continued in adult relationships either with that same person or with a love object.

Three things are needed to develop a phobia: (1) this was the first successful response to trauma as a child; (2) the ambivalent relationship continues now into adulthood in a different form, usually with a spouse or lover. The patient both wants to leave that person but is terrified of doing so; (3) in a situation where one's mind is in neutral gear, the unacceptable thought or feeling pops up and then is displaced.

For instance, the most common phobia in America is freeways. So many hours are spent on the freeway in traffic when things slow down. Imagine being a prephobic person sitting in a traffic jam. His/her mind is in neutral gear, and suddenly the thought "I want to leave my spouse" jumps out and is displaced onto the freeway. The traffic is stopped. The person can see the exit a quarter of a mile up, but can't leave, and feels trapped. The phobia replicates the trapped feeling in the ambivalent relationship. It is a reflection of the feeling of being trapped in life with some significant person. The phobia allows the individual to escape the terror of facing his/her ambivalence. "It isn't my spouse, it's the freeway I'm afraid of."

Next while in a bank line waiting to cash a check, one's mind is in neutral gear, and the thought flashes again. Now the fear is displaced onto banks, next to supermarkets, then to the post office. It never occurs to him or her that the real fear is leaving his/her spouse or lover, or parent. With each phobia, the world shrinks and eventually one is a full-fledged agoraphobic who can't leave the house.

Such debilitating phobias must not be confused with normal phobias. Everyone has a phobia acquired around the age of three. A successful normal phobia is one that does not restrict your life. A phobia of leopards, for example, is a very successful phobia because the chances of encountering it in the course of daily life is nil. A healthy phobia bounds certain very strong feelings in your childhood. For example:

I (Nick) discovered my phobia on a mission in World War II that required evacuation by submarine. Those who have never been aboard a World War II submarine have no idea how small and confining it is. When submerged, it becomes hot, stuffy, and smelly. I had jumped out of airplanes; it never scared me. Even in combat I wasn't as terrified. In those three days I was aboard this submarine, I thought I was going to die. On a scale of 10 my anxiety was at 9 or 10 for those three days and nights. I didn't sleep a wink. I had a phobia. In my analysis, I found out where my phobia started. My mother used to punish me by locking me in a closet. It was dark, but I was a pretty clever kid and had stashed away a flashlight and reading material in the closet. She always picked one special closet because it was the darkest. I'd sit there with my flashlight, reading by the hour. She could never understand why I wasn't crying, but apparently it had its impact on me.

When I suddenly realized that they didn't expect us to get back, it replicated the hours I must have spent in that closet thinking how cruel and rejecting my mother is for doing this to me. Now the Army suddenly became my mother, and my feelings from childhood crystallized in a phobia about submarines. It has been a successful phobia, because I've lived my life very successfully for the past 50 years without going near a submarine.

Entry

The entry point in treating phobias is to train the patient to retreat before desensitization. It is imperative that the therapist remain cognizant that the entry point for phobias is to remember the concept of retreat before desensitization, with desensitization being the ultimate goal of treating the phobia or multiple phobias that most of our patients come in with. The case of Doris, a severely housebound agoraphobic, is an excellent example of how the retreat/desensitization sequence is continued throughout the treatment and becomes part of the patient's way of life after treatment.

Case Illustration: Housecall to Doris

Doris had been housebound for three years, the last six months of this in bed. She complained of 29 distinct phobias, ranging from television newscasts to the dark. She had not been out of bed for six months without the presence of her husband, upon whom she had become totally dependent. She was a full-blown, housebound agoraphobic.

As stated earlier, the entry point for treating phobics is *retreat* before desensitization, with desensitization being the ultimate goal. This approach becomes clear in the first session with Doris, which, of course, had to be a housecall because she was housebound. The therapist, on a prearranged appointment, was ushered by the husband into the bedroom where Doris greeted him with an ultimatum: "If you are here to get me out of the house, you can leave now." She was assured that not only would the therapist not attempt to get her out of the house, but if she, herself, attempted to do so, *he* would leave. In fact, he was not even going to help her leave the room, as he was there just to assess the extent of her disability. The patient's response signalled her skepticism as she pulled the bed covers tightly under her chin.

As Doris and the therapist talked about her condition and its duration, the therapist wondered if she could remove her right leg from under the covers. The patient, who was modestly dressed in pajamas, said she could, but as she did so she hastily asserted "but I'm not getting out of the house." She was again assured that no attempt would be made to even get her out of the room, and she was asked to quickly put her right leg back under the covers. This is known as "retreat before desensitization." After she had relaxed, the therapist wondered if she could do the same with the left leg. When she did, she was asked quickly to put her left leg under the covers. This procedure with one leg and then the other was repeated several times to the point of boredom. The patient was now desensitized to removing each leg from under the covers. The therapist explained his requests on the basis that after so many months in bed, it was important to determine whether she had developed any muscle weakness.

The therapist then wondered if the patient could remove both legs from under the covers. When she complied, the same procedure of retreat and eventual desensitization to the point of boredom was followed with that behavior. Each time she was reassured that no attempt would be made to get her out of the house and if for some foolish reason she attempted it herself, the therapist would leave.

Following the same tedious sequence, she successfully draped both legs over the bed without touching the floor, and then, with desensitization, touching the floor. There followed a long series of retreats and desensitizations where she was asked to stand on the right side and then on the left side of the bed. Eventually, she was walking around the room, and with each brief foray retreating back to the bed. She was doing all of this for the first time in three years without the presence of her husband. The housecall took slightly over one hour.

On the second housecall two days later, the same retreat and desensitization was applied to getting her to every room in the house. The retreat was always back to the bedroom. During these retreat-and-desensitization housecalls, it was learned how Doris, who had been housebound for two-and-a-half years but was comfortable in her kitchen, lost the ability to sit in that room. She was given some books on phobias that she began to read in the kitchen. She was overcome with extreme panic, retreated to her bed, and there she remained the six months just preceding the first housecall. Her multiple phobias included any suggestion of violence, so Doris had been reduced to watching only game shows on television. Her husband faithfully taped these programs so she could rewatch them at a time when no game shows were being broadcast.

Again meticulously following the procedures of retreat and desensitization to the point of boredom, the third housecall succeeded in getting Doris out of the house and eventually to the nearest corner on her block. The fourth session was in the therapist's office.

The phobic displacement in Doris's case was her wanting to leave her husband. In every case of phobias the therapist must look for the ambivalent relationship. It will usually be found with someone on whom the phobic person is dependent: parent, spouse, lover, close friend, employer. This person will usually have some dominant behavior toward the phobic patient, heightening the anger. But even without this, no one can accept dependency without anger toward the person on whom one is dependent. The dependency/hostility is resolved by the phobia, which makes it impossible to leave the relationship. This is why, if one does not add sufficient psychodynamic treatment along with the desensitization, the recovered phobic patient will regress back to the incapacitated phobic state when subsequently the ambivalent relationship is exacerbated by life events.

Doris had begun her adult life as a very attractive fashion model, a career that was interrupted when she married and dutifully followed her husband to his next job assignment. She had always somewhat resented her subordinate role, but this was continuously exacerbated through the years as she was asked to move 22 times, each move representing a career advancement for her husband. And each time she was asked to acquire a new home and decorate it in a manner befitting a rising corporate executive. In all these moves, her husband was so insensitive that he had not an inkling that each was a trauma for his covertly angry, but overtly dutiful, wife. The desire to leave him seemed to double with each of the 22 moves, until finally the desire was so overwhelming as to threaten to break through her own denial. A new phobia would occupy her thoughts and bolster the denial. Doris' phobias grew over the years until finally in her late fifties she manifested 29 distinct phobias and eventually was housebound and even bedridden. The tables were reversed, as now her husband was her devoted nurse.

The final outcome in this case was not only the desensitization of Doris's 29 phobias, but the complete sensitization of her husband. Beneath the neglecting behavior of a rising corporate star too busy to attend to his wife's needs was a potentially warm and loving man. With a few counseling sessions for him, he became a very attentive, caring man with whom Doris fell in love all over again.

After the first several individual sessions, Doris was treated in an agoraphobia group program, which included regular field trips and pairing with a "buddy" for practice on her own. The first three or four phobias took longer to disappear than the last two dozen, as there is an accelerated rate in recovery. Doris had expected that her worst fear, that of the dark, which had forced her most of her married life to sleep with a bright light, would be tenacious. She was pleasantly surprised when she noticed inadvertently that it was gone. Her recovery has remained stable because the ambivalent relationship, the significant dynamic in her life, had been resolved.

This case further demonstrates the melding of behavioral and dynamic forms of therapy into one treatment approach. It was important not only to desensitize Doris to her multiple phobias, but also to resolve her ambivalent relationship to her spouse. Desensitization would have proceeded without the latter, but without the resolution of the ambivalence a future relapse would be very likely.

LEGEND

Psychological Mechanism:	Displacement, Perfectionism
Diagnosis:	Agoraphobia (Multiple Phobias)
Operational Diagnosis:	Housebound and now bedridden
Implicit Contract:	I do not want to leave my husband
Personality Type:	Onion
Homework:	Desensitization practice
Therapeutic Techniques:	Housecall
	Desensitization insight
	Special agoraphobia program

Depression

After a diagnosis of depression is made, a further differentiation must be made between endogenous depression and reactive depression. Endogenous depression may be influenced by external events, but is primarily determined by biological factors. The depression in bipolar disorder is endogenous; bipolar disorder is an inherited condition, with a higher incidence among people of Eastern European Jewish origins. The disorder is best managed with a combination of medication and psychotherapy. Depression diagnosed as dysthymia or major depression must also be carefully assessed to determine whether it is fundamentally endogenous or reactive.

Reactive depression is exogenous, which means it is determined by events outside the body. Reactive depression may be masked or associated with bereavement, but the fundamental dynamic is anger directed toward the self. Patients suffering depression are onion, but depression can also typify a personality disorder. A depressive character is a garlic person who uses his/her depression as a weapon. Their "woe is me" is all over the place, and they must be treated as garlic.

The withdrawn schizophrenic and the depressed patient can present similarly and will both say, "I feel depressed." To make the differential diagnosis between schizophrenia and depression, ask the patient, "Does your mind feel like you're trying to walk in molasses up to your neck, like you're swimming in molasses. Or are your thoughts racing so fast that you can't keep up with them?" If they say, "It's like molasses," they're depressed. If they say, "My thoughts race so fast I can't keep up with them. I'm speeding," it is schizophrenia.

Dynamics

The defense mechanism in reactive depression is introjection. The goal in therapy, in dynamic terms, is to expel the introject. A reactive depression is intrapunitive. The patient is angry at someone else, but either circumstances or his psychological make-up preclude this feeling. For example, he may imagine that getting angry at his boss or spouse will result in dire consequences, or anger may have been equated with irrational violence in his childhood and thus must be avoided at all costs. Thus the only way this anger can find expression is for the patient to psychologically swallow or introject the other, and then punish the other by causing himself to suffer. We miss the mark if we try to comfort depressive patients by assuaging their guilt or shoring up their self-esteem. The real issue is their anger towards the introjected person.

Entry

The entry point with reactive depression is to expel the introject. There are two ways to do this: One is to become like the person who has been internalized and the other is to articulate to the patient what he or she is saying to him/herself. The next two cases respectively illustrate these techniques.

Case Illustration: John—Still Angry at His Father

John was a young man who dropped out of college when his father died of a heart attack. He was very depressed. This was not bereavement; this was depression. He was furious with his father. As I began to understand where he was coming from, I found out that this young man and his father had never gotten along. He had just begun working through his father–son struggle when his father dropped dead of a heart attack. This totally aborted the father–son relationship, and the son internalized the hostility and became very depressed. I learned that his sister had been the apple of his father's eye. His sister could do no wrong; he could do no right. When he graduated from high school, he was told that his father was on a business trip. He didn't find out till several years later that his father was playing golf across town. He didn't want to cancel the golf date to go to his son's graduation.

His father never had time for him. His father had time for everything else, especially his golf and his sister. This all came out in bits and pieces. He didn't sit down and tell me he hated his father. This was my surmise.

In this case, the operational diagnosis was "I got cheated! My father died before I could fix him, before I could tell him off." The implicit contract was "I'm not going to let my father get away with it!" And the only way this man had of not having let his father get away with it was to internalize his father and then beat up on himself. So, you have to understand that this man is going to resist any efforts to make him nondepressed because this is the way he's beating up his father.

I had the advantage of knowing enough about his father to intervene by acting like the father. I never take phone calls when I see a patient, but I instructed the patient coordinator to call me 15 minutes into the hour. I picked up the phone and said, "Oh, yeah. Yeah, what do you mean you can't play golf tomorrow morning? Of course we're going to play golf tomorrow morning." I stayed on the phone for 10 minutes talking about golf, this at a time when John was absolutely spilling his emotions over the floor, telling me how terrible he is, and how he doesn't care about anybody.

I got up, went out to, over to the window, and started staring out the window. He said, "What are you doing?"

I said, "Oh, I'm wondering if it's ever going to clear up, because I want to play golf later."

He complained, "You didn't hear anything I said."

I responded, "Oh, what were you saying?" Even though I had heard everything, I would systematically make comments that told John I hadn't heard anything he'd said. He would tell me something, and then five minutes later I'd say, "You know, I've always wondered about such and such," and he'd look at me and say, "I just told you about that, five minutes ago."

One day, I constructed a fake chart. I made sure that a woman's name was very prominently on the chart. In the middle of this session I reached into my desk, pulled out this chart, and started going through it. Finally, after about 10 minutes, he said, "What are you doing?"

I said, "Oh, this woman's a very difficult case. I'm really concerned about her." I was replicating John's relationship to his sister. John increasingly got angrier and angrier and angrier. I did this for several weeks.

If you use this intervention, don't stop it until the anger's all out. John had a great deal of anger. He started saying, "You know, you're the worst psychologist in the world. How in the world did you ever get to where you are? You know, I'm going to call up the ethics committee and report you. You're outrageous." He started accusing me of all the things that he'd accused his father of: "You care more about your women patients than you do about men. You care more about golf than you care about me. You don't give a damn about me."

After several weeks, he was talking about how he wasn't ever going to go back to college and building up in a crescendo to climax. He shouted at the top of his lungs, "Why should I ever go back to college, if I should ever be lucky enough to graduate, you'd play golf instead of coming to my goddamn graduation!"

At which point, I yelled back at him, "I'm not your goddamn father!"

He sank back in his chair and said, "My God, that's what this is all about, isn't it." Then we started very effective and rapid treatment. John did not quit therapy prematurely despite his anger because when you connect with the patient's problem, your unconscious connects with your patient's unconscious. Patients know something important is happening. They're building up their rage and won't quit. Let me give you an example.

On my ranch we've always had collies as sheepdogs. Collies have very long snouts. In the summertime in California when all the grass is dry, there are foxtails. Foxtails look like the top of oats, and they go only one way. If they get up the snout of a dog, they will eventually puncture through the sinus and get into the brain, causing an infection that will kill the dog. I noticed one of our collies must have had a foxtail because I saw some bleeding. She sat for almost an hour while with my wife's tweezers from a cosmetic kit I reached way up the snout and, piece by piece, pulled out this foxtail. It was very difficult because it won't go backward. This dog was whimpering with pain, but she never once tried to leave. She knew I was doing something healing for her. And it occurred to me while I was doing this, "If our dogs know, our patients must know." Our patients surely know when we're doing something for our egos. They also know when we're doing it for them. After the fact, John was able to comfortably verbalize how the therapist's emulating his father was what put him in touch with the anger he had been determined to deny.

LEGEND

Psychological Mechanism:	Introjection
Diagnosis:	Reactive Depression
Operational Diagnosis:	My father died before I could get even
Implicit Contract:	Help me fix my father without continuing to hurt me
Personality Type:	Onion
Homework:	Continue to hate yourself
Therapeutic Technique:	Expel introject by mobilization of anger in the interest of health

In the case of Lenore, rather than play the role of the introject, the therapist verbalized what the patient was saying to herself. By so doing, the therapist is already beginning somewhat to expel the introject by externalizing the internalized thoughts. It is almost an unconsciuos ritual with some reactive depressives to counteract any attempt to break through the resistance by repeating the internalized guilt thoughts silently and often without consciousness. By siding with the patient's guilt/punishment resistance, the therapist can have a profound effect where direct attempts at guilt reduction fail.

Case Illustration: Lenore—Guilty As Charged

Lenore was a 52-year-old woman who 15 years ago left her husband. He did everything to get her back, including threatening suicide. She refused to take him back. Three months after the separation, he killed himself with a bullet to the head. Almost immediately thereafter, Lenore began experiencing severe, intractable headaches. One might speculate that had her husband shot himself through the heart, she might well have begun experiencing "heart trouble" instead of headaches. In the 15 years afterward, she visited every physician in her community many times and received every evaluation and pain reliever known to modern medicine; however, the headaches not only persisted but grew worse. She also saw every psychologist and psychiatrist in her community, as well as visiting two chronic-pain centers. And when psychotherapy did not bring relief, she received several courses of biofeedback training.

Lenore was a very gentle woman whom everyone liked intensely. All those who attempted to help her were too kind. Repeatedly she was told that her husband's suicide was not her fault. For 15 years Lenore would nod agreement, but it was apparent that she was not accepting the good-intentioned attempts to help her. Her headaches became so severe that she could not work, and she was on total disability. In fact, the pain was of such intensity 24 hours a day that Lenore did little else but several times a day visit physicians and psychotherapists. Now that she was on welfare, the state was paying for her ineffective treatments.

Finally, after 15 years, Lenore came to our center because this was a new service available for the first time in her community. She was desperate to get relief and her therapist, as had all of the therapists before him, misinterpreted her desperation for motivation to get well. He treated her in the same kind way, repeating that her husband's death was not her fault. She continued to get worse, and her psychologist came to the senior author for a consultation. The advice, after hearing the facts in the case, was that she should be told that she was guilty of murder and that her sentence was to suffer headaches for the rest of her life.

This intervention was chosen because Lenore, at least on an unconscious level, was saying this to herself. It is important to externalize the life sentence. In analytic terminology, its purpose was to expel the introject. The psychologist, a very kind man, found this intervention to be repugnant. But he was asked whether he wanted to help the patient or whether he just wanted to be nice. He agreed to the intervention, but he had to write it down, and he role-played it with another staff member for the several days before Lenore's next appointment.

The psychologist went ahead with the intervention, and Lenore lapsed into silence. It was stated to her several times. The following week she returned for her appointment in a state of subdued anger. She protested that the therapist did not understand the sufficient reasons for leaving her husband, and she criticized her husband for the first time since his death. She told the therapist that her husband had ongoing affairs and brought these women into her own marital bed. When she protested, he beat her unmercifully. It was noted that her headaches had subsided in intensity, and she had two days when she was actually symptom free. The psychologist made a grievous error. He returned to his usual kind demeanor and pointed out that if anyone had the right to leave her husband, she did. Lenore welcomed the statement, but when she returned the following week her headaches were worse than ever.

Now, in his own desperation, the psychologist telephoned for another consultation. It was pointed out that he had accepted prematurely the patient's protests that her husband was no good; at the next session he should state that he had thought it over and she was still guilty of murder. However, since there were extenuating circumstances as evidenced by her husband's infidelity and beatings, she was guilty of only second-degree murder. She did not need to have the headaches for life. The question now was whether she should have them for five or 10 more years.

This time the psychologist stuck with the strategy, and over several weeks Lenore persisted in relating a long litany of abuses and saying that she had no alternative but to leave him, all the while becoming increasingly and overtly angry at the therapist for insisting on the sentence of second-degree murder. Week after week Lenore's headaches dramatically decreased, and after she was totally free of them for several weeks she decided to discontinue the appointments because the therapist simply did not understand. But this psychologist had succeeded where all other therapists had failed. This is another reason why brief therapy is hard work. It is the long-term patient who heaps gratitude and gifts on us. In brief therapy, the reward often is only in the patient's recovery.

LEGEND

Psychological Mechanism:	Introjection, Denial (Rage)
Diagnosis:	Reactive Depression
Operational Diagnosis:	Welfare required visit to new counseling center
Implicit Contract:	I am guilty and will not be helped
Personality Type:	Onion with interspersed garlic
Homework:	Determine sentence for murder
Therapeutic Techniques:	Expel introject
	Mobilization of rage in the interest of health

The case of John illustrates how the introject is expelled through anger mobilized against the therapist in the transference. The therapist becomes the person who has been internalized and thus enables the patient to externalize the hostility turned inward. In the case of Lenore, the therapist articulated what the patient was saying to herself unconsciously. The first way was to become the introject. Either way, the internalization is externalized where the patient can start directing anger outward at the therapist. Despite eliciting psychic blood, the patient hangs in there because he knows intuitively there's something real going on. When this anger has been purged, the process itself can be discussed and resolved.

These interventions must be done within the context of the therapist's own style. Even when assuming the patient's context, the therapist must formulate and deliver the intervention in a manner befitting his or her own style.

Chronic Depression

Sometimes the loss and rage can occur so early in life that they become immutable. These are people who go through life depressed. They present as low-energy people and may be misdiagnosed as schizoid because they have impaired social relationships. They have a lifestyle of depression, but come in when something happens in their life to make the depression worse. When they get over that, they go back to being their old depressive selves. Very often, the therapist does not realize that such a person now has gotten the maximum benefit. This person is never going to change; their lack of energy has become a way of life. These people often cope with their depression with drugs or alcohol. Some become daredevils because cheating death is the only way they can feel alive.

A woman may become this kind of person as a result of having been sexually molested by her father at an early age. A man cannot sexually molest his daughter and still be her father. That little girl's father dies at that moment. So, if this molestation happened when this girl was five, six, seven, eight, she may suffer from anhedonic, nonclinical depression throughout her life. Molestation by another adult is traumatic enough, but molestation by one's father is devastating. To protect themselves from overwhelming feelings, these women have reduced their energy so stimuli cannot penetrate them and they hibernate through life.

Cognitive-behavioral approaches are appropriate with these people, but the therapeutic goals are limited. In Carmel there is a tree on Cypress Point that is the most photographed tree in the world. It is a gnarled, wind-blown, wave-swept cypress growing on a rock protruding into the ocean. No tree surgeon on earth could ever straighten that tree out. These chronic depressives are like that tree. They cannot be straightened out, but that tree is beautiful, and they need to realize the beauty of their own struggle against the trying circumstances of their lives.

There are instances of chronic depression happening in adulthood, but these are treatable. They may occur when children die before parents. Nature has no provision for the death of a child before the parent. It may also occur when the person has suffered severe trauma, as in the case below. Many survivors of the Holocaust manifest this almost intractable form of chronic depression.

Case Illustration: Rachel, The Chicken Lady

There existed in San Francisco in the 1950s and 1960s a condition affectionately labelled by the psychotherapists involved as the "Petaluma Syndrome." Petaluma is a city about 50 miles north of San Francisco that at that time was the chicken farm center of California. Oddly enough, a sizeable number of Holocaust survivors had taken their reparations money and bought chicken farms. This behavior was paradoxical for a group of Polish Jews who had never before seen an unplucked chicken. Once a week the women survivors boarded a chartered bus to San Francisco where each saw her respective therapist. Then they had lunch together and did a bit of shopping. Thereafter, they reboarded the bus back to Petaluma, only to repeat the trip the following week and each week thereafter. A group of therapists who were individually seeing these women considered it their obligation to render supportive therapy to these victims of the Holocaust. This had been going on for about a decade when the senior author was asked by a leader in the San Francisco Jewish community to replace a psychiatrist who had died.

Rachel came to her new psychologist after 10 years with her now deceased psychiatrist. She questioned his non-Jewish status, but felt satisfied when she learned her new therapist had fought in World War II and had a hand in liberating the Buchenwald concentration camp. The psychiatrist continued the supportive therapy he was told was indicated, although this kind of treatment was not natural to him. Rachel came in week after week with the same litany. She regularly whined, "Oh, the chickens have caught cold and are not laying enough eggs. Oh, the price of feed has gone up and I'm losing money. And Sammy don't love me no more." This kvetch was recited as if it were a script. The psychologist was properly supportive but felt nothing rewarding was taking place. After all, this survivor had earned the right to complain.

Within six months, the psychologist begged the community leader who had assigned him the case to be excused. The result was the heaping upon him of centuries of Judeo-Christian guilt, under which the psychologist buckled and agreed to continue to be therapeutically supportive of Rachel. But he could not get rid of the nagging feeling he should do more for her. Within another two months, the constantly repeated phrase, "And Sammy don't love me no more," came crashing on him.

In response to this insight, he asked Rachel a number of questions and learned that Rachel and Sam were married in September, 1939 and were on their honeymoon in Poland when Hitler's forces invaded the country. They fled for the Soviet border, having been separated when volunteers interceded to help. Sam went with a group of men, got to the Soviet Union, then to Sweden, and finally to the United States. Rachel fled with a group of women and was captured. She spent the next five years in a Nazi concentration camp. At the end of the war Sam went to Poland and searched until he found the emaciated survivor who was his wife. This is a heartrending story, and one that would have to be put aside if Rachel were to be helped to get on with her life.

The psychologist asked gently, "Rachel, have you ever resented that Sammy escaped while you spent five years in hell?" The flash in her eyes revealed her hidden feelings. The therapist was then emboldened to ask abruptly, "Rachel, is Petaluma Sammy's concentration camp?" The patient sat quietly for about two minutes and then she smiled, "You're pretty smart for a goy."

The therapist then wondered out loud why the 10 years she had the chicken ranch did not punish Sammy enough to compensate for the five years she was in the concentration camp. She replied, "Ah, but how many years of Rachel are necessary to make one year of the Gestapo?" The therapist immediately recognized this as Rachel's implicit contract, and a treatment plan complete with homework was constructed accordingly. He advised Rachel that her job would be to ascertain how many more years Sammy must remain incarcerated on the Petaluma chicken farm.

Rachel was beside herself with fury. Week after week she would refuse to do her homework. The therapist remained unrelenting in the demand she do the homework. She would yell and call him, *Goyishe Kopf*, and he would yell back *Yiddishe Kopf*. She accused him of being insensitive to the plight of the Jews. He accused her of being ungrateful since he had helped liberate the Jews. This was tough love, indeed.

Overlooked in embarking on supportive therapy with this chronically depressed Holocaust survivor is that as in all depression, the appropriate treatment is to help the patient expel the introject (Sammy) and externalize the tremendous hostility she harbors. In her depression, she was hurting herself more than her husband, who had adjusted fairly well to the unwelcome role of chicken farmer.

Finally, Rachel began to make estimates of how long Sammy should be incarcerated. Her first estimate of three years of Rachel for every year of the Gestapo was promptly rejected by the therapist who extolled that Rachel was really a cream puff and proffered a ratio of five to one. This would mean 15 more years in Petaluma. Within a couple of weeks Rachel began arguing that Sammy had suffered enough. She feared she might be almost as bad as the Nazis. The therapist exploded! After all, he had fought the Nazis, and a ratio of two to one was unacceptable. Rachel said little in the next four sessions. She seemed preoccupied but not sullen. Then she came in and said, "To a housewarming you should be coming."

Rachel had sold the chicken farm and prevailed upon her fellow survivors to do the same. And they all had bought condominiums in the same upscale building in San Francisco. The psychologist eagerly attended the housewarming, where he met all the "girls," as Rachel called her fellow survivors. It was apparent that Rachel was the group's leader, both in the Nazi camp and in Petaluma. Her fellow survivors had followed her into chicken farming. Then the psychologist was surprised to learn that he was the only guest. He had been invited so Rachel's friends could meet him. The "girls" all affectionately embraced him. "Two concentration camps you liberated, one in Poland and one in Petaluma."

The deep-rooted introject had, indeed, finally been expelled. Although her hate for her Gestapo captors still and always will remain partially introjected, remanding her to the scars of a lifelong depression, at least Rachel was finally freed to rebuild her life rather than to continue the incarceration. On a final note, this case demonstrates that in spite of all the hostility that is expressed toward the therapist when the anger is being externalized, there is an unconscious recognition that some very real and important healing is going on. Depressives do not quit therapy at such times.

LEGEND

Psychological Mechanism:	Introjection and Denial
Diagnosis:	Chronic Rage, Depression and Post-Traumatic Stress Syndrome
Operational Diagnosis:	My previous therapist died

Implicit Contract:	Don't tamper with my solution
Personality Type:	Onion and garlic mixed
Homework:	Determine husband's sentence
Therapeutic Techniques:	Mobilization of rage
	Paradoxical intention

Anniversary Depression

Both mourning and depression can be postponed to a day of reckoning. Sometimes, this can be for many years. Typical would be the man who never mourned his father's fatal heart attack, but when he reaches the age his father was at his death, the man becomes convinced of an impending heart attack. Or, a woman who never resolved her feelings toward her deceased mother may experience an anniversary depression every year on the date her mother died. Many forms exist, and although they are treated as chronic depression, additionally some detective work may be involved.

In 90 percent of cases in which the depression is triggered by the anniversary of the death of a parent, it is the death of the same sex parent that elicits conflicted feelings. In most American families, fathers are patsies for their daughters, mothers are patsies for their sons, and the frustrating parent is the parent of the same sex. To resolve this conflict, the child identifies primarily with the frustrating parent. Thus, in cases where the process of bereavement has gone awry, an anniversary depression can be triggered by the guilt the child feels over his hostility towards the parent he has identified with. The patient postpones a reactive depression and then, a number of years later on, experiences the depression. Thus, Ernest Hemingway put a gun to his head and killed himself at the exact age that Hemingway's father had put a gun to his head and killed himself. Other significant losses can also serve as the basis for an anniversary depression. Whatever the etiology, the treatment is simple: Connect the present situation to the postponed situation. Generally, people who can postpone something for long periods are resilient and respond well. Below are two cases of anniversary depression. The first of these on the "due date" resulted in physical crippling; the second was about to cause death.

Case Illustration: Cheryl and the Witch's Curse

At the age of 50, Cheryl came down with gnarled, crippling arthritis within 60 days. Her physician who had referred her was absolutely astounded by the speed with which such severe crippling arthritis had gnarled her extremities. He was baffled, but he didn't refer her for her arthritis; he sent her because she was such a difficult, demanding, impossible woman.

As I worked with her, I realized that Cheryl had an anniversary depression. She hated her mother. They had fought incessantly. When her mother was dying, Cheryl said to her mother, "I'm glad you're going, you witch." Whereupon, her mother said, "I'm going to damn you. At 50 years old you're going to have crippling arthritis and you're going to become a witch just like me." Cheryl forgot the whole blasted conversation. When she reached 50, Cheryl developed crippling arthritis just like her mother, who had always used this condition as an excuse to not be a mother and to not be there for her daughter. At 50, Cheryl not only got the fastest crippling arthritis her PCP had ever seen, she became a witch like her mother. This woman was awful!

Cheryl was assigned to go up to Boise where her mother was buried and redo the final conversation. Cheryl resisted and resisted, but I told her that it was a condition of treatment. I wasn't going to fool around with her any more. She had to go to Boise or end therapy. Finally, she decided to go up, mainly to please me.

When she came back, she told the following story. She flew in and landed about 11:00 A.M., rented a car at the airport, drove out to the cemetery, went to the office, and found the plot. She had a 3:30 P.M. flight back to San Francisco. She intended to stay for a few minutes at the cemetery. As she approached her mother's gravestone, she noticed that it was the only gravestone that the pigeons had left droppings on, and she started laughing. She said, "Even the pigeons don't like my mother." She sat down in front of the mother's grave and started talking. She said, "I kept talking and talking, and when I came to again, it was dark. It had rained. My clothes were soaking wet. I don't remember when it rained. I don't remember how long I was there. I got back to the car, looked at my watch, and it was after 9:00 at night. I told my mother everything I had wanted to say in my entire life." And that's where her arthritis was reversed.

The PCP called up and said, "I can't believe it. I never saw anything like that come and go so fast in my life."

It had been an anniversary depression. Her mother had damned her from her deathbed. Cheryl had forgotten the incident, but it wasn't enough to just connect the arthritis with the damnation. The life long history of conflict with her mother had to be resolved and it finally was by the graveside in Boise.

LEGEND

Psychological Mechanism:	Inrojection and Displacement (Somatization)
Diagnosis:	Anniversary (delayed) Depression
Operational Diagnosis:	Payment is now due
Implicit Contract:	Help me escape payment
Personality Type:	Onion
Homework:	Talk to mother's grave
Therapeutic Techniques:	Expel the introject Mobilization of rage

Case Illustration: Dan's Date with Death

Dan was 21 when he came for death and dying counseling. He was suffering from lymphoma and had come to this distant city to be treated at University Hospital by one of the nation's leading experts. When first seen, he had lost all of his hair from radiation and chemotherapy. He did not respond favorably to treatment and he had been told to get his affairs in order.

The patient had moved into an apartment built on a hill, as is common in San Francisco. In the basement was an unfinished room, which the landlord planned to have excavated and made into a storeroom. Dan decided to help. Every morning on his way out he would fill a small paper bag full of dirt and then deposit it in the nearest public trash can. The patient was practicing a kind of magical behavior typical of those who know they are dying. At the rate of one paper bag a day, the large mound of dirt guaranteed that Dan would live a long life. The denial, of course, is that he cannot die until the task is completed.

Death and dying counseling was abruptly interrupted when something Dan said alerted the therapist. Almost as an aside, Dan tossed out the statement, "I feel as if I've made a pact with the Devil." He was unable to account for this statement and, under questioning, dismissed it as his pessimism in the face of death.

Dan had lost both parents at age eight in a tragic freeway auto disaster. Dan and his three-year-old sister were staying with grandparents, where the family gathered upon hearing the tragic news. He was awakened in the middle of the night by the crying and wailing of the family members. One by one, his four grandparents came to Dan's bedside and expressed the wish that God had taken them instead of his parents. Each stated, "I've had most of my life. Their death, on the other hand, leaves two orphans." This is all Dan remembers.

There followed a series of intense questions in which the therapist unrelentingly insisted that the patient recall whatever it was he was hiding. Dan reacted with increased violent behavior, often writhing on the floor, screaming there was nothing more. This behavior only convinced the psychologist there had to be more. Eventually, in a particularly intense session during which Dan kicked a chair across the room, he remembered.

On each of the occasions when his grandparents expressed a wish that they had been taken instead of Dan's parents, the patient recalled with much emotion how he thought to himself that he was glad he was not taken. He also recalled thinking that his parents, whom Dan now recalled as quite cold and rejecting, really deserved to die. Then one night, either in a nightmare or in a childhood hallucination, he was awakened by the Devil who came to claim the life of this ungrateful son. Dan recalled crying and pleading with the Devil, "I'm only a little kid. Let me live until I'm 21 and I'll go willingly." The Devil agreed to what seemed a lifetime of reprieve to an eight-year-old. But shortly after his 21st birthday, Dan was diagnosed as suffering from lymphatic cancer. The day of reckoning had arrived.

On learning of these powerful events, the therapist made no promises, but stated that the therapy could well question a contract to die made by a distraught child. The next several months were spent in examining his hostility toward his parents. Dan's mother was a self-centered woman. He could be doing his homework, and when she drove up, she would honk. He would have to come out to open the garage door so she wouldn't have to get out of the car and open the door herself. There was incident after incident like this in which nobody else's time mattered but hers. His father was "out to lunch" and never around either physically or psychologically.

Often, as Dan externalized his anger, the therapist was the recipient of stormy, hostile emotions. At other times, to facilitate expelling of the introjects, the therapist mimicked what he learned had been typical parental behaviors. The stormier the therapy sessions, the stronger Dan became physically. Eventually, the patient, who had been declared terminal, was found by his physicians to be in remission. His oncologist was skeptical and insisted Dan see him weekly. Dan resisted, but the therapist pointed out that the skeptical oncologist was his best friend: "If there is even one cancer cell in your body, he will find it." Finally, it became obvious to his oncologist that the patient was in full remission. Oncological treatment was terminated. Therapy was also interrupted, with the admonition that if he ever felt a swollen node to call immediately for an appointment.

Dan called three years later. He had since been married and had a daughter. His wife was in the process of divorcing him, and in his distraught state Dan noticed a swollen node. He came in for more therapy, during which time he was helped to separate from his wife and to reconcile himself to the visiting privileges he would have with his daughter. His cancer did not recur.

Over two decades passed before he was seen again. He had read a profile of his therapist in the newspaper and became aware for the first time of the psychologist's advanced age. He came in saying, "I hope you live many more years. But I did not have the opportunity to say goodbye to my father, and I want to make certain I say goodbye to you." He then went on to tell the psychologist about his successful second marriage, his children by that union, and the fact that his first daughter had elected to live with them instead of with her mother. He then went on to tell of his successful and innovative career. He confided that he had followed from afar his therapist's lifelong innovations and he confessed how proud he, himself, was to have innovated in a totally different occupation. It was striking that Dan did not seem to be talking to his therapist, but to his father.

LEGEND

Psychological Mechanism:	Introjection
Diagnosis:	Anniversary (delayed)
	Depression
Operational Diagnosis:	Help me die peacefully
Implicit Contract:	You can't change the inevitable
Personality Type:	Onion
Homework:	Renegotiate death contract
Therapeutic Techniques:	Mobilization of rage
	Expel the introject

Anniversary depressions are so pervasive that on the "due date" the person's life is at stake. The abreaction that Cheryl experienced at the gravesite and Dan upon recalling his pact with the Devil are important, but they mark the beginnings of therapy. There must follow often stormy and always painful sessions in which the aborted relationship with all its postponed hate is understood and resolved. But without the patient's often sudden realization of the anniversary reaction, therapy remains blind, undirected, and usually unsuccessful. The ultimate entry point is the acceptance of the postponed day of reckoning.

Hysteria and Conversion Neurosis

Dynamics

The main defense mechanism in hysteria is pure repression. The hysteric operates on the level of a three-year-old child caught taking a cookie when told not to. The child can innocently say, "Mommy, I didn't take the cookie. My hand did it." Hysterical symptoms can appear as childish and ludicrous, but hysterics believe their symptoms and are not conning you. The therapist must resist the temptation to even hint at an, "Oh, come on now!" reaction. To do so is to drive the patient away. The failure to keep sexual conflict repressed, along with the fear of intimacy, is at the roots of the anxiety experienced by the hysteric. The failure of heretofore successful repression has been triggered by recent life experiences or circumstances.

In hysteria with a conversion reaction, the primary mechanism of repression is complicated by the displacement of anxiety or hostility onto a body organ. Well educated people, especially in the health field, can replicate just about any neurological disease. Doctors and nurses can do it to a fine detail because they know the neuromatomy of the body. Unsophisticated people can get anesthesias that are impossible because the configuration of the nerve paths do not follow the commonsensical view.

Entry

The entry point in psychotherapy with hysterics is to reinstate the repression and to reframe the problem as not one of intimacy or sexuality, thus allowing the hysteric to save face. Strong-arming the resistance by forcing the hysteric to confront the content of her repression will lead to greater resistance and perhaps increased symptoms as the hysteric fights to preserve his/her self-image.

The case of Melody illustrates to what extent the therapist must go to avoid implying that the problem might be sexual. This involves joining the resistance. When equilibrium is established, the patient signals this as Melody did, indicating to the therapist she was ready for the next step.

Case Illustration: Melody, the Honeymooner

Melody was referred by the emergency room staff following a thorough neurological workup, the results of which were negative. She had gone to the emergency room with her husband with the complaint that she had awakened in the middle of the night to discover she was suddenly unable to read. After several hours of exploration, the emergency room staff's provisional diagnosis was hysteria. Wife and husband arrived at the psychologist's office as a couple, expecting to be seen together.

When an appointment is made for an individual, if that person arrives as a couple or a family, it is important to interview that person first. Otherwise, the therapist is committing prematurely and without foundation to couples therapy or family therapy. It is always imperative to ascertain the operational diagnosis and the implicit contract before agreeing to a treatment plan. The therapist advised Melody's husband that he wanted to meet with the wife first. Should it be indicated, he might very well wish to meet with the husband later. He offered no resistance.

Once in the office, Melody gave the following story. They arrived at their honeymoon destination four days ago very late at night and much too exhausted to consummate the marriage, so they decided to wait until morning. At 2:00 A.M. she awakened momentarily, looked at the hotel information card on the bedside table, and panicked when she realized she could not read it.

In fear, she jumped from the bed and attempted to read other materials to no avail. She then awakened her husband, who tried all kinds of reading material with her, but again with no success. She simply and inexplicably was unable to read a single word.

The therapist handed her a clipboard with a pad on it and asked her to write her name, address, telephone number, and date of birth. She complied, but when asked if she could read what she had written, she said, "No." The therapist interjected, "This is very interesting. You can write but you cannot read." She agreed this was, indeed, interesting.

One is tempted to convey a feeling, "Oh, come on, you don't really believe this. You must be pulling my leg." The other temptation is to make the obvious connection between her symptoms and her fear of sex. Even though the baffling symptom had effectively prevented any kind of sex, to point this out would be to strong-arm the resistance. She was complimented on her very understanding husband, who had the sensitivity not to attempt to make love to her when she was so distraught. She beamed as she began the bonding process with the therapist.

The subject of sex was avoided as the therapist purposely talked with her about her wedding, saying, "You must have planned it for months." She said, "I planned it for over a year." There were 350 guests invited for a sit-down dinner at this large and expensive wedding. She agreed with the psychologist that this was a wonderful, but exhausting experience.

Near the end of the session, the therapist shared his suspicion that she could be suffering from some kind of exhaustion syndrome. He also confided that he did not fully understand this, but until they could together get to the bottom of this exhaustion syndrome, he wanted her not to exacerbate the exhaustion. He called in the husband and enlisted his cooperation in helping Melody refrain from three things. The first request was that she discontinue her daily habit of jogging as this was potentially too tiring under her present condition. She was also to refrain from alcohol, inasmuch as that beverage can complicate many neurological problems. And, finally, she was to refrain from sex. The latter was the critical feature; the first two were thrown in to make certain the patient did not think the psychologist was anticipating a sexual problem.

The husband, who was virtually as hysterical as his wife, practically saluted the therapist in his eagerness to be of help. The couple left determined to abide by the prescribed regimen.

When they returned the following week, they assured the psychologist that they had followed the prescription to the letter. The therapist complimented both of them and added that Melody was fortunate to have such an understanding husband.

During the second session, the diagnosis of hysteria was confirmed along with both the operational diagnosis and the implicit contract. Melody had a limit to the intimacy she could tolerate. She could engage in sex before they were married because there was not the commitment of marriage. Once she was married, the commitment was so unconsciously overwhelming that something had to give. So it was either sex without marriage or marriage without sex. To have both together constituted the breaking point of too much intimacy. Despite the so-called sexual revolution where premarital sex is usual, this is far more prevalent a syndrome than many therapists appreciate. Melody was able to present all of this in the characteristic fashion of hysterics who can talk about sex as long as the therapist does not.

At the end of the second session, the therapist confessed, "You know, we still haven't gotten to the bottom of this. So again next week no jogging, no alcohol, and no sex." Once again, the eager husband's cooperation was solicited, and they left with Melody still unable to read. But the operational diagnosis was clearly the inability to have sex, which was created by the honeymoon. The implicit contract was that the therapist would help her avoid sex. To not strong-arm the resistance required that the therapist help her do just that. And it had to be presented in a plausible, face-saving manner.

On the third session, Melody reported there were two periods, one for about 15 minutes and another for only 10 minutes, during which she could read. The therapist admonished that although this was encouraging, the prescribed regimen should be maintained. Too many therapists make the mistake of prematurely accelerating a treatment plan, only to find the patient has regressed as a result. She was not yet ready to confront her real problem.

By the fourth session, Melody's reading ability had amazingly and suddenly returned. The abandonment of the symptom is the sign to the therapist that the patient is now ready, ever so gently, to begin talking about the real problem. She was now far enough removed from the terror of the wedding and she was with a therapist/parent figure she trusted, so she could talk about it. But the therapist steered her to the subject of intimacy and postponed the terror of sex until a later session.

In not strong-arming the resistance and by offering a rationalization of exhaustion, therapy was effective. Brief therapy most emphatically does not mean using a battering ram. This woman improved very rapidly and by the sixth and seventh sessions she was talking openly about the terror of intimacy in her original family.

In summary, the entry point with hysteria is to help reinstate the failed repression. As in this case, the symptom was reframed so as to allow her to save face and to bond with the therapist. Ultimately, the therapy allowed her to regroup and adjust to the new level of intimacy the marriage entailed. But it must be pointed out that her overall identity was still that of a hysteric, albeit a more successful one.

LEGEND

Psychological Mechanism:	Repression, Displacement (Conversion)
Diagnosis:	Conversion Hysteria
Operational Diagnosis:	New marriage
Implicit Contract:	Help me avoid sex and deny fear of sex
Personality Type:	Onion
Homework:	No jogging, alcohol, or sex
Therapeutic Technique:	Joining the resistance (symptom)

It is quite common in practice today to be confronted by an angry, resistive person with conversion hysteria whose exasperated physician has told her, "It's all in your head; go see a shrink." This usually occurs after many months in which the physician has exhausted all laboratory and other procedures looking for a physical explanation of the symptom. The therapist now has the added problem of counter-acting the damage done by the physician, because it is still important at the entry point to join the patient's resistance. It is not fruitful in this kind of situation to join the patient in scapegoating the well-meaning, but exasperated, physician. The therapist needs to exercise special skills and inventiveness to repair the therapeutic damage, as in the case of Nancy.

Case Illustration: Nancy's Paralysis

When a patient is told by a physician that her condition is all in her head and she should see a psychologist, she naturally comes in feeling angry, betrayed, and defensive. Such was the case with Nancy, a 27-year-old woman married for two years. She was in a wheelchair, but her neurologist had told her in exasperation that the "paralysis" of her legs did not fit any neurological condition. She interpreted this as meaning she must be crazy. In this kind of case, it is particularly important not to strong-arm the resistance and to give the patient the opportunity to save face.

The husband brought his wife in her wheelchair and did not protest when the psychologist indicated he wished to see Nancy alone. Inasmuch as an individual session was scheduled, to see the patient as a couple would prematurely commit to a treatment modality. As it developed, Nancy would have been unable to say much of what she said with her husband present.

Nancy's entire posturing suggested she did not wish to see the psychologist, but was complying with the physician's referral. Much later, it was elicited that one implicit contract was that she would return to the physician with the complaint that psychology was not helpful. She would by that time also have found a physician who had established the physical cause of her paralysis. Before bonding could occur, this patient's hurt would have to be overcome.

Early in the session, the therapist joined her in a lament that neurology was still a relatively inexact science. She agreed to enter counseling to help her adjust to her paralysis. Hastily, as if to anticipate any questions, she insisted that her marriage was a very happy one. She and her husband loved each other, and he was very sympathetic and patient. But she worried that her inability to have sex because of this paralysis might eventually pose a threat to the marriage. For these issues, she agreed counseling could be helpful.

Near the end of the first session, the therapist set the stage for saving face. But first it was important to go with the resistance and emphasize that even though a lack of sex could pose a problem in their marriage, it was important to her physical well-being that she for the time being dismiss all such considerations from her mind. Then he launched into an elaborate and seemingly unrelated explanation that baffling neurological conditions can have unexpected remissions. The psychologist used multiple sclerosis as an example of a condition in which the paralysis can come and go inexplicably. The foundation was laid without further comment, while she agreed she would not only not attempt sex, but also not worry about the lack of it.

At the second session, she began to talk about the cramping in her legs during sexual intercourse and several weeks before the onset of the paralysis. She wondered if these cramps might be the precursors to her paralysis. The psychologist agreed that these could well have been prodromal signs and complimented her on her astute analysis. She ended the session with confirming that counseling was, indeed, helpful and she felt much better emotionally after each session.

At the third session, she reported that she had been able to get out of the wheelchair as much as a half hour at a time on three different days during the preceding week. On each instance, she returned to the wheelchair when she experienced the beginnings of cramps in her leg. She thanked the therapist for telling her about this prodromal sign, seemingly forgetting that the idea was first hers. The psychologist expressed pleasure at her improvement, but strongly cautioned her against attempting too much too soon. Even if she felt up to it, she should limit her time out of the wheelchair. He further reminded her of her promise to refrain from sexual activity, pointing out that this would be far too strenuous. She reiterated her agreement.

In the fifth session, she came without the wheelchair, saying she had not needed it for the past six days. Occasionally, she would experience slight cramping of her legs and she would sit down until it subsided. She was grateful to the psychologist for her improvement, and attributed it to therapy's helping her relax enough to permit the spontaneous remission. At the psychologist's insistence, she agreed to continue abstinence from sex until the baffling neurological condition was better understood.

During the next several sessions, the patient was able to face the feelings that had accompanied the initial cramps, which had first manifested themselves during sexual intercourse. She admitted that she did not enjoy sex, but felt guilty and hid this feeling from her husband. He enjoyed sex tremendously, and soon her guilt feelings turned to resentment toward her husband and his pleasure. She eventually recalled that she began to experience the fantasy during the sex act that she would raise her leg abruptly and kick her husband in the scrotum. It was not long before the fantasy advanced to a strong temptation, which disappeared from consciousness when the cramps appeared. The cramps were a struggle to keep from kicking her husband in the groin and the paralysis was the resolution of that conflict. Not only was she unable to kick her husband, but the paralysis put an end to their sexual life. Her husband was too concerned and sympathetic to even entertain the thought of sex.

With the disclosures, the patient was able to address her fear of intimacy and her fear of letting go in the sex act. Treatment was now fully underway. Her homework, which up to this time had been to refrain from sex, now became a series of small excursions into trusting herself and her partner. As she allowed sexual pleasure to happen, she also permitted herself the luxury of a letter to her neurologist in which she pointed out that his bedside manner had all the professionalism of a runaway bus. This case illustrates how, by abandoning the presenting symptom, the patient signals her readiness to explore her underlying problems.

LEGEND

Psychological Mechanism:	Displacement (Conversion), Repression
Diagnosis:	Conversion Hysteria
Operational Diagnosis:	Increased aversion to sex
Implicit Contract:	Prove that my condition is physical

Personality Type:	Onion
Homework:	Remain in wheelchair; go slow
Therapeutic Technique:	Joining the resistance
	(symptom)

Obsessive-Compulsive Personality Disorders

Dynamics

At the opposite end of the neurotic spectrum from the hysteric is the obsessive-compulsive. The defense mechanism for obsessive-compulsive neurosis is isolation, isolation of affect from thought or from events. Emotions have to be expressed, but the obsessive-compulsive will express emotion when it has nothing to do with the event or the thought.

One obsessive-compulsive patient had a little daughter who almost died. She was in the hospital with an incredible fever for several days, teetering on the verge of dying. This man never shed a tear or showed a bit of anxiety through the whole ordeal. After his daughter was recovering, and recovering very rapidly, he was watching "Lassie" on television one day. Timmy and Lassie are separated and running all over trying to find each other. The patient dissolved in tears for an hour. Obsessive-compulsives have to protect themselves because they can't handle feelings, so they amputate themselves at the neck.

An obsession or compulsion is a distraction. It distracts you from what is bothering you. It allows you to isolate your affects. We all experience an obsession at times like a tune that reverberates through our heads. The more you try to get rid of it consciously, the more the tune stays in your head. Instead, you should ask yourself honestly, "What am I trying to avoid facing right this moment by having this tune reverberate through my head?" If you are courageous enough to answer that question, the tune is gone.

Entry

To break up the isolation of the obsessive-compulsive, the entry point is the magical system by which they isolate their affect. If patients report washing their hands 50 times a day, don't strong-arm the resistance by attacking that symptom. You must identify the magical system that is empowered by other ritualistic behaviors. A very common one is getting out of bed in such a way that both feet touch the ground at the same time. If one foot touches the ground before the other, the obsessive compulsive has to get back into bed and get out the other side of the bed, making sure that both feet touch the ground at the same time. If again he fails to do that, he must get back in bed and try a third time on the other side of the bed, and keep going until he gets it right. Other obsessive-compulsives have to have the right foot touch before the left foot. The conflict underlying the ritual is so layered and long lost in the patient's isolation that it may not be possible to discover. In the case below, the patient illustrates this ritualistic behavior.

Forbidding the ritualistic behavior is not strong-arming the resistance; the resistance is in the repetitive behavior, as in the case of the hand washing. For example, in the following case, Walter has been wearing white socks since he was about five years old and this was not connected to the symptom. It was a successful way of life, a defense mechanism that successfully isolated this man's affect. The symptom that bears the resistance is the hand washing, or the repetitive behavior. The identified symptom, which has become ego dystonic and brings the obsessive-compulsive in, should not be the focus of therapy. Rather, the magical behavior, which is ego syntonic and a part of the way of life, offers a more potent, undefended entry point into undermining the patient's isolation and facilitating the integration of affect into the personality.

The magical system employed by the patient to keep affect and thought separated is usually so seemingly insignificant that it is almost overlooked by the therapist. Yet this trivial behavior is the keystone to treating the obsessive-compulsive patient. This is keenly apparent in the case of Walter, whose white socks were the bulwark of his defenses.

Case Illustration: Walter, the Cathodic Engineer

Walter, 42 years old, came to therapy because his indecisiveness was becoming too much of a problem. He always had trouble making up his mind, but it seemed as he got older that it was more and more difficult to choose. He gave as an example the fact that he had been going to the same restaurant for lunch for almost two years. He knew the menu by heart and was tired of the same old food. He would look longingly across the street to another restaurant and determine he would go there for lunch tomorrow. But the next day he would begin to obsess, "What if it is worse than the one I am going to?" In the end, he would return each day to the same old restaurant.

Walter was approaching a midlife crisis which he avoided by his interminable array of obsessions. He was a cathodic engineer for an oil company and he would walk the several blocks that separated his office from the commuter train station. He lived in the suburbs where his wife cared for their three children and was deeply involved with church work. On his walk to or from his office, he had elaborately constructed in his mind that it was permissible to cross against a red light at some intersections, but not at others. The system made sense to him: On small alleys with little traffic, it was all right to ignore the stoplight, while on larger thoroughfares it was not. What irked Walter was that other pedestrians did not abide by his rule and he would find himself getting inwardly furious with them. However, unbeknownst to Walter, the degree of his fury had nothing to do with the number of pedestrians who violated his rule, but rather with the number of times this mild-mannered man had suppressed his anger with his colleagues that workday. Or, if this was in the morning walk to the office, his annoyance with the pedestrians was directly proportional to his unrecognized anger at his wife. Walter was an obsessional neurotic. This was only one of scores of obsessional systems.

Walter was unaware that he was angry with his wife, but he could discuss difficulties with her without much feeling. He told the story of the time his wife was freezing peaches. She had run out of aluminum foil and asked him to drive quickly to the store and buy some before the peeled fresh peaches turned brown. Walter dutifully drove to the supermarket where he discovered there were two kinds, one quilted and the other not. His wife had not told him which one she wanted, and after 40 minutes of vacillation during which he made several aborted trips to the checkout stand, Walter returned empty-handed. By this time, the peaches were spoiled and his wife blew up with exasperation. Neither was aware, however, how passively hostile Walter's indecision had been. Walter was genuinely disturbed that he had upset his wife, but he was isolated from his feelings of anger.

In fee-for-service practice, obsessional neurotics are bread-and-butter patients. They never express anger at the therapist, they do not call after hours, they keep their appointments, and they pay their bills on time. These advantages do not pertain to capitated practice, where their intractableness and interminability are disadvantages. Yet the therapist's best intentions to move the case along are seldom successful. Even Freud, who was comfortable in long-term therapy, told an obsessional patient in his 10th year that whatever the outcome they would terminate in three more years!

The defense mechanism by which the obsessional neurotic avoids the anxiety that would result in facing the real problem is called "isolation of affect." The patient can talk about the actual problems in his life, but since feeling is absent, no change or real understanding occurs. Feelings are isolated and discharged later. Just as Walter discharged anger at the pedestrians on his walk, he discharged affection by crying during mushy television programs. In fact Walter could overlook his cold, detached manner toward his family by recalling how sensitive, warm, and tender he would be watching a movie. In treatment of the obsessional neurotic or the compulsive neurotic, the therapy must create a situation where the event and the feeling are simultaneously present.

Strong-arming the resistance by forbidding the obsession is a frustrating experience for both therapist and patient. The therapist is foiled, while the patient experiences an increasingly broader obsession. The entry point for the obsessional is through the magical system that enables the neurosis to exist. Every obsessional has at least one magical behavior, and usually two or three. The therapist will not learn what these are without probing.

Walter was well dressed in a dark suit and dark tie, but his white socks were startling in this context. On the second session, he was dressed the same way, suggesting this was not a one-time aberration. When asked, Walter responded that he wore white socks only. He would not feel comfortable with colored socks. Suspecting the "foot magic" often found in many obsessionals, the therapist asked if Walter had a certain way he would get out of bed each morning. Indeed he did. Both feet would have to touch the floor at the same time. If one foot touched first, the patient would get back under the covers and emerge from the opposite side of the bed, making certain this time that both feet touched the floor simultaneously.

The therapist waited two more sessions until the patient had bonded with him. Then he advised Walter that it was important to his therapy that he wear black or dark blue socks and that he get up in the morning with either foot touching the floor first. Under no circumstances should both feet touch first. If inadvertently they did, he should get under the covers and emerge from the other side of the bed, this time making certain only one foot touched the floor.

Walter was silent and noticeably uncomfortable for over 10 minutes. He eventually broke the silence himself, asking why he was being asked to do this. The therapist replied, "This is one of those times in therapy when the *why* is not important, but the *what* is." The patient was silent for another 10 minutes, and then wondered whether or not he could do this. "It would be like getting started all wrong every morning. And I can't explain it, but the white socks make me feel protected." The therapist interjected, "Would insulated be a more accurate word?" Walter nodded, "Yes, that's the right word." The therapist insisted and the patient agreed, but thought it would be "very hard" to do. The therapist countered that if the patient found it too difficult, he should telephone for an appointment earlier than the one scheduled the following week.

Walter called two days before his scheduled session and was seen that day. He was very anxious, but had kept his promise on both counts. He had been too tense to sleep and had trouble concentrating at work. "I'm a nervous wreck." It was in sharp contrast to the emotionless man who had come in the previous sessions, insisting his only problem was indecisiveness. His obsessional systems had disintegrated. Now, when he talked about his problems, both the event and the affect were present.

He did not know what to do, as he felt he was constantly on the verge of blowing up at his co-workers. In fact, to his chagrin, he had exploded with anger on two occasions, and it seemed he was perpetually angry at his wife. He was clearly anxious and was sweating profusely. The therapist interjected, "Walter, this is the way you have been feeling for a long time, but you've covered it up with stoplights and aluminum foil. Let's talk about what has been really bothering you."

The following sessions continued to be filled with anxiety and emotion. His previously dormant midlife crisis was now overwhelming him. He hated his job, he was bored with his wife, and, above all, he was tired of having been "proper" all of his life. He was able to admit for the first time that he had fantasized how it might be with another woman. He had even focused upon one of the women at work who had noticed that whenever she was near him Walter would become red-faced and uncomfortable. Finally, she asked him to stop as he was making her self-conscious. In exasperation she had said, "Either ask me out on a date or quit acting like a sick calf." Walter was mortified and would make sure he was never near her again.

Little by little, Walter learned to express himself appropriately. As a result, he became more comfortable with both his anger and his lust, and learned that neither was inevitable or fatal. Throughout, he kept his promise to wear colored socks and to abstain from his morning ritual. His indecision all but disappeared and he became assertive and happy with his wife and a real father to his children. He thanked the therapist for getting him through the midlife crisis and particularly thanked him for "getting me over my lifelong obsequiousness."

LEGEND

Psychological Mechanism:	Isolation of Affect, Intellectualization
Diagnosis:	Obsessive-Compulsive Personality
Operational Diagnosis:	Entering midlife crisis
Implicit Contract:	I am not angry
Personality Type:	Onion
Homework:	Wear dark socks; refrain from morning ritual
Therapeutic Techniques:	Forbid the enabling magic
	Turn up the heat (anxiety)

6
Garlic/Analyzable

Addictions

Dynamics

The main defense mechanism in addictions is denial. The denial is pervasive, and addicts are likely to come to treatment only because there is external pressure on them or because they seek to recapture the halcyon days when the addiction worked, and not because they are motivated to achieve abstinence.

Their implicit contract is likely to be, "Turn me into a social user." There is no such thing because addiction results in physiological tissue change and drug tolerance. The more you take of a drug, the more you need in order to get the kick, and the more cells in your body are committed to neutralizing that drug. The body turns addictive substance into a food or a necessity. To express it as an axiom: The highest level of a chemical needed to bring about the high becomes the minimum daily requirement for life. It may take an alcoholic 20 years to build up to a quart of whiskey a day. That alcoholic can be dry for 10 years. If he starts drinking again, within days or a couple of weeks, he will be back to a quart of whiskey a day.

Addiction is not merely popping something into one's body, but a constellation of behaviors that constitute a way of life. An addict can be likened to an unfinished house that has only an attic and a basement. Addicts understand this metaphor exactly because they know only two moods: elation and depression. They do not experience the limited, normal mood swings common to other persons because as they start to fall out of the attic, they run quickly to the bottle, the pill, the needle, anything to prevent falling clear down to the basement. The first thing we have to teach them is how to build a floor in that house, because you cannot live just in elation or depression. As one philosopher put it, "Those who are chronically depressed are damned to pursue pleasure constantly."

Addicts are damned to this fate because insight is soluble in alcohol, in calories, in cocaine, in amphetamines, or in whatever addiction the addict uses to escape anxiety and depression. Patients may be addicted not only to drugs but to food, gambling, sex, or work. Additionally, the orgiastic nature of an addiction allows the addict to stay in perpetual denial by relieving the anxiety and depression that might otherwise force him or her to change.

Entry

The entry point in psychotherapy with addicts is to refuse treatment, thus avoiding conflict with the patient's denial and engaging the addict's own characteristic obstinacy to challenge. In this technique, the therapist skillfully verbalizes the patient's own denial, while at the same time withholding treatment as something not worthwhile for that particular addict. For example: "You can beat this yourself." "You have been conning your wife for over 10 years and with a little effort you could con her into taking you back." "Your boss is a softy and we can figure out a way to get him to hire you back." Hearing his covert beliefs expressed by the therapist, the patient begins to talk like the therapist. For example: "I can't continue to fool myself." or "My wife (or boss) deserves better." The person who came in determined not to continue is likely to demand to be seen. More details of treatment, including the need for skilled triage along a continuum of care and the games addict play, can be found in "Psychotherapy with Substance Abusers" (Cummings, 1993).

The technique of reducing the impenetrable denial found in chemical dependency must be modified in addictions other than alcohol and drugs. Yet the overall approach is also useful with food addicts, defined as persons who eat when depressed, anxious, or lonely. This modification is illustrated in the case of Mary.

Case Illustration: Mary, The Foodaholic

Mary was a 25-year-old, 347-pound single woman who was first seen with her even more obese identical twin. She was not seen again for several months, when the operational diagnosis was that her sister had just died of the complications of morbid obesity. This event had a profound effect in motivating Mary to lose weight, but not nearly as much as another unexpected event that occurred early in her therapy.

The patient had failed in a number of food addiction programs and her implicit contract was that she would change her eating habits just slightly enough to avoid dying like her sister. She was not prepared for the abstinence approach of this program.

All addictions are garlic and must be treated as such. No addict can recover as long as the denial is fueled by the addiction. Abstinence is the pathway into the program, and continued abstinence is required for continued participation. But where alcoholics and drug addicts can be asked to completely abstain, the foodaholic still has to eat. Therefore, the approach to abstinence needs to be modified. As a prerequisite to entering the program, foodaholics must lose a modest amount of weight, continue to lose more weight each week, and refrain from eating their nemesis foods. The latter are defined as those foods that the person will binge on if she/he eats just a little of it. These foods differ from individual to individual, and every foodaholic knows his or her own nemesis foods. Any pounds lost above the weekly requirement go into a bank, to be drawn upon at times when no loss occurs. Failure to maintain the prescribed regimen results in varying degrees of exclusion from participation.

Without going into great detail, suffice it to say that Mary succeeded through one 20-week addictive group program in which she lost 55 pounds, and was granted a second 20-week program in which she lost an even greater amount of weight. But midway into the first program Mary began to falter, and it appeared she would fail the program. Then the unexpected happened.

Mary arrived for her group session in a state of agitation. A small, wiry young man began talking with her at the bus stop and within five minutes proposed marriage. He got on the bus with her and in the 35-minute ride to the therapist's office he proposed marriage a half dozen more times. Once off the bus, he followed her into the waiting room, where he continued to plead with her to marry him. Mary was noticeably upset. She had met her first "chubby-chaser," men who have an irresistible compulsion to be with very obese women.

The psychologist ordered him out of the building, but he waited outside for her. He began to appear everywhere in her life. Complaints to the police were of little avail as the chubby-chaser ignored orders to stay away. Mary, who was just about to fail the program, declared she would lose weight so as to get this man and any others like him out of her life. She made good her promise, and when she dropped below the critical level that triggered this man's perverted eroticism, he disappeared as suddenly as he had appeared.

Mary eventually stabilized her weight between 170 and 180 pounds, and maintained that level for years. She always joked that she was driven to fitness by a chubby-chaser.

LEGEND

Psychological Mechanism:	Denial
Diagnosis:	Food Addiction
Operational Diagnosis:	Sister died of morbid obesity
Implicit Contract:	Reduce weight only enough not to die
Personality Type:	Garlic
Homework:	Lose modest weight; Avoid nemesis foods
Therapeutic Techniques:	Humor the resistance
	Special addictive program

There is controversy as to whether what has been termed by many psychotherapists as "sex and love addiction" is actually an addiction. On the one hand, the behavior fits many of the characteristics of addiction: A high followed by a low (crash), with the urgency to repeat the behavior. Abstinence reveals an underlying depression. The behavior, like alcohol and drugs, "protects" against intimacy and rejection. Despite these shared characteristics, others say that calling such behavior an addiction has led to the label being attached to such varied and farfetched activities as "compulsive shopping" and "compulsive

Nintendo playing." In the authors' view, such nonchemical highs such as those derived from compulsive sex and compulsive gambling create biochemical conditions in the body that resemble to some extent those induced by excessive alcohol, drugs, food. Yet, without coming down on either side of the controversy, a case of so-called sex and love addition is given here because of its frequency in our society and the extent to which psychotherapists tend to treat it as if it were onion rather than garlic.

Ted's search for the perfect woman was appropriately treated as garlic, in spite of the fact that beneath the exterior there was hidden a frightened little boy terrified of being rejected by women.

Case Illustration: Ted, In Search of the Perfect Woman

Ted was a 29-year-old, single lawyer, working for the government, who came in complaining of a "bathroom problem." Upon explanation, this was a symptom that had developed over the past year in which Ted would experience sudden abdominal cramps and diarrhea. This would occur at the most inopportune times, and he would have to interrupt whatever he was doing to rush to the restroom. In fact, this occurred twice during the first session. This was very obviously a symptom of anxiety.

The patient was referred by a young female psychologist whom he had seen several times. She believed he had an erotic transference with which he did not wish to deal openly, so she recommended he be transferred to the care of a male. The patient agreed, but denied any romantic interest in her and stated flatly, "She was not that good looking." The psychologist remembered the woman therapist to be exceptionally attractive and asked the patient why he did not think so. He responded emphatically, "She's too skinny." As if to justify his conclusion, he went on to state that he had spent the past 10 years studying the perfect female form and was thus an authority.

Eventually, Ted brought in an extensive collection of charts, beginning with the foot. He had constructed the "golden mean" of how a woman's foot should look, so that the size was proportionate to her height. There was a "golden mean" for each height, by half-inch increments, from 5 feet to 6 feet. He did not regard a woman under 5 feet or over 6 feet as attractive, so for the range he chose there were 24 drawings of perfectly proportioned feet. As if this were not complicated enough, he had had drawn by an artist 24 specifications, according to height, for the ankle, knee, thigh, hips, buttocks, waist, bust, shoulders, and neck. In order to display the "golden mean" for a woman, 240 drawings were thus necessary. He could never bring all of these in at one time, but to demonstrate the process he brought in for a woman of 5 feet 6 inches the 10 drawings for the perfect foot, ankle, knee, thigh, hips, buttocks, waist, bust, shoulders, and neck. Realizing he had overlooked the arm, he was in the process of constructing drawings for both the forearm and upper arm. This would add 48 drawings.

Ted confided that once he found the woman who had all of the golden means, he would marry her. Unfortunately, he had found only near-perfect women so far. "Even the best of them will be imperfect in just one part." Then he added that the perfect woman would also have to have a big "bush." Although this was not on the drawings, it was the last criterion of perfection, and one that would have to be ascertained by going to bed with the woman.

In his search for the perfect woman, Ted was always "on the make," because only in total nudity could he fully assess how perfect or imperfect the woman's form was. He meticulously kept an annual diary of all the women he slept with for the sake of his quest. He would record each woman's name, proportions, and other pertinent data. Two years ago, he had his best year, having slept with 93 different women during that 12-month period.

Beneath all of these rituals, Ted was a sex addict. In time, it was also learned he was a pornography addict. Each weekend, he would rent 15 to 20 pornographic videos to copy. Being impatient with any activity other than the orgiastic sequences, he would fast forward the tapes until he had reduced 15 to 20 videos to 2 hours of concentrated visual orgasms. He bragged that years of such effort had resulted in the finest and wildest library of pornography in the world. The psychologist named him the Duncan Hines of pornography. Ted relished the appellation.

All of this did not come out at once. Rather, this information was revealed in small pieces over a number of sessions. Eventually, it was also discovered that Ted was a compulsive masturbator. His greatest pleasure was obtained through onanism, and even his sex with women was both pornographic and masturbatory. His thrill was to watch a woman perform oral sex on him. At the critical moment, he would pull away and masturbate on her face. Ted's thinly disguised embarrassment was not hidden by his bragging that he was the heir to the crown left by Don Juan, Casanova, and Errol Flynn.

Ted's presenting symptom, his "bathroom problem," began when he decided to study for the state bar examination. During that year, he developed so much anxiety that studying was futile. He wanted the psychologist's permission to not take the bar examination. After all, he did not need it as a government lawyer and he planned to remain in government service. He could not make the decision on his own, as his father was urging him to become a member of the bar. Within the first 10 sessions, he had formed a strong transference and accepted the therapist's permission as a substitute for his father's disapproval. Almost immediately, Ted's "bathroom problem" disappeared, only to return a few months later, bringing him back to treatment.

When he returned, he stated that the reappearance of his "bathroom problem" was interfering with his ability to seduce women, as it would disrupt his activity at the critical moment. It was also apparent that the patient liked the psychologist and enjoyed the closeness he had never experienced with his father. He wanted to continue therapy.

The patient acknowledged that he was a sex-pornographic-masturbatory addict, but he seemed to want the therapist's stamp of approval for his behavior. He attempted in many ways to manipulate the therapist into seeing his sexual activity as positive. Failing to get it, he decided he would achieve a compromise wherein he would be in charge of his addiction, rather than his addiction driving him. He announced that he was going to be the first patient to "beat the addiction without abstinence." His "bathroom problem" grew worse.

Ted staunchly denied that his search for the perfect woman was a rationalization for his fear of intimacy with women. Since he would never find the ideal, he could avoid forever his fear of an ongoing relationship. As if to prove the therapist wrong, he announced at his appointment that he had all but found the perfect woman. A date at the beach revealed a bathing suit-clad figure that was perfect. All that remained was to determine if she also had the required thick pubic hair. He threatened the therapist, "If she has a big bush, you'll see how wrong you are. I'll propose to her."

The following week, Ted came to his session dejected. The woman in question did have a profusion of pubic hair, but she had no navel. It seems that when her umbilical cord was removed the infant developed an infection which resulted in deep and extensive scarring. At age three her pediatric surgeon covered the area in plastic surgery. Ted dramatically displayed anger, crying, "I finally found the perfect woman and she has no belly button!" The therapist had difficulty stifling a laugh. The patient hesitated and then also laughed.

To attempt to prevail upon Ted to abandon his seduction of women or his use of pornography would be to strong-arm the resistance. The entry point in his treatment would be forbidding the gratification derived in masturbation, either alone or with a partner. After considerable argument, Ted agreed. It was also agreed that if he broke his abstinence he would come in for his appointment, briefly tell the therapist how it happened, and then forfeit the session. With the blocking of this gratification, some surprising changes began occurring. But even more surprising was that Ted had to forfeit only one session over the next several months.

Ted found himself in a three month relationship with a woman, a period that was like a lifetime for this man who specialized in one-night stands. At the end of three months, she broke off the relationship. Ted was devastated. His "bathroom problem," which had abated with abstinence from masturbation, returned with a vengeance. The patient berated the therapist, for it was he who got the patient into this. Then, Ted developed a severe neurodermatitis, which persisted for several weeks. He continued to blame the psychologist.

During this time, Ted began to have important insights. His father was in the Vietnam War when Ted was two to three years old and his mother, grandmother, and several aunts doted on him as "the man of the house." The day came when his father was coming home. Ted was dressed in a specially tailored and authentic little soldier suit as he and his mother met the father's troop ship. His excitement turned to disappointment over the ensuing several days and into the following weeks. Mother and father became absorbed with each other, ignoring him. He could have tolerated losing his status as the "man of the house," but his father was incapable of truly relating to Ted or his two brothers, who were born when he was four and five. He had lost his mother without gaining a father.

As he grew older, he became an excellent athlete in an attempt to gain his father's approval. Not only did his father continue to ignore him, but with puberty when all his fellow athletes began growing tall, Ted remained short. His athletic career was over. Ashamed, Ted discovered elevator shoes and pornography. The first made him feel tall, the second made him feel strong. No longer did he have to trust a woman who would betray him as did his mother. With pornography, he was in charge of his gratification and his self-esteem. When he became sexually active with young women, he continued his masturbatory attitude, remaining romantically aloof as he was successfully seductive. So angry was Ted at his mother (and subsequently all women) that he did not attend her funeral.

As these insights unfolded, Ted volunteered that he had destroyed all of his pornography tapes. "What good are they if I can't masturbate?" A few weeks later, he realized he also had to destroy his cherished diaries. "I never wanted to admit it, but those diaries were supposed to make me feel adequate in my old age and after I'm impotent. I don't want to end up being that lonely old man."

Ted has now been in a relationship with a woman for almost two years. When he is being honest with himself, he admits he loves Laura. But most of the time he complains that she fits none of his criteria for the perfect woman. He has not masturbated for over two years, but he continues kicking and screaming as he drags himself deeper and deeper into intimacy.

LEGEND

Psychological Mechanism:	Denial
Diagnosis:	Pornography Addiction
Operational Diagnosis:	Sudden anxiety diarrhea
Implicit Contract:	Don't touch my pornography and compulsive masturbation
Personality Type:	Garlic
Homework:	Abstinence
Therapeutic Techniques:	Blocking gratification
	Special addictive program
	Humor the resistance

Personality Styles and Disorders

Dynamics

In personality disorders, impairment has occurred early in life, thus coloring the personality generally. The earlier the impairment, the more garlic a personality is likely to develop. Personality disorders can be of any neurotic type. For example, there are depressive personality disorders. In contrast to a depressive neurotic to whom one might offer encouragement to be assertive, a depressive personality disorder would be flattening everybody in the family. Again the axiom of garlic before onion applies.

In clinical practice, it is useful to distinguish a level of impairment resulting in a distorted style of personality but which may not meet the DSM-IV criteria for a personality disorder. Although the impairment is more severe with the personality disorder, in both the patient denies the effect of his personality in interpersonal interactions and his or her responsibility for consequences. The entry to treatment is also the same.

Entry

The entry with personality styles and disorders is to turn up the heat. The anxiety that motivates the patient to seek treatment must be maintained to sustain the therapeutic leverage for change. This must be done without narcissistic blows to the patient's ego, an approach that requires considerable sensitivity.

Roland has been chosen as an example because most therapists would treat him as onion, noting that treatment is necessarily protracted because the condition of a schizoid lifestyle is intractable. It is our contention that this is therapist error, and that personality lifestyles are amenable to change if the interventions take into account that the life style is denial, and thus garlic.

Case Illustration: Roland, the Pretender

Some personality disorders seem to be suffering so much on presentation that it is often difficult for the therapist to keep in mind the fact that the patient is garlic. This can be especially so if the personality disorder is at the moment displaying the anxiety that often accrues from the consequences of one's own garlic behavior. Such a patient was Roland, a schizoid 35-year-old man who in spite of being married, was very isolated from people and generally insulated from life. It never would have occurred to him to seek psychological help were it not for his wife's preparing to leave. This impending change in his life had generated considerable anxiety in a man whose usual demeanor was one of distance and aloofness.

Roland had constructed his life in accordance with his schizoid isolation. His home was built in two wings, one in which he lived, and the other housing his wife and two children. Whenever he wished, he could enter the family wing, but his wife and children were forbidden to enter his wing without his express permission. In fact, the door into his wing was kept locked and only he had the key.

His occupation also reflected his isolation from people. As a telephone installer, he could harbor the illusion that he was interacting with people, where actually the brief encounter with no subsequent contact with the customer suited Roland's aloofness.

The wife complained that at no time had Roland ever kissed or embraced his children. Sex with her was mechanical, conversation was shallow, and any semblance of warmth was completely absent. Originally a naive farm girl whom Roland had brought to the city, in the following years of marriage this woman had grown up and wanted more than this cold man could offer.

Clearly, the patient was here now (operational diagnosis) because his wife was about to leave him. The implicit contract was: Keep my wife from leaving me without my having to change. His resistances were all toward preventing closeness at all costs. The wife sincerely believed Roland to be so fragile that without help he would collapse when she left. So she decided to remain in the marriage until he was able to rely on his therapist. Thus, Roland's implicit contract was initially fulfilled and he cooperated in treatment on that basis.

Roland was not pleased at being assigned to group therapy, but he went along with it. This treatment plan reflected the patient's need for socialization, but, as painful as the group process was to him, it was preferable to the potential terror of having to relate to a therapist in individual treatment. As a schizoid, Roland was more likely to respond to a diluted group transference, while he would have distanced himself from any possible individual transference. Accordingly, when the group assigned homework within the framework of that which was doable, Roland would wince, but comply.

Responding to the fact Roland had never kissed either of his children, the group assigned the homework of kissing each child on top of the head when he arose from the breakfast table each morning to go to work. His protests turned to surprise when he reported within two weeks that he was also kissing the children each evening when he returned home. He had not been asked by the group to do this, and he grudgingly confessed that he enjoyed the children's positive response. With a multitude of such small steps, Roland was finally displaying more and more affection to his wife and children, and was even relating slightly to co-workers. His wife was seriously reconsidering her decision to divorce him. All was going well until Roland's life myth, which enabled his isolation, was revealed in the group.

Roland was born in a small midwestern town and never knew his father. He was aware he was born out of wedlock. While he hated his mother for it, he sustained an elaborate fantasy from his early childhood. He believed his father was either the president of the Chase Manhattan Bank or the United States ambassador to the United Nations. This startlingly specific fantasy further stated that this father, on his deathbed, would recall this bastard son and send for him. Upon seeing Roland, he would be so overcome with guilt and remorse for having abandoned him that he would change his will, leaving Roland the bulk of his multimillion-dollar estate. While awaiting the fulfillment of this prophecy, Roland would not have to succeed at anything: occupationally, socially, or domestically. All would be given him at the appointed time. This fantasy was the core of his personality disorder, and it both justified and enabled his aloofness.

The group assigned the homework that Roland would visit his mother and ascertain from her exactly who his father was. The patient resisted the idea for weeks. Finally the group, at the suggestion of the therapist, made it a condition of continued treatment. It is therapeutic to do so in limited and well thought through instances where treatment would be stymied if it were not insisted that the patient take that step. Roland went to the Midwest and confronted his mother.

At the next group session, Roland was a stunned, anxious man. He was floundering, as his well-constructed schizoid personality with its cold aloofness had fallen apart. His denial (garlic) was shattered. He was pleading for help. He had learned his father was a musician who had come through town on a one night stand.

Subsequently, Roland entered individual therapy, established for the first time a deep emotional attachment in the transference, and succeeded in making a number of remarkable changes.

LEGEND

Psychological Mechanism:	Withdrawal
Diagnosis:	Schizoid Personality Disorder
Operational Diagnosis:	Wife is divorcing me
Implicit Contract:	Prevent divorce without changing me
Personality Type:	Garlic
Homework:	Pretend to love children; confront mother
Therapeutic Techniques:	Group therapy
	Prescribing the resistance (i.e., verify famous father)

Impulse Neuroses

Dynamics

Impulse neuroses, which include such varying conditions as peeping toms, exhibitionists, and compulsive gamblers, are often called compulsive disorders because the individual builds over time to an anxiety level that is relieved only by acting on the impulse. Because of this confusion of terminology, it is important for the psychotherapist to be reminded that whereas obsessive-compulsive disorder is onion, impulse neurosis is garlic. It becomes even more imperative since the impulse neurotics are almost never seen unless they are in trouble. The situational anxiety will be so intense on presentation that patients will appear to be onion. The psychotherapist must be mindful that successful therapy with such cases requires ignoring the situational stress and treating the garlic. This is not easy, as the patient will manifest a great deal of obvious distress. Reducing this stress results in the patient's feeling better and concluding that treatment is unnecessary. Garlic is denial, and impulse neurotics, as with all personality disorders, do not regard themselves as abnormal.

Entry

The successful treatment of such patients involves the often difficult triad of (1) raising the patient's anxiety by raising the "heat," (2) blocking the gratification usually experienced by acting on the impulse, and (3) taking advantage of the profound increase in emotional distress created by the first two. This approach can be demonstrated in the case of Oscar.

Voyeurism as an impulse neurosis is so prevalent and the recidivism so complete that society feels helpless to reduce its incidence. Most authorities regard it as a nuisance, for with our jails clogged with violent criminals, our criminal justice system metes out probationary period after probationary period. Psychotherapists have been of little help as our usual therapeutic interventions are unsuccessful. The key to treating voyeurism and all impulse neuroses is to (1) see it for the garlic it is and (2) turn up the heat by forbidding the primary gratification. In voyeurism, the primary gratification is compulsive masturbation, an activity that the usual forms of turning up the heat (jail, probation, fines, loss of job or reputation) do not touch. Consider, for example, a prison system that attempts to forbid masturbation, surely an inappropriate restriction for all but the impulse neurotic. On the other hand, a skillful therapist can use the threat of the justice system, coupled with denying treatment, as motivation to impose abstinence from masturbation. As shown in the case of Oscar, this is really turning up the heat.

Case Illustration: Oscar, the Voyeuristic Optometrist

The patient was a 31-year-old married optometrist with two children. He had been arrested while on business away from home. Oscar had actively been a peeping tom since early adolescence. He had been apprehended a number of times, but regarded by an overworked police force as a nuisance rather than a threat, charges would be dropped or probation with the requirement of treatment would be ordered by an equally overworked court. Follow-up had been sloppy, and Oscar never continued therapy beyond the first few sessions. Before seeing his new therapist, he had gone for treatment four different times, only to discontinue once the "heat" was off. This time the charges were serious, and Oscar was worried and upset.

While on a business trip in another part of the same state, Oscar positioned himself on the hotel fire escape and witnessed two women in a lesbian act. He denied at first that he masturbated while peeping, but it was soon established that masturbation accompanied all of his voyeuristic acts. The women discovered Oscar, who in his excitement had thrown caution to the wind, and he was apprehended by the hotel's security force and turned over to the police. Similar discovery had occurred on other occasions and Oscar expected to be only inconvenienced. He had not anticipated the militancy of the two women he had victimized. They demanded Oscar be prosecuted and they sued the hotel for damages due to their neglecting to protect its guests. There was considerable publicity and the trial promised to be a major media event in that city.

Following his lawyer's recommendation that Oscar should avoid a highly publicized trial, he pleaded no contest. He was awaiting sentencing and a hearing with the state's Board of Optometry already had been scheduled. It was rumored that the judge would "throw the book" at the defendant and Oscar could well have his optometric license revoked. He needed and sought a prominent practitioner who would vouch that Oscar was in successful psychotherapy and well on his way to being cured.

In the first session, Oscar put his best foot forward. He described his successful practice and his devoted wife who was sticking by him, and he downplayed the extent and duration of his peeping tom behavior. The psychologist was direct and straightforward. He pointed out to Oscar that not only was his story full of inconsistencies, his description of his behavior did not fit the syndrome. He had the privilege of consulting another therapist, but if he were going to work with this one, he would have to come clean. Oscar hesitated for a few minutes, then told the entire story. As a child, he found ways of spying on his mother when she was undressing, and after puberty he became the neighborhood peeping tom. He was involved in several skirmishes in which irate husbands almost caught him, but he escaped detection until adulthood. He was arrested several times and always managed to get through the ordeals with a minimum of damage to himself and his practice. He described how a steady buildup of anxiety would eventually drive him to seek the only relief possible, and he boldly asked the psychologist to testify to the court the helpless nature of his behavior, his sincerity in seeking treatment, and the assurance he would never do this again.

The psychologist countered that the best he could do was to ask the court to delay final sentencing for 90 days while treatment proceeded. During those 90 days, the patient would keep semiweekly appointments, refrain from both voyeuristic and *all* masturbatory behavior, and diligently apply himself to his therapy. The restriction was so stringent that he could not even look at female underwear or bathing suit advertisements, and masturbation was forbidden even without voyeurism inasmuch as the patient was adept at conjuring vivid mental images. Violation of these conditions would result at the conclusion of the 90 days in the termination of further treatment and the rendering to the court of a report indicating Oscar was a poor rehabilitation risk. The patient was very upset, but realized he had no choice.

Over the course of the next several weeks Oscar's anxiety grew at times to almost intolerable proportions, but he abided by the rules of treatment. He began to learn alternative ways of discharging anxiety, the first of which was a clumsy heaping of anger on the therapist. Later, he learned to refine his anger. He also learned that turning to his wife in a needful attitude invoked in her a caring that was very helpful. He also began to enjoy his two children in a more meaningful way. But treatment was turbulent, and Oscar was never totally without his denial. One manifestation of his resistance when an interpretation was made or an insight was looming was for this optometrist to remove his glasses, and then declare, "I just don't see that." Therapists often overlook the magical fulfillment in such symbolic denial and fail to forbid the behavior. Doing so in Oscar's case both curtailed the denial and facilitated understanding. Whenever he would begin to remove his glasses, he would stop, laugh at himself, and say, "There I go trying not to see something again."

At the end of the 90 days, the therapist and Oscar agreed that therapy should continue. The court placed him on two years probation, and his license was placed by the board on three years probation. Recidivism is high among impulse neurotics, but Oscar never again engaged in voyeuristic behavior. He had learned other means of handling his anxiety before it reached volcanic proportions. This did not mean he was not tempted, and he considered himself not "cured," but in recovery. During periods of unusual stress in his life when Oscar was strongly tempted, he would make an appointment to see his therapist. The key to his recovery is his continued abstinence from any masturbatory behavior.

LEGEND

Psychological Mechanism:	Denial
Diagnosis:	Impulse Neurosis
Operational Diagnosis:	Fear of incarceration
Implicit Contract:	Get me out of trouble without changing me
Personality Type:	Garlic
Homework:	No voyeurism and masturbation
Therapeutic Techniques:	Turning up the heat
	Blocking gratification

Hypomania

Dynamics

Hypomania is always garlic and exhausting to treat. Hypomanics are very, very emotional and infectious people. They are ebullient, happy, and self-confident, and people love them. But, in reality, they are very depressed people. Hypomania is depression turned upside down, and treating it successfully is likely to plunge the patient into a profound depression.

Entry

The treatment of choice for bipolar disorder is lithium carbonate, which effectively controls most cases. However, the need for psychotherapy for these patients is not necessarily counterindicated. Bipolars can feel their subdued elation and depression cycles behind their medication, and some, welcoming the elation, temporarily stop taking the lithium. They enjoy the initial hypomania, but as the condition progresses they desperately overdose on lithium. When seen, the patient is not only manic, but also suffering from lithium toxicity. Other patients stop their lithium for 10 to 12 months so as to have a baby without risking the possible and severe cardiovascular side effects on the fetus. During this time, they must be supported by psychotherapy. Still other patients suffer kidney failure or other physical complications and must discontinue their lithium.

Psychologically, the entry with patients suffering from hypomania is to assign an enormous task appealing to their narcissism. In this way, they are kept occupied until arrangements can be made for hospitalization, as in the following case.

Case Illustration: Eleanor Flying High

Eleanor was a 39-year-old bipolar patient whose lithium was effective as long as she took it. On three occasions, however, being mildly aware of her elevated mood that was being kept under control, she decided to allow herself that "wonderful feeling." She stopped her lithium ostensibly for a couple of days, but as she became more hypomanic she was enjoying the experience too much to resume taking her medication. Interestingly, her husband did not see the warning signs even though she had done this on three previous occasions and with devastating results. One morning, she awakened feeling very high and, after her husband had left for work, she went to a travel agent and bought a first class airplane trip around the world. She charged this on credit cards and was gone when her husband arrived home from work that evening. She had left him a note saying she would see him in three weeks.

Four days later, Eleanor was remanded by the airline to the authorities in Hong Kong. She had not slept for many days and her behavior on the flight from Honolulu was so outrageous that the pilot had called the Hong Kong police by radio. They were waiting for her when the airplane landed. The husband was contacted and he made arrangements for his wife to be returned under heavy sedation and in the care of an accompanying nurse.

Once back home the effects of the sedatives wore off and Eleanor was once again in a manic state. She resumed her lithium, but in very heavy doses, and she convinced her husband she had her medication and would be all right. She did not wish to go to the hospital. He unfortunately agreed, and by the next three days Eleanor was not only still manic, but also toxic. He called the psychologist who had treated the patient several years earlier, as he was the only one Eleanor would agree to see. She threatened to run away if the husband attempted to take her to the hospital or to another practitioner. She was brought to the office.

Anyone who has not seen a manic turn from an elated state to an abusive, belligerent state cannot appreciate the extent to which the manic person can be hateful and physical. They can destroy every object around them, attack others, and require several people to restrain them. The husband, who had seen his wife in such a state, knew better than to attempt to force her to go somewhere she did not wish to go.

As a psychologist, the therapist could not prescribe medication or treat her lithium toxicity. He also had the goal of getting her to the hospital without her running away or becoming abusive and uncontrollable. In the meantime, she was everywhere in the suite of offices, talking volubly, and disrupting all activity. The therapist sat her down in a vacant office and asked her to write her autobiography, with particular emphasis on all of her talents and successes. She was to think of this as the manuscript for a book that could be entitled "Eleanor, A Very Remarkable Woman." The receptionist would keep her supplied with paper.

The next two hours, while arrangements for hospitalization were completed, Eleanor had written on two full reams of typing paper. She thanked the psychologist for helping her get in touch with the special person that she was and she went willingly, but noisily, to the hospital.

LEGEND

Psychological Mechanism:	Denial
Diagnosis:	Mania
Operational Diagnosis	Failure to take lithium
Implicit Contract:	Help me stay high

Personality Type: Garlic
Homework: Write autobiography
Therapeutic Technique: Increase compliance with
         lithium regimen

Narcissistic Personality Disorder

Dynamics

The narcissistic personality strongly resembles the borderline personality, but with one important difference that renders the patient more accessible to treatment. Both manifest the mechanism of splitting and projective identification. Like the borderline personality, the narcissistic personality is self-centered, susceptible to a variety of addictive behaviors, and given to sexual aberrations and perversions. Neither is capable of bonding and the transference is always tenuous. Both have been denied loving parenting and do not expect to find it in either life or psychotherapy.

However, where the borderline personality was abused, the narcisstic personality was indulged in childhood. This indulgence was a substitute for real parenting, but the patient became dependent upon it. This dependency is repeated in adulthood with persons who can supply the patient's narcissistic needs, but the attachment to such an individual is entirely egocentric and is based on "what he/she can do for me." Failure to meet the patient's expectations triggers the same kind of berating and derogating of the person that is found in the borderline. This is the projective identification: The person becomes the projected "bad part" of the patient. However, in contrast to the borderline personality, the narcissist is highly vulnerable to losing the person who is meeting his/her needs. This mitigates the immediate rejection that is characteristic of the borderline personalities, since the narcissistic personality desperately clings to the needed person in a panicky attempt to continue the narcissistic supplies. This feature renders the narcissistic personality more accessible to understanding his/her own behavior and adjusting it so as not to lose the object. Consequently, where the borderline personality must learn almost solely from painful experience, the narcissistic personality, though still mainly dependent on experience, is capable of some insight and anticipation.

The narcissistic personality shares with the borderline personality the lack of bonding, the self-centeredness, the propensity to addiction and sexual perversion, the hysterical acting out, the inability to tolerate stress, and the tendency to go in and out of psychotic-like states. But in contrast to the borderline, the narcissist has an extreme vulnerability. Whenever there is the threat of losing the therapist, the narcissist will become compliant and even pleading.

Entry

The patient with narcissistic personality disorder is extremely dependent on the therapist for narcissistic gratification, and the therapist must use this to set limits and consequences for the patient.

The treatment of Neil was complicated by a previous therapist who for 11 years acceded to the patient's every demand. This is not unusual, as many bright, gifted narcissistic personalitites are witty, affable, and successful. They are admired by many of their acquaintances, who aspire to emulate their success. When their vulnerability does show because of a rejection or a setback, they can be ingratiating and receive the attention and help they desperately need. Many are able to hide for long periods the contempt for others that is a part of their self-centeredness. When they are vulnerable, they appear as onion, but actually the appropriate treatment is to regard them consistently as garlic. All of this is illustrated by Neil, who unfortunately typifies to many the dashing, successful, affable, and handsome American male.

Case Illustration: Neil's Life in the Fast Lane

Neil came to the West Coast from the Midwest when the cable television industry saw him as a rising star. He had been in charge of advertising sales for a small television station. With his new job came a six-figure salary, a large expense account, and the "big time."

A 38-year-old, single man, he was referred by his therapist who had been seeing him for 11 years. He did not make contact until he had been on the new job for several weeks and had encountered his first difficulty. Neil epitomized the stereotypical man of the eighties:

successful, egotistical, self-indulgent, and greedy. On his first appointment, he asserted that his only interests were fast money, fast women, and fast cars, in that order. He pushed the envelope to the edge and when he ran out of energy, there was cocaine to provide the necessary boost. He lived hard, worked hard, and cared only for himself.

The patient had people he admired, but the admiration was based on their usefulness to him. He liked knowing celebrities and flaunting his acquaintance with them. However, his tenuous admiration was dramatically illustrated by his mildly contemptuous description of the therapist he had relied upon for 11 years: "I was his life's work. He was always available, any time of the day or night. I wonder what he's doing without me."

To describe the patient as demanding would be an understatement. He wore his self-esteem on his sleeve, and if a woman he hit on rejected him, he would be so devastated he would call the psychologist in the middle of the night from a bar for a psychological Band-Aid. He liked to be the one who left the woman and he took pride in how many lovers he had "trashed."

After ignoring the referral for several weeks, he called in a state of extreme agitation. He had demanded that the car the company provided him be replaced by a Jaguar. When his boss refused, he yelled at him and, after a one-hour battle, the boss fired him. Neil saw himself as blameless and was bewildered with the boss' refusal to give him the Jaguar. "Please do this for me," was a legitimate demand to Neil. He asked the psychologist to contact the boss on the patient's behalf and was angry when the therapist explained why he could not do so. After all, Neil's previous therapist "did these things for me all the time." On his own, the boss reconsidered, rehired Neil, and bought a Jaguar for him. But Neil expressed his contempt for his boss by having sex late one night with the boss' secretary on the boss' desk.

Neil was a "menopausal" baby and was doted on by his older parents. For 11 years he had a doting psychologist and now he had found a doting boss. The reality check in his life would have to be his therapist, who informed the patient of this in terms he would understand and remember. Pulling open his suit jacket, the therapist said, "See, I have no tits." This became the shorthand between patient and therapist. Whenever the patient made vociferous and unreasonable demands, without saying a word the therapist would pull his suit jacket open. Usually, the patient would resign himself to the reality. The few times that Neil would continue his demands, the therapist would remind the patient of their agreement and invite him to get another therapist.

Limits were set for the patient consistent with the structure of therapy: The treatment would help the patient anticipate the consequences of his reckless narcissism, but if he ignored the warnings and got into trouble, it would be his sole responsibility to extricate himself. This simple therapeutic contract was subjected to every possible test by the patient each time he got into trouble.

Despite his outrageous personal behavior, Neil was very good at his work, which was selling advertising on the cable network. This is not unusual for narcissistic personality-disordered persons if they are in jobs where their affability, good looks, extraversion, breezy self-confidence, and ingratiating manner are assets. Throughout all the turmoil of Neil's therapy, his employers were pleased by the sales record and amused by his playfulness.

There were innumerable instances where Neil tested the limits, of which the following was illustrative. The patient was driving away from the trendy bar in which he was known as the "mayor" when he had an automobile accident. The police, who regularly patrol that fashionable part of the city as the trendy bars are closing, were there instantly. Neil had been drinking and he had done a line of cocaine as he was leaving the bar. He was also in the company of the wife of a member of the city council. Neil called the psychologist in a panic at 2:30 A.M. on his car phone, but in keeping with the therapeutic contract the psychologist refused to take the call. He learned the details at Neil's next appointment. By that time, the entire matter had been hushed up, ostensibly because the city councilman's wife also had cocaine and alcohol in her bloodstream. The matter did not escape the attention of the news media, however.

The councilman and his wife were in a messy divorce a few weeks later. Neil was dragged through the media spotlight and, although he appeared confident and likeable on television, he responded with his usual inability to tolerate stress. He was refused his whining requests for a sedative, which persisted for several weeks. In accordance with the therapeutic contract, had Neil obtained sedatives or tranquilizers elsewhere, his therapy would have been terminated. Also in accordance with the therapeutic contract, Neil forfeited the two sessions following the one in which he reported the incident. This was for having used cocaine, as all illegal substances were forbidden in his therapeutic contract. Neil protested loudly that at the time he needed the therapist the most, "Your dumb rules forbid me to see you."

Neil continued to cling to the therapist as his lifeline and, with each test, he seemed to become a bit more responsible. Neil is still a narcissistic personality, flashy, self-possessed, and affable. But he is considerably more responsible. He no longer sells television advertising, having become a station manager. On his new job, extraversion remains an asset, but the distinguished look of a senior broadcaster is required. He is playing his role of a responsible community leader well. So well, in fact, that Neil no longer gets into any kind of trouble. He sees the psychologist infrequently, and *before* he gets into difficulty.

To the idealistic therapist, this may seem insufficient. In response, attention can be called to years and years in analysis expended to change basic personality. The patients are happier and more successful, and this is commendable. But so is Neil. No one can make a redwood tree out of a magnolia. The best we can do is eliminate the aphids in the magnolia.

LEGEND

Psychological Mechanism:	Denial and Projective Identification
Diagnosis:	Narcissistic Personality Disorder
Operational Diagnosis:	Replace my doting previous therapist
Implicit Contract:	Fulfill my narcissistic needs
Personality Type:	Garlic
Homework:	Abstinence
Therapeutic Techniques:	Setting limits
	Taking advantage of vulnerability

Borderline Personality Disorder

Dynamics

Every borderline is a five-year-old who has managed to terrify his or her parents and is enjoying every minute of it, but underneath has the terror of feeling, "My gosh, what if I need somebody? Who's going to be there for me, because I'm stronger than my own parents?" The borderline relishes the fantasy and the victory of being stronger than you and vanquishing you, but the moment they do vanquish you, they hate you because they also harbor the hope that you will be strong enough to be the parent they never had. The borderline needs your strong ego.

Borderlines are the product of dysfunctional families, are increasing geometrically, and may come to dominate caseloads in the future. Parents of borderlines are likely to have been drug dependent, and as a child the borderline has experienced neglect and/or abuse from birth. Thus, the borderline never learned to bond and cannot develop healthy interpersonal relationships. Their defenses are characterized by projective identification and splitting. In order to survive their abusive childhood, they learned to be manipulative and destructively hostile, and rejecting. In therapy, they project this "bad" self onto the therapist and test the therapist's strength and honesty. In their social environment, they alternately seduce or infuriate people, thereby splitting groups and pitting members against each other. These dynamics are further discussed in the protocol of the borderline group found in the appendix.

People with borderline personalities do not have schizophrenic overlaps. The greatest event that can befall a borderline is to be diagnosed as schizophrenic, which then gives him or her a pass to all the wanted hospitalization. Borderlines dive into psychosis like one dives into a pool and comes out at the other end. A schizophrenic doesn't come out the other end. The borderline jumps into primary process and comes out at will. The schizophrenic cannot come out at will. Borderlines want hospitalization when it's going to suit their purpose. Once they've accomplished their purpose, there's no reason to keep hearing the voices, so they stop all of this primary process. One question that can differentiate between the borderline personality and the schizophrenic is, "Are the voices inside your head or outside your head?" The schizophrenic will look at you and say, "Huh?" The borderline will say, "Oh gosh, I've got to get the right answer." To the schizophrenic, there's not a right or wrong answer. The voices just are. The borderline will try to outguess the examination. Borderlines are so named because they are on the borderline of suffering a thought disorder, but their etiology of their impairment is psychosocial and not physiological as in the thought disorder of the schizophrenic.

Borderlines are survivors. Borderlines do not do themselves in. Borderline patients are remarkable human beings. They survived dysfunctional families that would have flattened all of us. Borderlines kill themselves only in despair, if they no longer can play the game. A borderline remanded to the back ward of a state hospital will kill themselves because they can no longer engage the world in their game.

Entry

Rapid changes can occur with borderline patients when they are properly treated. They should not be allowed to muck around in their childhood, but instead should be corralled in the here and now with structure and props that will make them less and less like leaves in the wind. They are best treated in groups, and a protocol for doing this is found in the appendix.

With borderline patients you can be as outrageous as they are, but not one iota more and certainly not less. When you have outwitted a borderline, you will see something very interesting: a little flicker of a grin, just a little bit on the edge of the mouth, or a glint in the eye. If you want to become successful, use the same outrageousness they use. But when they are being absolutely impossible, you say, "You're really obnoxious today. What the heck is this all about? Why are you so obnoxious today? You really trying to drive me up the wall? What's going on?"

They love you for it. They'll think, "This person is not a hypocrite. Every therapist I've had was so busy being nonjudgmental that they would tell me I was good when I was terrible." You can be very, very straightforward with borderlines as long as you're not angry with them. The moment you get angry with a borderline, you've disqualified yourself as a therapist. Borderlines set out to make you angry. They set out to prove you're no better than their parents were. They're out to disqualify you as a therapist. As they get angrier and angrier with borderlines, most therapists think that they do not have a right to be angry with the patient, and so they suppress it. In suppressing it, they respond to the borderline with more and more kindness. That's when the borderline absolutely destroys you with your hypocrisy. Ultimately, what the borderline is searching for is honesty. They'll try to knock your honesty down, because they don't believe that there's any such thing as an honest human being. After all, their parent's weren't and you can't be any better than their parents. But they need you to be there for them. The key to treating borderlines, especially, and all character disorders is not to get angry at them, but to be very straightforward instead.

Borderlines are particularly adept at becoming whatever they discern is of interest to the therapist. And because so many therapists are intrigued by multiple persoalities, survivors of incest or other sexual abuse, and so-called victimization in general, the borderline personality disorders will emulate these conditions. This does not mean that multiple personality disorder or victimization does not exist, but the conditions do not need the well-meaning, inept therapist to proliferate iatrogenic simulations. Preventing a borderline from acquiring a syndrome is illustrated in the case of Sandra.

Case Illustration: Sandra et al— A Case of Multiple Personality

When the nation's first psychotherapy benefit was implemented at Kaiser-Permanente in San Francisco during the late 1950s and early 1960s, the psychotherapists were startled by the high percentage of multiple personality disorder in their female patients. Before psychotherapy was included as an insurance benefit, it was largely the penchant of the upper middle class which was both highly educated and able to pay out of pocket. It was hypothesized that in the less educated general population for whom psychotherapy was now available dissociative disorders were far more prevalent. This did not prove to be the case, for as the glamour of multiple personality disorder wore off, the syndrome all but disappeared.

The implementation of the nation's first comprehensive psychotherapy benefit had coincided with the movie, *The Three Faces of Eve*, after which Joanne Woodward received the Academy Award for her portrayal of Eve and subsequently married Paul Newman. These events popularized and glamorized multiple personality disorder, which, as all fads must do, faded in time. In recent years, glamorization of the disorder has been revived by a series of books and made-for-television movies, but particularly by psychotherapists who seem to encourage its emergence. There are findings that suggest that although real multiple personality disorder exists, it is rare, and most instances are iatrogenic. Borderline personalities are particularly adept at mimicking any fad disorder. When agoraphobia was the glamour condition in the 1980s, borderline patients became housebound and were admitted to agoraphobic group programs, which they disrupted. Whereas agoraphobics are the epitome of onion, the borderline is unrelentingly garlic. Many a psychotherapist learned the hard way that buying into a borderline patient's pretense at being agoraphobic spelled failure for the group program.

With these concepts in mind, it would be useful to review the case of a rapidly emerging multiple personality disorder. Sandra was 23 when first seen by a therapist who specialized in that condition. Within two sessions a second personality emerged, and by the time the therapist was promoted and transferred to another state, she had four personalities. All of this had occurred within three months, and within 11 sessions. The therapist who inherited the case was suspicious that Sandra was really a borderline personality who had taken her cues for dissociation from her previous therapist. She prevailed upon the senior author to see the patient on his upcoming visit. The patient seized the opportunity when she was told of the visiting psychologist's reputation, and she confirmed the exhibitionism expected of a borderline personality. She knew the entire staff would be watching through a one-way mirror.

Once in the office with the visiting psychologist, the patient plunged into her abused past as a child. Everything she described was consistent with the background expected of a borderline personality. It was also consistently embellished and highly dramatized. The psychologist seemed markedly disinterested, at which point the patient became flirtatious and seductive. In response to the question, "And who are you?" she replied, "I'm Terry." The psychologist then asked, "How did you get in here?" Sandra, now as "Terry," tossed her head back and defiantly stated, "I come out whenever I want. Nobody tells me what to do." The psychologist then looked the patient intently in the eye and stated emphatically, "Psychotherapy is a confidential relationship between the doctor and the patient. No third person is allowed to intrude. If you do not leave now, the session is terminated." The patient, still in the role of "Terry," seemed stunned, but she remained—whereupon the therapist stood up, announced the session was over, and began to leave the room. Suddenly the patient, as Sandra again, pleaded, "Don't leave. It's only the two of us here."

The patient and therapist spent the remainder of the session talking about the patient's so-called multiple personalities. It was clear that Sandra was aware of the other three personalities, something that she had not revealed to her previous therapist. The psychologist took the position that all of these personalities were no more than aspects of Sandra, and Sandra was aware and responsible for all of them. The correct diagnosis now having been established, Sandra agreed to enter the borderline group program as described later in the appendix.

LEGEND

Psychological Mechanism:	Projective Identification, Dissociation
Diagnosis:	Borderline Personality Disorder
Operational Diagnosis:	Perform/Impress visiting supervisor
Implicit Contract:	I'll convince you I'm a multiple personality
Personality Type:	Garlic
Homework:	Keep therapy one-on-one
Therapeutic Techniques:	Limit setting and confrontation Special borderline program

Extreme borderline patients are intent upon proving that the world is just as unworthy as their parents. They will grab control and maintain it by threats of suicide, malpractice suits, or whatever will intimidate a therapist or a clinic. The longer they are successful, the longer will be the time required to create that psychological structure they so desperately need. Such an extreme case was Peggy.

Case Illustration: Peggy, The Borderline Center Director

When the senior author arrived at one of the busy staff model centers in the South for its annual clinical audit, he found that the entire staff was eagerly awaiting his help with a patient who had literally exhausted, one by one, each of the psychotherapists except one. The one who survived her onslaught was the one therapist she refused to see again.

Peggy was a woman in her early thirties who was very obviously manifesting a severe borderline personality disorder, but knowing the diagnosis did not shield the staff from her incessant demands. To complicate matters, she was married to a master's level licensed counselor who supported her in all her acting out and constantly challenged the treatment and diagnosis accorded his wife. Peggy attained health plan eligibility in February. By early July, she had succeeded in all but paralyzing both the health plan and its mental health contractor. In those five months, she was hospitalized six times, treated in the emergency room 23 times, usually late at night and sometimes twice the same night, and given 17 emergency, daytime drop-in sessions. She was also scheduled for semiweekly regular appointments, of which she kept only two. Whenever a staff member tried to set limits, she responded with either suicidal threats or gestures. Her counselor husband was always by her side to challenge the therapist's behavior as colleague-to-colleague, adding each time a not-so-subtle threat of lawsuit. Together, they had filed over a dozen formal complaints to the health plan, and the person in charge of patient relations spent most of her time attempting to mollify this one couple.

The center director took the liberty of scheduling Peggy as a therapy demonstration patient, an opportunity Peggy seized. As the staff and patient filed into the conference room, Peggy immediately took the center director's chair and presided over the meeting as if she were queen rather than patient. The center director, on the other hand, unwittingly found herself in the chair that had been designated for the patient. Peggy's current therapist, the most recent of a succession of therapists, began the session by asking Peggy to describe for Dr.

Cummings the problems that brought her to treatment. The patient launched into an articulate history of the abused childhood, embellishing every detail as she wallowed in her self-pity. Clearly, Peggy relished every moment of an exercise that was not only unproductive, but deleterious. The more a borderline is allowed to wallow in self-pity, the more likely he/she is to regress.

The senior author gently but insistently brought her back to the present until finally she defiantly refused to talk about anything but the past. She was unable to ignore the reasonable request that it was important to understand her situation today, so as a last resort she lapsed into determined silence and began rocking in her chair. Apropos of all Peggy's acting out, it was pointed out to her that she had initial control of this rocking behavior, but if she continued beyond a certain point she would be unable to stop. She was asked whether she preferred to be in control of herself or to punish Dr. Cummings for not allowing her to dwell deliciously on her abused childhood. Momentarily, she stopped, but then made the decision to be defiant. She resumed her rocking motion and soon she was in a trancelike state. From then on nothing got through to her. At the end of the time allotted for the case conference, she refused to leave and Dr. Cummings announced adjournment. All but Peggy left the conference room.

Once alone, Peggy did three things. She sat on the floor and wedged the full force of her 6-foot, 2-inch frame and 240-pound weight against the door. Then she began banging her head against the door in perfect cadence. Then, while continuing the first two, she telephoned her husband, who appeared within an hour, and notified the office of patient complaints at the health plan, which called the center director telling the staff Peggy was in the process of slashing her wrists in their own conference room at that very moment.

Peggy was definitely in control of the situation. The center staff, on the other hand, was near panic. Attempts were made to push the conference door open and rescue the patient before she ostensibly bled to death. But Peggy dug her heels into the carpet and pushed her back against the door with all her might. It became apparent that to attempt by sheer numbers of staff to push the door open could cause Peggy serious bodily harm. The staff looked to Dr. Cummings for a solution. The question was put as follows: If you had a four-year-old throwing a temper tantrum, what is the best response? Everyone agreed that the four-year-old should be ignored, but this was easier said than done since the staff—who were by now clearly the real patients, sought for ways to rescue Peggy. Again, this was true of all but the one aforementioned staff member.

All but one of the psychotherapists at this center, including the center director, were women whom Peggy had manipulated by getting them to believe she was truly dangerous to herself. The one male therapist had not been taken in by the manipulation, even when he saw her for the first time late one night in the emergency room. This male psychologist happened to be on call, but he knew a great deal about Peggy, as she had been the subject of almost every clinical case conference since her first contact with the center. He refused to hospitalize her since his clinical findings counterindicated inpatient treatment. She angrily left the hospital and called at 4:00 A.M. Still on call, the same psychologist responded. Peggy described how since leaving the hospital and for hours she had been wandering in the middle of the streets in a trance. She was awakened from her trance by an automobile horn from a car that in the dark almost ran over her.

The psychologist asked in a calm voice what kind of car it was, and then responded, "That's a very expensive car, Peggy. You are such a big woman you could have done great damage to it if he had hit you." Peggy hesitated for a few seconds, then slammed the phone down in a rage. But the important thing is that from then on, before going to the emergency room, she would first telephone the center to ascertain who was on call that night. If this particular psychologist was on call, Peggy would postpone her "emergency" until his time on night duty was completed. She steadfastly refused appointments with him when the center director, having now recognized that this psychologist was the one whom she should see, tried to transfer her to his care.

This case thus far demonstrates that when a borderline personality disorder seems most out of control, within the chaos created the patient is really running the show. Furthermore, research has shown that the stature of the therapist diminishes each time he or she is successfully manipulated. While the patient seems to delight in dethroning the therapist to the same rubble to which the parents are assigned, deep inside is a frightened child who is begging to be stopped. The terror stems from an inner realization, "If I can defeat everyone, who will be there for me?"

After about an hour of refusing to come out of the conference room, Peggy heard her husband outside and dashed into the waiting room where she grabbed him and they hastily departed. It was soon to be learned that they reported to the emergency room to have her "slashed" wrists stitched. She had left behind several slightly blood-stained pieces of tissue.

Much of the time during which Peggy was closeted, both the center director and Dr. Cummings were on the phone with an extremely critical patient complaints clerk. It had become apparent during these conversations that this clerk was, herself, a borderline and for the past five months had unwittingly been enabling the patient's acting out. Fortunately, the medical director was a competent, thoughtful man who agreed with Dr. Cummings' strategy for managing the patient. He had examined the superficiality of the cuts on the wrists and concurred with both the diagnosis and the treatment plan. Peggy was told she had no choice but to return to the center. If she refused to cooperate, she would be dropped from the health plan rolls.

There ensued two hours of negotiations on the telephone between the center, on one side, and Peggy and her husband on the other. Ostensibly Peggy had her lawyer on another line, insisted on quoting him profusely, but no one else actually talked with him if, indeed, he existed. Finally Peggy agreed to come in with her husband after the center backed away from insisting that they be seen separately. Peggy even voiced the fear; "I won't give you the chance to win him over." By agreement and seeing them as a couple would be her most recent therapist and Dr. Cummings.

Before they arrived, her therapist and Dr. Cummings had agreed on a strategy and the need to maintain firmness. Peggy was presented with a treatment plan that involved semiweekly regular appointments that must be kept. Also, since she was fearful she could not be seen in case of an emergency, she would be permitted five emergency sessions during the next 30 days. This figure was arrived at by a careful examination of her pattern of presenting herself in "emergency" conditions. It was apparent that about one emergency per week was actually legitimate. So, on the basis of not asking a patient to do more than she can, one emergency each week was acceptable, with an additional one thrown in for good measure, to five for the month. She could use all or none, immediately or spaced, but once they were used up she would be eligible for no more mental health services until the 30 days had passed. Peggy accepted the conditions with a defiant smirk, then promptly used all five of the emergency visits allotted for the month within the following three days. She then embarked on a series of so-called suicide attempts, appeals to the health plan, telephone calls from a lawyer and several community leaders, and the involvement of the police. Peggy had mobilized and was manipulating the entire community.

This time her therapist remained steadfast. At the end of the 30 days, it was Peggy and not the psychologist who was exhausted. She returned to the center and for the first time entered treatment. Her admiration for her newfound strong, firm, and reliable "parent" was the basis for a new and productive therapeutic relationship. This did not mean that Peggy did not occasionally test her therapist to reassure herself that the therapist was strong enough to be there for her. But the therapist consistently met the tests and Peggy continued to settle down and make use of the treatment, which now disregarded her very abused childhood, but concentrated on helping her meet the problems of daily living without regressing to a helpless, temper tantrum–driven, terrorized little girl. And the designated center director resumed her rightful role as the real head of the center.

LEGEND

Psychological Mechanism:	Denial, Splitting, and Projective Identification
Diagnosis:	Borderline Personality Disorder
Operational Diagnosis:	The boss is coming to town
Implicit Contract:	I shall continue to run the center
Personality Type:	Garlic
Homework:	Get self expelled from treatment
Therapeutic Techniques:	Paradoxical intention Setting limits

It cannot be reiterated too often that borderline personalities are such because they actually were abused. Their stories are so heart-rending that therapists fall prey to emotions of sympathy, throwing therapeutic effectiveness to the winds. It cannot be overemphasized that feeling sorry for a borderline is antitherapeutic. It is in the worst interest of the patient and may help to eventually destroy him or her. Being caring people, psychotherapists are easy prey to what are most often spigot tears that are turned on and off. To help a borderline, the therapist must have a mental image of a huge neon sign that flashes GARLIC whenever the borderline begins to cry. Andrea is typical of thousands of borderline patients who receive more sympathy than help, and eventually are rejected by an exhausted therapist who is totally unaware of his or her own anger toward this frustrating patient that "I gave so much to."

Case Illustration: Andrea and the Abuse Excuse

After 11 years of therapy, Andrea's therapist left the state to accept an impressive professional position. The social worker, a very dedicated and caring woman, wanted to make certain Andrea was left in expert hands. She hounded the new therapist until he agreed to accept the patient in an already overburdened schedule. When he met the patient and became aware of the tremendous demands she had been making on her former therapist, the psychologist could not help but wonder if this ostensible promotion might have been her way of extricating herself from an ever engulfing vortex.

Andrea was an intelligent borderline personality whose manipulative ability was enhanced by years of training in well-meaning psychotherapy. She was the only child of affluent parents who were more interested in their successful business than in their daughter. Unable to give her love, they showered her with gifts, which fell short of Andrea's expectations. She became the epitome of the love-starved "spoiled brat." The family lived in Southern California's wealthiest community, and although they were well-to-do, their income was in the low range for the residents. Consequently, they could not afford to give Andrea the car and the Rodeo Drive clothes that her friends took for granted. As a teenager, Andrea became very adept at shoplifting whatever she wanted, getting caught only once in her high school years. This was hushed up in the manner typical of upscale residents who can afford expensive lawyers.

Now age 31, Andrea was estranged from her parents, who had all but disowned her. Spectacularly beautiful, she was always able to make a good living in marginal executive positions where attractiveness, charm, and manipulativeness were the key ingredients. At the same time, and at three different periods of her life, she also supplemented her income by being "kept" by wealthy men. Nonetheless, no income could satisfy Andrea's ravenous appetite for expensive clothes and jewelry. Her other career was shoplifting.

Early in the 11 years of therapy, Andrea and her therapist, through hypnosis, uncovered repressed memories of sexual abuse by both parents during her childhood. And six times during those same 11 years the therapist testified in court on behalf of Andrea when she had been arrested for shoplifting. In all six cases, the defense was the same: Andrea was the victim of incest. The transcriptions of the court cases, all meticulously preserved by her previous therapist, were instructive. The therapist was eloquent and persuasive. The defendant (patient) was better than a trained seal. At just the right moments and in just the right amounts there were tears, contrition, and victimization. A judicial system, already overburdened with shoplifting cases, and with jails overcrowded with violent offenders, found it easy to grant probation and order more therapy all six times!

The court transcripts were revealing on another dimension. The incest had grown in 11 years of therapy from a simple case of a father sneaking into the daughter's room and the mother refusing to believe it, to rape with a broom handle by the father as the mother held the child down, to the parents sexually sharing their daughter with their adult friends, and finally to Satanic rituals. It seemed that the elaboration of the original alleged incest over 11 years more closely approximated newspaper and television headlines than any uncovering of repressed memories. The new therapist could not help but be reminded of daytime television shows in which a group of borderline personalities tell their stories of abuse, which, by the end of the hour, have been elaborated to include details from all the guests' stories.

It was important to set limits early. The previous therapist had been available to Andrea without limit, a potentially destructive approach in an adult "spoiled brat" syndrome. For example, a cocaine-spiked spat with her boyfriend at 1:00 A.M. warranted a two-hour telephone therapy session. An agreed-upon system of when and how the therapist would be available was formulated and put in writing. The shoplifting was put in abeyance, waiting for the moment the patient would bring it up. The therapist did not have to wait long.

On the fourth weekly session, Andrea sought assurance that if she were caught shoplifting the therapist would come to her aid. She feared that arrest was probable and acknowledged that for every time she had been caught she had shoplifted 50 times or more, but she couldn't help it. The therapist made it very clear he did not regard the patient as a kleptomaniac (kleptomaniacs are persons whose compulsion typically drives them to steal things they cannot use). He recounted the example of one of his patient who could not stop stealing bobbie pins even after she had stolen over 100,000 of them. Persons who steal very expensive clothes and jewelry are thieves, not kleptomaniacs, and he would say that in court. The patient first attempted to inundate the therapist with her history of childhood sexual abuse. When that failed, she quickly agreed to take responsibility for her shoplifting rather than have her overly elaborated history of abuse called into question. The stage was set for a showdown and the curtain went up early.

Three days later, Andrea was arrested for attempting to steal an $18,000 fur coat. She screamed at the psychologist, "See how wrong you are. I *am* a kleptomaniac. As an animal rights activist, I would *never* wear a fur coat." Some garlic is truly of gourmet quality!

The therapist remained faithful to the agreement, and Andrea went to the county jail for 90 days. She was placed back on continued probation and remanded to the psychologist for psychotherapy. The court order had enough leverage to make therapy possible and the psychologist was very open with the patient about how he intended to use it therapeutically. Falling off the wagon (shoplifting) would mean increasing jail terms. Not atypical of borderline personalities, Andrea seemed relieved and began to engage in her therapy. She was placed in the special borderline group program where, through therapy and advancing age when borderline personalities run out of steam anyway, she learned to control many of her impulses, including shoplifting. Interestingly, there came a time when she repudiated *all* of her so-called repressed memories and reconciled with her now aging parents.

LEGEND

Psychological Mechanism:	Projective Identification, Splitting
Diagnosis:	Borderline Personality Disorder
Operational Diagnosis:	Therapist leaving
Implicit Contract:	My incest/abuse history justifies all
Personality Type:	Garlic
Homework:	No shoplifting
Therapeutic Technique:	Setting limits with consequences for antisocial behavior

7
Schizophrenia

In the Onion–Garlic chart on page 111, schizophrenia is divided into schizophrenias controlled by individual suffering and schizophrenia controlled by attacking the environment. The discussion in this section pertains to both categories.

Schizophrenia is not the end of a continuum of severity of emotional distress. A schizophrenic is qualitatively different from a neurotic because of the thought disorder resulting when the primary processes of right brain thinking are not mediated by the logic and reason of left brain thinking. Physiologically schizophrenia is an inheritable condition characterized by a defect in the mediating function of the corpus striatum of the corpus callosum which connects the two hemispheres of the brain.

Many great artists and writers have the ability in their creativity to dive into right brain thinking and create. Whether creating the art of a Picasso or the poetry of a Gertrude Stein, these people have the ability to dive solely into the right-brain thinking unhampered by left-brain mediation, but when they create, they are able to merge uninhibited processes with learned forms. They come out of purely idiosyncratic right-brain thinking.

As many as 5 percent of all Americans have schizophrenic thought disorder (Fromm-Reichman, 1929, 1950), but only a small minority will manifest a psychosis or be hospitalized. Sullivan (1927, 1940) called this form of thinking parataxia, and derived much of his knowledge from his own schizophrenic thought disorder, about which he was quite candid. Rorschach studies (Schafer, 1948), which are particularly able to detect parataxic thinking, tend to confirm that a benign thought disorder is far more common than we are comfortable in admitting. It depends how life treats them, how heredity endowed them, what kind of a family they grew up in, how lucky they are in life. The interplay among the severity of the thought disorder, the familial environment, and happenstance in life determine whether the schizophrenic succeeds. At one extreme, the thought disorder can overwhelm any familial influence or fortune. At the other end, if the thought disorder is slight, a great family or luck can result in impressive accomplishmets.

Only about 1 percent of the estimate 4 to 5 percent of the persons having the thought disorder will ever manifest a schizophrenic psychosis (Rosenham & Seligman, 1984). Many will contain their peculiar thinking by joining cults and other groups that structure and direct their thoughts and behavior. Some who are charismatic may become cult leaders, and once they have followers who believe their peculiar thoughts can no longer be deemed "crazy." Others learn to compensate for the thought disorder and use it creatively, as renowned psychiatrists Harry Stack Sullivan and Carl Whitaker have candidly described about themselves.

The people most overly sensitive to rejection are schizophrenics. They are 100 times more sensitive to rejection than people of low self-esteem. This is only to be expected, however, since schizophrenics have been rejected all their lives. As children, they've been seen as strange. The other kids pick on them. They're called FLK's in school, "Funny Looking Kids." If they get nervous, they walk funny. There's something going through their minds that's making them very nervous. Repetitive movements, athetoid movements, repetitive speech, all of these hit the poor schizophrenic when he or she is nervous. If they're nervous about the first day of school, or starting a new year in a brand new school where they don't know anyone, with the last school having been a disaster, schizophrenic children are terribly nervous. When the teacher goes around the room and asks the childen to say their names, the schizophrenic child just falls apart and starts doing repetitive movement. "My name is Tom. My name is Tom. My name is Tom." All the kids laugh, and it's downhill from then on. A life filled with such humiliation and rejection naturally results in the extreme sensitivity of the schizophrenic. For example:

I was driving with a patient across a bridge with a toll booth only on one end so that the fee is collected only once for a round trip. We got on the bridge and were driving on when the patient

said, "You didn't pay the toll." I said, "This is the free direction."
He said, "You must pay the toll!" I said, "No, no. This is the
free direction."

He got repetitive and said, "You must pay the toll. You must
pay the toll. You must pay the toll. You must pay the toll." And
he's screaming by this time, and I'm getting desperate.

I start doing foolish things. I'm being logical. I reach in my
pocket, get a bunch of change, open the window, throw it onto
the bridge, and say, "There, I paid the toll."

He said, "You did not pay the toll. You did not pay the toll.
You did not pay the toll," and continued to decompensate.

I'm struggling, and think, "This has nothing to do with the
damn bridge. What does the toll have to do with his feeling
rejected?" When a schizophrenic patient gets like this, 99 times
out of 100 they feel rejected. I look over and on his lap he had
a novel that he'd been reading. The title of the book is *Love is
a Bridge*. I turned to him said, "Do you have the feeling that if
I don't pay the toll on this bridge I don't love you?"

He looked at me and said, "It's not true?

I said, "No. It has nothing to do with it. I love you."

He sank back in the car seat and said, "Thank you."

With the advent of psychotropic medication the importance of de-
lineating and understanding the *prepsychotic* schizophrenic thought
disorder that afflects many persons has been forgotten or neglected.
Our approach, with its emphasis upon reducing therapeutic failures,
has extended the Onion–Garlic chart to include the prepsychotic
schizophrenic who decompensates into full-blown psychosis when
subjected to uncovering (analyzing) psychotherapy.

Recognizing this thought disorder is particularly important because
the nonpsychotic schizophrenic, being very close to primary process
thinking, presents a richness of pathological material that is tantalizing
and seemingly begging for analysis. As the layers are peeled off, the
therapist feels rewarded by an ever-increasing gold mine of pathology.
Then suddenly the patient is overwhelmed and engulfed in psychosis
and requires hospitalization.

Persons with a schizophrenic, but nonpsychotic, thought disorders
come into psychotherapy because adverse circumstances are eroding
the boundaries that contain the potentially psychotic thinking, and

the patient feels vunerable and threatened. The treatment of choice for these patients is a type of covering therapy, or a restoration of controls before the patient is overwhelmed. This requires special skills that concentrate on the here-and-now, helping the patient restore equilibrium by coping with the adverse events. Of considerable importance is the strength of the therapist, for as the patient's ego weakens, he or she can rely on the therapist's ego strength.

In addition to the decompensation that can be precipitated by uncovering therapy, a patient suffering from a nonpsychotic schizophrenic thought disorder can suffer an equally adverse effect from certain anxiolytic and antidepressive medications. Typically psychotherapists do not concern themselves with medication issues, but this is an area in which a competent diagnostician can be of immeasurable service to the patient and of help to the prescribing physician. Very few psychiatric and nonpsychiatric physicians are trained to recognize this thought disorder, which is so recognizable to psychologists on Rorschach testing. Such patients with this thought disorder may become anxious or depressed as they struggle with circumstances that are threatening their stability, they are often given otherwise appropriate medications. With these patients such medications disrupt emotional stability and often accelerate decompensation to the point where psychotherapy is difficult or impossible, and hospitalization is necessary. The medications with the greatest deleterious potential are the benzodiazapines and their more recent pharmaceutical second cousins.

The nonmedical practitioner, in discussing with physicians the potential deleterious effects of certain medications on his or her patients, should be particularly sensitive to the physician's authority and preeminence in psychopharmacology, which must be unquestioned. The role of the psychotherapist is to alert the physician to psychological problems that would not have come to the physician's attention. When the interprofessional relationship is a comfortable one, the physician is eager to have the benefit of the psychotherapist's intense contact with the patient.

Although all schizophrenics are nonanalyzable, some can be considered onion and others garlic. The latter are the more difficult to treat because, in addition to having a thought disorder, they are also antisocial. As will be seen, for some garlic schizophrenics such as serial killers, there currently exists no viable intervention other than a type of quarantine called incarceration.

8

Schizophrenia: Onion /Nonanalyzable

Onion/Nonanalyzable: Schizophrenia as a Thought Disorder (Anastasia)

The thought disorder, not delusions and hallucinations, is the essential feature of schizophrenia. Delusions and hallucinations are the schizophrenic's attempt to heal, just as a fever is symptomatic of the body's fight against an infection. The fever is not the disease; it is the body's immune system fighting the disease. People with AIDS get infections but not fevers because their immune system is so compromised they cannot fight back. The same is true with decompensating schizophrenics overwhelmed by their thought disorder and unable to make sense out of the universe. Delusions and hallucinations are their attempt to explain what is happening to them, to bring order into the chaotic reality their thought disorder has thrown them into. The restitutive nature of delusions was well illustrated in the cases of Dennis and Sam in the preceding section on Joining the Delusion in Chapter 3. The totally decompensated schizophrenic in the back ward of a state hospital is a vegetable without delusions, without hallucinations, and with an overwhelmingly apparent thought disorder.

Functioning in schizophrenia varies according to the degree of severity of the disorder. When schizophrenia is latent, the individual is able to contain his or her anxiety and hostility in a viable delusion that enables him or her to function in society. Schizophrenics often present as neurotics until the process of psychotherapy or increasing stressors undermine their defenses and the thought disorder emerges. For example, after five or six sessions, an obsessional character who has a compulsion to brush his teeth may say, "I have to brush my teeth 25 times a day because I can't use the toilet brush to brush my teeth in the morning." Or a hysterical woman may say, "The reason why I can't have an orgasm is because at that moment the next door neighbor sends radio waves through our bedroom."

Another form of latent schizophrenia is the pseudoneurotic schizophrenic who looks like a neurotic but whose neurosis and personality traits keep changing. The pseudoneurotic schizophrenic may present as the perfect hysteric, but then looks like the perfect obsessive-compulsive and then perhaps the perfect phobic. Because of this lability, pseudoneurotics are often misdiagnosed as borderlines.

Many latent or patent schizophrenics have harmless propensities that would be inconsequential if it were not that the missing of their diagnosis often renders them victims of iatrogenic exacerbation of a mild condition. This is illustrated by the case of Olga, whose mother and next door neighbor desperately sought the psychologist's help.

Case Illustration: Anastasia, Czarina of Russia

Olga was a 16-year-old who had refused to get out of bed for almost all of the past year. Originally she agreed to see the psychologist, but on the day she was to come to the office she characteristically refused to get out of bed. Her mother, who had been bringing meals on trays to her bed and in all other respects had been waiting on her was at her wits end. The mother was an apparently passive woman who had difficulty expressing herself. A neighbor had taken the initiative and pushed the reluctant mother, who feared her daughter would be found to be "crazy," to make the appointment with the psychologist. Seeing their desperation, the psychologist agreed to see them even though the appointment had been made for Olga. A determined woman, the neighbor did most of the talking while the mother sat ringing her hands.

Olga was born in the United States, but her parents were born in Harbin, China. She was the youngest generation of a large group of émigrés' who fled to China following the Bolshevik Revolution in 1917, remained there for a few decades, and eventually entered the United States. She was part of a group of people who lived in fantasy and in the past. Setting aside their menial occupations, at the community functions they revelled in the glory of obsolete titles and elegantly tailored costumes. If one's grandfather had been a count or a general, one affected that position on the frequent Russian holidays that were occasions for these adults to "dress-up," pathetically childish as this may have appeared to outsiders. A fry cook by day, a man would don a general's uniform at night and receive all the deference accorded his grandfather in Czarist Russia. Olga grew up in this atmosphere, ostensibly the granddaughter of an ambassador. Her father, who simulated that role until he deserted the family, had not been seen since Olga was age 10.

Seeing no other effective way to engage Olga, the psychologist arranged for a housecall. The home was modest, as were most homes in the district the Russian émigrés had settled, but Olga herself was elegantly dressed as she sat propped up in bed among satin pillows and sheets. She extended her hand, splendidly jeweled with the fortunes of her grandmother's generation. The psychologist felt as if he were in the presence of royalty.

Olga spoke in a deep throaty voice and with a decidedly Russian accent. It was difficult to keep in mind that she had, indeed, been born and reared in the United States. She also had a number of repetitive and manneristic motions that were schizophrenic rather than affected royalty. Initially, Olga was very skeptical of the psychologist, but spoke with him politely, if not haughtily. She explained that she had decided to be waited on in a manner befitting her position and she berated her mother for not insisting on the deference she deserved from her surroundings. She even hinted that her mother was actually a woman to whose care she had been entrusted. Instant rapport was established when the psychologist bent down and whispered in her ear, "Are you Princess Anastasia?"

Students of history as well as devotees of Ingrid Bergman movies will recall the legend that the Czar's daughter was smuggled out of Russia as a very young child. Not only was she the heir-apparent to the Czarist throne, but she also was the rightful owner of the Romanoff fortune that had also been smuggled out of Russia. There have been many pretenders to that position, none of whom had been authenticated. In her own mind, Olga was the latest pretender, no matter that the real princess, if she did exist, would be an old woman by now.

She began addressing the psychologist as Czar Nicholas, playing off his real first name and ignoring the fact the real Czar had been dead for more than half a century. Seizing the windfall rapport, the psychologist extended an invitation that she visit him in his office. She did so and never became bedridden again. In the privacy of her individual sessions, the psychologist addressed her as Anastasia, and she reluctantly agreed to address him with a simple Nicholas rather than the full title she believed was his. The sessions were very practical, pointing out that until the empire was restored and restitution made, she and all Russian émigrés would have to finish school, get a job, and survive. She agreed. After all, as she pointed out, even Czar Nicholas was working as a psychologist. She graduated from high school, attended a business school, and obtained a job as a secretary. She was seen infrequently and at her request, usually two or three times a year.

During the sessions, the psychologist would review her intervening activities since the last session, and helped her sort out inappropriate behavior. Olga could be very inappropriate. At one session, she asked immediately upon entering the office if she could have a drink. The psychologist went to the water cooler in the waiting room, and when he returned to the office with a paper cup of water, Olga had taken a bottle of red wine and a crystal wine glass from her purse and was sipping an expensive vintage. When it was explained that this was inappropriate behavior for a doctor's office, she complied but responded that exceptions should be made for a princess.

In her late twenties, Olga married a contemporary she had known all of her life but paid no attention to until she saw him on leave and in his army uniform. At the same time he was both her handsome "soldier boy" and a general. The bubble burst when he returned from the Vietnam War and donned civilian clothes. She became extremely anxious and would not allow him to touch her. She called for an appointment, but the psychologist was out of the country. In the emergency room that night, she was given a benzodiazapine by the psychiatrist on call. Three days later, Olga was hallucinating, created a scene in a large downtown bank as she demanded Anastasia's wealth, and was taken to the psychiatric ward of the county hospital.

Schizophrenics respond negatively to benzodiazapines, as well as to most antidepressive and anxiolytics. However, in an era where schizophrenia is not seen as a thought disorder and the condition is reserved for the blatant schizophrenic with obvious delusions and troublesome hallucinations, the latent and patent schizophrenics are misdiagnosed in accordance with the presenting symptoms. Schizophrenics can become very anxious, on occasions, but their behavior is qualitatively different if one observes the thought disorder that is just beneath the anxiety. A nonphysician therapist experiences considerable difficulty questioning a prescribing psychiatrist's choice of medication. It is seen as an inappropriate response by a nonphysician. But it is not the physician's unquestioned authority to prescribe that is being challenged, but the inability to diagnose schizophrenia that is latent or patent. Once the medication has pushed the patient into blatant schizophrenia, there is no longer any question whatsoever as to the correct diagnosis.

Olga divorced her husband and continues to work. She calls for an appointment when she feels she needs one, sometimes going more than a year without contact. But she has had four hospitalizations, each following the prescription of an anxiety-reducing medication. In these instances, the psychologist was not available and she saw an emergency room physician. The problem has been eliminated by giving her a prescription for antipsychotic medication that she takes infrequently and around episodes of what she calls being "very nervous." She relies upon this appropriately and has not been hospitalized again. Her greatest crisis came at the time of "glasnost" in the Soviet Union. Olga, who had patiently waited all these years, became agitated as she thought the time to ascend the throne had arrived. She and her therapist worked through the crisis. She is quietly living her life, and although she still believes she is Anastasia, she also believes she will never be acknowledged as such. In a sense, she has given up the throne.

LEGEND

Psychological Mechanism:	Withdrawal (Patent Delusion)
Diagnosis:	Adolescent Schizophrenia
Operational Diagnosis:	Mother will no longer care for me
Implicit Contract:	Accept my Imperial Royalty
Personality Type:	Onion
Homework:	Behave as royalty
Therapeutic Technique:	Joining the delusion

When a schizophrenic patient decompensates, the treatment plan must focus on shoring up the defenses and covering up the thought disorder. Otherwise, interventions will precipitate a psychotic episode.

In blatant schizophrenia, there are prominent psychotic symptoms. Blatant schizophrenia most frequently emerges between the ages 18 and 25 and thus was once known as dementia praecox or the dementia of youth. The inability to make a transition from adolescence to adulthood results in a breakdown of coping and the schizophrenic's thought disorder overwhelms him.

Schizophrenias Controlled by Individual Suffering

Dynamics

Schizophrenics who control their anxiety and anger by individual suffering sacrifice a portion of their functioning in order to achieve a reality they can cope with. When logic is sacrificed, as in paranoid schizophrenia, delusions of various kinds are prominent. There are several common types: somatic, world-reconstructionist, grandiosity, and persecution, to name a few.

When emotion is sacrificed, as in hebephrenic schizophrenia, the person avoids life by jumbling the emotional response. Informed of his mother's death, a hebephrenic will laugh uproariously. Informed of winning a lottery, he or she will cry for hours. Hebephrenics blunt a world that they cannot handle by giving up appropriate feelings.

When intellect is sacrificed, the simple schizophrenic presents as mentally retarded. The movie *The Rain Man* paints a beautiful portrait of a simple schizophrenic. This type of schizophrenic can add seven digit numbers virtually instantaneously, but would not be able to calculate the change if he or she bought a loaf of bread for a dollar and a candy bar for a quarter and gave the clerk a five dollar bill. The difference is that the first situation is abstract; the other is living. They withdraw the intellect from living. By giving up their intellect, simple schizophrenics control their anxieties and their anger but will score in the mentally retarded range on simple I.Q. tests. Unfortunately the diagnosis of mental retardation precludes effective treatment.

When motility is sacrificed, the result is catatonic stupor. In one way, this is the most successful schizophrenic mechanism of all because it literally immobilizes the schizophrenic from acting on his desire to kill out of rage, but it is also the most devastating if the mechanism breaks down. The most dangerous schizophrenics are not the paranoids, but the catatonics whose loss of control over motility ends in mania rather than stupor. These are the people who would walk into a McDonald's or a schoolyard and kill all the people because their immobility is no longer extant. Before demonstrating blatant symptoms, an emerging catatonic will display frozen positions or repetitive movements or verbal expressions. Diagnosing a catatonic at this stage can preclude the serious deterioration.

Entry

In working with schizophrenics, don't challenge the delusion. Don't do uncovering. Stay with the here and now. In the blatant schizophrenic, join the delusion as an ally as in the example of Dennis, the CIA menace in the section on psychojudo. This case illustrates an axiom: A delusion occupies psychological space for which there is room for only one person. If you can get into the patient's delusional space, if the patient lets you in, the patient has to leave it. He can leave it, however, because he has identified with your ego. You cannot communicate with schizophrenics until they let you in. Schizophrenics cannot bond, but once they let you in to their psychological space, it is like glue more than any bonding you'll ever experience. They absolutely cling to your every word. You become their eyes, their ears, their brains. But every once in a while, because you don't think like they do, you'll do something that leads them to conclude you're rejecting them.

Somaticized responses, usually among latent or patent schizophrenics, often follow fads. There are alleged "syndromes" that can suddenly appear, become epidemic among a sub-group, and then disappear almost as dramatically as they appeared. Such is the case of so-called yeast infections, a concept prevalent 10 years ago to explain all kinds of seemingly emotional difficulties. This "syndrome" has all but disappeared, but it has been replaced by multiple chemical sensitivity (MCS) which has prompted some communities (e.g., Marin County in California) to ban perfumes and other common chemicals from public meetings. The unproven theory is that a small chemical exposure can "sensitize" certain individuals to not only that chemical, but also a huge number of other chemicals and products found throughout the environment. Examination of the histories of these patients suggests that almost anything can trigger the sensitivity.

As in all epidemics that occur and then subside suddenly, it is important that the therapist bear in mind that any actual syndrome can be mimicked by a person in emotional distress. We have seen how borderline personalities simulate multiple personality syndrome. Similarly latent or patient schizophrenics can "acquire" MCS, making it virtually impossible for the therapist to differentiate this from the medical condition. For such a patient MCS fulfills all of the requirements of somatization where all interpersonal difficulties, social isolation, and fear of the world are explained by an ostensible physical condition. Yet the psychotherapist can treat a patient with MCS without having to either establish the medical criteria or challenge the belief, as the case of Samantha illustrates.

Case Illustration: Samantha: Please, No Perfume

Typical was the case of Samantha, a divorced woman, age 32, who was referred for psychological evaluation by her physicians. They had concluded an exhaustive examination following her complaint that she could not work in an office where her co-workers wore perfume. She had demanded that the employer ban perfume and, upon the refusal of the company to do so, she filed a disability claim, which put into motion weeks of medical investigation. All the results were negative and her claim was denied.

Samantha kept weekly appointments with the psychologist only because to not do so would have jeopardized the appeal of her denied claim for disability. Her behavior, however, was anything but cooperative. She harangued the therapist with "proof" that all of her symptoms were physical and not psychological. The therapist was careful not to reveal a belief one way or the other. He conveyed an open mind and confessed that he was not an expert on MCS. This is all Samantha needed. She deluged the psychologist with books, reprints, newspaper clippings and other materials intended to prove the theory of MCS. Over the course of four appointments, she grew steadily worse. When her appeal was denied, her sensitivities so worsened that she went to a "safe house" in Texas for several weeks.

The patient returned to therapy when her appeal was reopened and psychotherapy was made a condition for reconsideration. Fresh from Texas, Samantha was feeling much better and she was armed with a diagnostic work-up that indicated she was sensitive to no less than 80 common chemicals, and possibly more than 100. Sensitivity to perfumes was at the top of this list. She triumphantly presented these findings to the psychologist who, without challenge, accepted them in amazement. She resented having to see the psychologist, but apologized for her previous antagonism and seemed open to some kind of coexistence.

From the previous sessions, the psychologist had noted that Samantha's difficulties long preceded her MCS symptoms. She had manifested severe social problems throughout her life. In high school, she was very much the social isolate and particularly resented a clique of girls from well-to-do families who flaunted their clothes and other manifestations of affluence. Without ever connecting it to the present, Samantha once uttered, "I could smell them coming a mile away from their expensive perfume, and I would do anything to keep from seeing the haughty smirk on their faces."

Samantha had a series of brief, tumultuous relationships with men, which always ended with her breaking off the affair. Following each break-up, she would experience a period of several months where she sought isolation. She did not have any close female friends, either. When asked about this, she replied, "All the women I like wear perfume, so I can never really get to know them." It was very apparent, however, that Samantha's current severe symptoms began with her relationship with Harry, a dentist with three children from a previous marriage. Samantha and Harry had been sleeping together for two years and he wanted to marry her. She resented the occasions when she was required to play mother to Harry's children, and accused her lover of wanting to marry her so his children would have a mother. The more Samantha became attached to Harry, and the more he pressured her to marry him, the worse the MCS had become. However, the psychologist was meticulous in not making this connection.

Rather, the psychologist took his cue from Samantha's desire to coexist in a situation she did not want. He said, "Samantha, let's let the doctors fight over your chemical sensitivities while we stay out of that here. Why don't we do something they don't expect. We can take advantage of the situation and spend our time exploring your relationship with Harry. We know that has nothing to do with MCS and it is something I as a psychologist just might be able to help you with." She wondered if our exploration might reveal that she should leave Harry. The therapist pointed out, "If that is to be, better to know it early on." She agreed and plunged into the task with enthusiasm.

All of Samantha's life, except for the chemical sensitivities, became the subject of her therapy. Over the next several weeks, she slowly came out of her social isolation; as she improved, so did her MCS. Neither patient nor therapist made this connection. However, Samantha found she could tolerate the chemicals in the office when, at her request, her employer transferred her to a desk a short distance from her co-workers. She got the courage to approach a co-worker she liked and invited her to have dinner. She asked this woman whether she would mind not wearing perfume and received a positive response. In time, she was friendly with several women, all of whom volunteered for the sake of their new found friend not to wear perfume.

Harry and Samantha were married in a small, private ceremony. The patient quit her job and is enjoying being a full-time homemaker. She meticulously maintains a chemical free home, but she has an ever-expanding circle of friends. She is amazed that she can even tolerate perfume on the many social occasions she and Harry happily attend. For the first time in her life, Samantha is not a social isolate. The therapy was concluded with the connection between her symptoms and her interpersonal problems never having been made.

LEGEND

Psychological Mechanism:	Withdrawal (delusion)
Diagnosis:	Somaticizing Schizophrenic: MCS
Operational Diagnosis:	Denial of disability claim
Implicit Contract:	Prove my condition is physical and not emotional

Personality Type:	Garlic covering onion
Homework:	Keep MCS out of therapy
Therapeutic Technique:	Accepting the resistance

Whereas MCS can engender a great deal of sympathy from society and even interest from physicians, a blatantly paranoid somatization is rejected by both society and the medical profession. Yet the interventions follow the same therapeutic principles employed in other delusional formations. This is illustrated by the case of Ken.

Case Illustration: Stinky Ken

Somatization can be baffling to a physician who must order more and more tests in an effort to find the physical disease. When somatization reaches psychotic proportions, however, the physician quickly recognizes the mental illness. In this way, Ken was referred to the psychologist.

An 18-year-old freshman in college, Ken was referred by the emergency room physician when he appeared there complaining that one of his abdominal organs was rotting. He was not certain which one, but he knew this was so from the odor it gave off. This is a form of paranoid schizophrenia, sometimes called "organ psychosis," and the complaint is a delusion in every sense, and should be treated as such (see case of Dennis in Chapter 3). Having been alerted on the telephone by the referring physician, the psychologist prepared himself.

After Ken was ushered into the office and he and the therapist had exchanged greetings, the psychologist got up from his chair, saying, "Excuse me a minute." He then took a can of air freshener and extensively sprayed the room. The patient asked, "How bad is it?" The therapist replied, "Nothing I can't live with. How long has this been going on?" He responded that it began with a mild aroma about five months ago.

It is important to note that although the therapist joined the delusion, at no time did he specifically state that he smelled the odor. This is an important distinction in that behavior is more reassuring than words, and the therapist has not said anything he is not able to say with conviction. The paranoid is extremely sensitive to even the slightest hint of insincerity.

Ken was an overly protected son who lived in a devoutly religious home. Most of his contacts had taken place with his church group and he had attended Christian day schools all of his academic life. His family had hoped to send him to a distant Christian college, but the father's untimely death and a series of financial reverses made that impossible. His mother was a proud woman who did not want to accept charity. So Ken went to the state university where he had obtained a scholarship. This was his first experience living away from home.

The real world was both intriguing and frightening to Ken. His new friends teased him about his religious fundamentalism and embarked on a well-meaning campaign to get him to "loosen up." Ken tried alcohol and pot for the first time, and had his first sexual experience. Ken became more and more like the other men in the dormitory, until one day, as if he had rediscovered his religious convictions, he abruptly returned to his previously strict religious behavior. His former friends lost interest in him. Seeing him as boring and even embarrassing, they avoided him. Soon Ken began experiencing difficulty concentrating and he responded by skipping classes. He became increasingly withdrawn and isolated, but he recalled only that five months ago he developed a mild odor that was generating from his abdomen. The odor grew steadily worse until he realized one of his internal organs was rotting.

This delusion, as are all delusions, was restitutive. It accounted for his friends avoiding him and it spared him the turmoil of questioning his rigid upbringing. It also punished him for his brief period of alcohol and drug intake. Ken was certain that either alcohol or pot had damaged him physically, or that God was punishing him for transgressing. All of this was, of course, not directly discussed with Ken until after he had given up his delusion.

In the beginning, Ken agreed to use air freshener in his dormitory room so people would not be discouraged from visiting him. Also, he had to make every attempt to keep up with his classes. While in class, he would try to sit near an open window or away from the main group. Then, Ken was asked whether the rotting was physical damage or punishment from God. Ken thought it was probably the latter. The therapist agreed inasmuch as the rotting of the internal organ had not caused him to become seriously and systemically ill. The patient was asked to construct an elaborate penance, accompanied by prayers for forgiveness. Until he was forgiven, he was to use lots of air freshener and deodorant.

Each time Ken came in to the therapist, the latter sprayed the office with air freshener. And on each visit Ken reported on his religious recompensation. Each time they both learned a little more about Ken's problems. But the therapist was careful not to delve into them. In the fourth session, the patient announced that the therapist did not need to spray the office. Ken had given up his delusion, and this was a signal that he was ready to discuss the issues of an overly protected son who needed to grow up.

LEGEND

Psychological Mechanism:	Psychotic (Delusional)
	Somatization, Projection
Diagnosis:	Schizophrenia, Paranoid
Operational Diagnosis:	Leaving home to go to college
Implicit Contract:	I am not crazy
Personality Type:	Onion
Homework:	Use air freshener
Therapeutic Techniques:	Humor the resistance
	Enter the delusion

As is stated in the section on obsessive-compulsive neurosis, an elaborate obsessional system can often hide and mitigate an underlying thought disorder. The persons are potentially obsessional schizophrenics; as long as the obsessional system works and remains intact, the thought disorder is never manifest. Acquaintances and co-workers do find such a person a bit "peculiar" and "rigid," but an underlying potential psychosis is never suspected. If all continues in this vein, none will ever become manifest. However, often in such obsessionally defended individuals, there may occur events that cause the defense to decompensate. A latent schizophrenic may become patent, or even blatant. This is illustrated by the case of James, who was always regarded as a bit peculiar, but certainly okay by his fellow state employees. Then, one day all this began to change.

Case Illustration: James to the Rescue

An obsessional schizophrenic can for many years contain the thought disorder with an elaborate obsessional system that is plausible enough to escape being identified as psychotic. Such a system can be a world reconstruction fantasy, a psychological representation of the patient's attempt to reconstruct a fragile ego to keep it from crumbling.

James for over 10 years had worked for the state highway department as a surveyor. He had barely graduated from college with minimally passing grades in engineering and never attempted to obtain a job as an engineer. He was satisfied to work as a surveyor, a skill he learned in his engineering curriculum. He had settled for the security of a civil service job, and no one suspected how troubled he was with his self-image as an underachiever. He was regarded by everyone who came in contact with him as a fussy, meticulous man who had a slavish devotion to orderliness. He drove everyone to exasperation with his orderliness, so people just stayed out of his way. No one suspected that beneath all of this he was psychotic.

In his job as a surveyor in the highway system, James had witnessed the aftermath of many automobile accidents, some of them fatal. It was only natural he would be obsessed with highway safety. His solution to the problem raised a few eyebrows, but it was seen as well-meaning and, though unworkable, harmless enough. James had devised an elaborate system of stripes for the highways that would be color-coded to signify different speed limits for each lane. Each speed would have its own color, and a thin electrical wire imbedded in the paint had the capacity to change the color of the stripe from a central control panel. The colors of the stripes could be varied in accordance with traffic conditions. Speed limits would be decreased during congestion or bad weather, and increased when traffic conditions warranted it. James was convinced his system would prevent accidents and save lives. He would discuss his system with anyone who would listen, and he always had handy his briefcase with engineering drawings for the scheme. To everyone James was a "pleasant nut" to be politely avoided. It is not surprising that at age 36, James was still living alone.

Suddenly, James became more of a nuisance when he insisted that the traffic situation was soon to be out of control. To prevent the ensuing carnage, the state highway department had better implement his system before it was too late. He imposed himself on his superiors, and when they put him off, he went behind their backs to the highway department director. Soon he was sending urgent faxes to the state legislators and to the governor. James was no longer a "pleasant nut." His immediate supervisor was told to control him. James's world reconstruction fantasy had now become a world destruction fantasy, signalling the decompensation of his obsessional system and the crumbling of his ego. When James disobeyed his supervisor and even accelerated the number of faxes to important persons, he was suspended from his job.

James retreated to his apartment for several days, and on Sunday, when the road crews were not working, he went to the highway department yard and stole a truck loaded with highway barriers. He was closing off the third freeway entrance when arrested. When apprehended, he was severely agitated and incessantly screamed that the end of the freeway system was at hand. He was remanded to the psychiatric ward of the local hospital by the police. It was there that James, now in full-blown psychosis, was seen for the first time since his underlying, long-term schizophrenia had previously been contained by his obsessional system.

The precipitating event was an involvement with a woman that James met inadvertently in spite of his own shyness. It was she who took control and got them together over a period of weeks. When eventually they went to bed, James was impotent, experienced a heterosexual panic, and bolted. At home that night, he began having homosexual fears, which soon translated into his awareness that the end of the freeway system was at hand. James was treated in the hospital and released two weeks later. He entered outpatient therapy and began working back from his color-coded highway lane stripes to his real fears and concerns that had impaired his intellectual functioning and kept him isolated all of his life.

LEGEND

Psychological Mechanism:	Psychotic (delusional)
Diagnosis:	Schizophrenia (patent to blatant)

Operational Diagnosis:	Sexual affair for first time, with sexual panic
Implicit Contract:	I am not crazy
Personality Type:	Onion
Homework:	Refrain from sex
Therapeutic Technique:	Enter the delusion (highway codes)

Because in the current psychiatric nomenclature only blatant schizophrenia is recognized, psychotherapy can miss the early signs of decompensation and thereby also miss the opportunity for early intervention. The case of Sherrill is provided to alert therapists to early signs of catatonia in patients who, like Sherrill, would never ordinarily be regarded as a fast-approaching psychosis.

Case Illustration: Sherrill, The Catatonic Nurse

Because the stuporous symptoms of catatonia respond so well to anti-psychotic medication, most psychotherapists today have never seen a case of catatonic schizophrenia. Coupled with the fact that the catatonic's thought disorder is the least in evidence of all the schizo-phrenias, psychotherapists are very likely to miss a case of early catatonia. This is exactly what had happened with Sherrill, a 26-year-old registered nurse.

Sherrill's psychotherapist was baffled by the patient's complaints, which included a failed sexual relationship with a male physician and the threat of seduction by an ardent lesbian nurse, both of whom were on the same hospital staff with her. Yet Sherrill was really not very attached to the physician, although she talked a great deal about the brief, torrid affair. And even as she complained of the advances from the other nurse, she was distant, and even detached, from the so-called threat. Because Sherrill manifested no discerned thought disorder, schizophrenia was not considered a diagnosis, and her flat affect was misdiagnosed as major depression. The psychotherapist, an astute and experienced psychologist, was not comfortable with the provisional diagnosis of major depression and requested that she interview the patient behind the one-way mirror with the entire staff present on the other side. This was arranged, and the senior author happened to be present on a routine visit to the center.

The staff concentrated so much on what Sherrill was saying that they missed the cardinal symptom. They struggled to understand her interpersonal difficulties, her inability to adequately do her nursing job, and her desire to be alone most of the time. They did not question the misdiagnosis of her flat affect as major depression, and they did not even notice her catatonic posturing. For the entire 45-minute session, Sherrill's right foot was frozen six inches off the floor. A person has great difficulty maintaining such a position for more than one minute. Yet Sherrill's right foot remained suspended in midair for the entire session and no one even noticed. So much for nonverbal cues!

When the senior author mentioned this in the follow-up session, the staff was skeptical. Fortunately, the session had been videotaped, and a fastforwarding of the tape confirmed the prolonged catatonic posturing. The staff was stunned with its own nonperceptivity. Sherrill's diagnosis was changed to that of catatonic schizophrenia, she was started on antipsychotic medication, and the meaning of her symptom was addressed in therapy. In time, it was understood that Sherrill was giving up her motility so as not to physically attack the married physician who used her and then dumped her. Had she not been treated properly, in all likelihood the patient might have acted out her rage (catatonic mania), or more likely, she would have denied the rage by regressing into catatonic stupor. Sherrill was an onion catatonic and was unlikely to attack. A third possibility would have been a sudden, seemingly senseless running away. This, too, would have been an onion response.

LEGEND

Psychological Mechanism:	Withdrawal, Give Up Motility
Diagnosis:	Early Catatonic Schizophrenia
Operational Diagnosis:	Trouble at work
Implicit Contract:	I am not angry
Personality Type:	Onion
Homework:	Don't see your physician ex-lover
Therapeutic Techniques:	Antipsychotic medication
	Insight into sexual affair

It is not infrequent that an early schizophrenic is misdiagnosed as a depressive and prescribed an antidepressant rather than an antipsychotic. A withdrawn early schizophrenic can resemble a sloweddown depressive. When asked, "Are you depressed," a patient may erroneously report yes because he or she does not know the difference. The tragedy is more than the patient's being deprived of the appropriate treatment, for treatment with benzodiazapines and antidepressants can be often propel an early schizophrenia into fullblown psychosis. An example of such mishandling is the case of Randall, whose father's diagnosis was more accurate than that of his doctors.

Case Illustration: Randall, The Jumper

Randall, a 28-year-old unemployed single man living at home with his widowed father, was presented to the senior author because the patient seemed to be decompensating on the antidepressant regimen he had been on for the past three months. Since the patient was regarded as suicidal, the psychologist was reluctant to question the medication, but he asked for help in understanding this case.

The psychologist and the senior author interviewed the patient and his father together. From the onset of the interview, it was apparent that the identified patient's immobility and slow response were not manifestations of a retarded depression. His immobility was accompanied by repetitive, stereotyped, and highly manneristic movements when he did speak. Through most of the session, his left arm was suspended above his head. His speech, though infrequent, was circumstantial and manneristic.

Inquiry into the alleged suicidal attempt was revealing. Randall had been hospitalized with the diagnosis of psychotic depression. Early on his second day of hospitalization, he became increasingly more agitated until about 4:00 in the afternoon he jumped out of the hospital's third-floor window. He landed on both his feet and broke both ankles. In spite of this, Randall preceeded to walk over three miles. He recalled that there was absolutely no pain. He was apprehended when he attacked without provocation and with his fists three policemen who were guarding a visiting dignitary. This patient manifested a tethering of a feared garlic reaction. His jumping out the window was a substitute for attacking the hospital staff and his attacking the police was an expression of his rage in a way that would really not hurt anyone else.

Somewhat belatedly, the current diagnosis of catatonic schizophrenia was made. The antidepressants which were causing decompensation, were discontinued in favor of antipsychotic medication. In therapy Randall was treated as a schizophrenic and he rapidly improved.

Interestingly, the father had been aware of his son's schizophrenia for over a decade. He was comfortable with caring for his son, an activity that filled a void caused by his wife's untimely death 12 years ago. This father could not help but note his son's mental aberrations, and he read and informed himself as to better care for Randall. His entreaties to his son's psychiatrists that Randall was a schizophrenic were cavalierly ignored until now.

LEGEND

Psychological Mechanism:	Withdrawal, Give up Motility
Diagnosis:	Catatonic Schizophrenia
Operational Diagnosis:	Father's concern
Implicit Contract:	I am not angry
Personality Type:	Onion suppressing garlic
Homework:	Let father help you
Therapeutic Techniques:	Discontinued antidepressant in favor of antipsychotic
	Help father care for schizophrenic son

9
Schizophrenia: Garlic /Nonanalyzable

Schizophrenias Controlled by Attacking the Environment

Dynamics

In schizophrenias controlled by attacking the environment, defenses against acting out hostility have been overwhelmed. Catatonic mania occurs when the loss of control of motility leads not to stupor but to destructiveness, as in the following case of Alvin. Attacking paranoia occurs when delusions and personality types coalesce to make acts of destruction not only logical but necessary for salvation, as in the case of Ernesto below.

Entry

The potential of destructive violence must be carefully considered in attacking schizophrenia. The intensity of psychosis must be reduced by medication and the patient stabilized before psychotherapy is possible. Then, treatment should be focused on solving specific problems in daily living. A biopsychosocial plan of rehabilitation and access to the full continuum of care may be necessary.

Fortunately for those around him, Alvin turned his original attacking schizophrenia back onto himself. Although the result was grossly to his own detriment, the extent of the rage manifested could have produced drastic consequences had he attacked the environment. That the catatonic hears and sees while in a stupor is also dramatically illustrated by the case of Alvin. Therapy, patiently and painstakingly applied, can even have positive results with a person in a catatonic stupor.

Case Illustration: Old MacDonald Had A Son

Alvin, a 17-year-old adolescent who lived on a farm with his father and stepmother, was first seen after he had amputated both of his legs above the knees. He was also mute and in a total catatonic stupor. Had not the hired man found him lying in the barn shortly after the self-amputations, applied tourniquets, and summoned help, Alvin surely would have bled to death. The surgeon who stitched up the stumps marvelled at how skillfully the patient had amputated his own limbs. Examination of Alvin's blood revealed no alcohol or drugs of any kind that might have lessened what had to be excruciating pain. Many weeks later, after he came out of his stupor, Alvin stated that he absolutely felt nothing as he sawed both of his legs with an ordinary carpenter's saw. He was only acutely aware of the annoying, cutting sound and that the bleeding got in the way.

The patient was, of course, unresponsive to verbal psychotherapy, and his antipsychotic medication was force-fed, as was also his nutrition. The psychologist decided on a treatment plan in which he would visit Alvin daily during the lunch hour and conduct a one-sided conversation for about 15 minutes. The monologue each time was similar: "Hello, Alvin, I'm Dr. Cummings. This is your sixth day in the hospital and it's April 9th. It rained last night and this morning. You don't have to talk, but when you're ready, I'm here to listen." The remainder of the 15 minutes would be filled with news and other events of the last 24 hours. Then, the psychologist would conclude, "Goodbye, Alvin, I'll see you at noon tomorrow." If it were Friday, the goodbye would be modified to state the psychologist would see the patient on Monday following the weekend. All communications were brief, simple, but very precise.

For weeks Alvin remained unresponsive, staring into nothingness as he ignored the psychologist. Then, one day his lips moved almost imperceptibly, but what he said was inaudible. Attempts to get him to repeat what he had said were unsuccessful and were promptly dropped so as not to risk increasing the patient's negativism. Another week went by before Alvin spoke, this time quite audibly: "I'll get well if you don't send me home." Then he lapsed back into his mute, immobile state.

The psychologist now altered the content of the daily monologue to report progress in arranging transfer to a halfway house when Alvin was ready to leave the hospital. In due time, the psychologist reported that all the arrangements had been made and all that remained was Alvin's ability to leave the hospital. The patient remained unresponsive for several days. Then, one day when the psychologist came to visit, Alvin was in a wheelchair, transporting himself all over the fifth floor of the hospital, and talking with staff and fellow patients.

Psychotherapy now began in a more formal sense as Alvin was also fitted for and taught to use artificial limbs. It was then that the full story came to light. Alvin's mother died when he was age 14. The father was distraught, lonely, and depressed. The burden of seeing that all the farm chores were done fell on Alvin, as his father was too depressed to attend to what was necessary. Also, the father moved Alvin into his bed where he remained for two-and-a-half years. The father would have bad dreams and often embrace Alvin in his sleep, thinking he was the deceased wife. Just before Alvin's seventeenth birthday, the father met a woman, fell in love, came out of his depression, and married.

Alvin was returned to his former bedroom where every night he could hear the giggles and the lovemaking. The stepmother resented Alvin, and the father was too engrossed in his new life to pay the boy much attention. After several months, Alvin began experiencing, in the middle of the night, an uncontrollable urge to go into the adjacent room and murder his stepmother. One night, the urge was so strong that Alvin got dressed, went to his high school, broke in, and did thousands of dollars worth of damage as he smashed everything in sight with a sledge hammer. He was awaiting determination of his case by juvenile authorities when the uncontrollable urge to kill his stepmother occurred again. This time, instead of a garlic (attack) reaction, Alvin chose the penultimate onion reaction and amputated his own legs.

As is typical of catatonic stupor, Alvin was aware of and remembered everything he saw and heard during the more than two months he was in that state. He recalled all the details of the 15 minute conversations and described in the subsequent therapy his mute and motionless inner struggle as to whether he should trust the psychologist. During the stupor, the mind of the catatonic is very clear and insensitive remarks are remembered and resented.

LEGEND

Psychological Mechanism:	Withdrawal, Give-Up Motility
Diagnosis:	Catatonic Schizophrenia
Operational Diagnosis:	Father's remarriage
Implicit Contract:	I'll stay in my stupor
Personality Type:	Garlic retreating into onion
Homework:	Remain in stupor
Therapeutic Techniques:	Accepting patient's stupor
	Arranging halfway house

A case of paranoid schizophrenia, which was misdiagnosed and mishandled by professionals over a number of years, had a tragic ending that attracted much media attention and generated a great deal of hindsight. It is important that we as psychotherapists learn from a case as tragically mishandled as Ernesto.

Case Illustration: Ernesto the Constant Cuckold

Predicting violent behavior on the part of the paranoid schizophrenic is difficult, if not improbable. Yet observing the history of the paranoid behavior to determine whether it is onion (suffering) or garlic (attacking) can be extremely helpful. It should be assumed that all garlic paranoids have the potential to attack and appropriate precautions should be initiated and kept in place. Had this taken place with Ernesto, three small children and their mother might be alive today. With the visual acuity that accompanies hindsight, it might be helpful to assess how therapeutic ineptitude did nothing to avert a tragedy.

Ernesto, a man of 33, was seen for evaluation after a quadruple murder and attempted suicide. He had shot and killed his wife and three small children, and then critically wounded himself. His bungled suicide enabled the piecing together of a garlic paranoia that was abetted by therapy in its eventual deadly attack.

From the first day of his eight-year marriage, Ernesto was insanely jealous of his wife. On the first night of their honeymoon, he beat her for allowing too many male guests to kiss her on the cheek as they went through the wedding reception line. Inevitably, whenever they were out in public, he would accuse Louisa of making amorous eye contact with a total stranger.

About every three to four months, matters would come to a boil. Ernesto would "discern" that Louisa was having a sexual affair with someone they both knew, and he would slap her, badger her, and torment her for hours until she broke down begging his forgiveness. Whereupon Ernesto would tenderly wipe her tears, embrace her, and magnanimously forgive her. They would pray on their knees to God for another two hours, asking also for Divine forgiveness for Louisa. These episodes were repeated three to four times a year. They were always preceded by two to three weeks during which Ernesto would secretly follow her and otherwise spy on her. His job as automobile insurance claims adjuster gave him considerable leeway to leave his job during the day to spy on her. Invariably, once the torment session was over with the granting of Divine forgiveness, Ernesto would go through a 10-day to two-week period of insatiable sexual appetite in which he made love to Louisa three times a day.

In his early twenties, before he married Louisa, Ernesto had experienced a religious conversion in which he left the Catholic Church and joined a Pentecostal sect. He sincerely believed that a devil would possess Louisa, a naturally loving and chaste woman, and cause her to perform unspeakable acts with other men. He further believed that God's Providence had instructed him to cast out this devil.

Ernesto and Louisa sought psychological help for their marital difficulties on at least two dozen occasions during their eight years of marriage. Sometimes the children's nightmares, enuresis, and other problems were the excuse to seek this help. Unfortunately, the mental health service of the HMO to which they belonged provided only crisis intervention. This was also true for the community mental health center to which they presented themselves or their distraught children on a number of occasions.

The crisis workers concentrated on helping the couple in their marriage. Ernesto's behavior was attributed to a combination of cultural factors (Filipino), religious fervor, and deep personal insecurities and low self-esteem as a man. If medication was prescribed, it would be antidepressants. Only once was Ernesto given an antipsychotic. In his paranoia, Ernesto distrusted any medication and never took it as prescribed. No one followed up to see if he had complied. In all of this, no one listened or probed enough to discover that Ernesto had an elaborate, well-systematized delusion that sought constant corroboration. This delusion was on a collision course with tragedy.

The delusion was named Breckenridge. Although the first name was James, Ernesto thought and spoke of him only as Breckenridge. In the patient's mind, Breckenridge was a combination of James Bond, the Red Baron, and the Count of Monte Cristo. He was dashing, urbane, fabulously wealthy, and exceptionally virile. He had seduced Louisa when she was only 16, and she had been in love with him ever since. But God had informed Ernesto that Breckenridge was really the Devil in human form. He had the ability to possess Louisa because of her persistent love for him. It was God's plan for Ernesto to cast out this devil. If he failed, he would have to kill her and also the children since they, too, would be possessed. The ability to cast out the devil from Louisa was the key to the future. In the meantime, Louisa's infidelities, driven by Breckenridge, would be God's way of testing Ernesto's faith. None of this delusion was ever revealed to the various mental health professionals who had been seen; not surprisingly, they were not looking and probing for psychosis.

After years of struggling with Ernesto's periodic torments, Louisa announced she was leaving him. If she carried out her threat, how, then, could Ernesto continue his work of "purifying" Louisa? Within hours, Ernesto received his answer and instructions from God. He should kill Louisa and the three children, as well as himself. Then all five of their souls would be transported to Heaven where there is no sin and no divorce. The family would be intact through eternity and free of Breckenridge at last! Ernesto thanked God in his prayers for this deliverance, and set out to accomplish his Divine mission.

In eight years of mental health crisis contacts, Ernesto had never been properly diagnosed. The establishing of the diagnosis of paranoid schizophrenia would be only the beginning. The paranoid delusion, as well as his overt behavior for eight years, was clearly garlic, indicating the potential to be an attacking paranoid. The elicitation of the delusion would have made clear that the family needed protection and Ernesto needed antipsychotic medication with the follow-up to assure he was complying with the regimen.

LEGEND

Psychological Mechanism: Withdrawal (delusions), Attack, Projection

Diagnosis: Paranoid Schizophrenia

Operational Diagnosis: Wife announced divorce

Implicit Contract: I must join my family in Heaven

Personality Type: Garlic

Homework: Comply with medication regimen

Therapeutic Techniques: Antipsychotic medication Suicidal precautions

Impulse Schizophrenia

Dynamics

In impulse schizophrenia, the person cannot suppress the impulse to kill. This impulse is expressed in ritualistic serial killings. The ritualistic nature of the killing, like that of the Zodiac Killer who had to kill people in accordance with a certain progression in the zodiac charts, is a restitutive symptom. It is an attempt to keep from killing wantonly.

Entry

Impulse schizophrenics often have a long history of being seen in the mental health system, but they will not relate this to you. They will come in hoping that by some magic you will be able to fix them and they generally leave you wondering, "That was such a charming, healthy, normal human being. Why the hell did he come in?" They have looking normal down to a science and are even more clever than sociopaths. They come in hoping that somehow someone by magic can remove the impulse to kill.

There is no treatment for impulse schizophrenia; there is only incarceration to remove the possibility of acting on the impulse. Yet, even when the courts have removed such a person from society, our system of justice often releases the serial killer and the tragedy may be repeated.

Case Illustration: Harry, The Serial Killer

Within the confines of the state hospital, there was a 52-year-old silver-haired, distinguished looking man who had brutally killed eight women. His murders demonstrated the classic signs of both ritual and choice of women who fit certain criteria. Yet, during his past four years in the state hospital, his behavior belied his psychotic brutality. Harry was charming, especially toward women. He had ingratiated himself with nearly everyone, was accorded freedom of the grounds, and had been assigned to the library as patient-assistant. Whenever anyone, staff or patient, needed help, Harry was there. His silver tongue matched his silver hair. Everyone seemed to have forgotten who Harry was and what he had done. Then, Harry filed a writ to be released from the hospital as cured. The hospital contested the writ and Harry became his own advocate.

The psychologist was asked to administer a battery of psychological tests in anticipation of the court hearing. Harry cooperated fully and yielded a surprisingly healthy profile. The psychologist was uneasy: Harry's responses were too normal. Either he was the healthiest person alive, or there was something odd about the test results. In thinking through the matter, the psychologist was struck by the answer. Harry had access in the hospital library to all of the tests and pertinent books. A highly intelligent and resourceful man, he had memorized both the tests and a set of responses.

A technique known as "testing the limits" was then applied. Harry was asked to respond to a second administration of the Rorschach inkblots without repeating any of his previous responses. Harry complied with an incredibly healthy profile. He had memorized a back-up set of responses! The Rorschach was administered a third time and with the same restriction. Harry finally revealed himself, but only momentarily. He described card III as a wood carving of two men and stated the red was the bleeding from the carving. When asked how wood could bleed real blood as it was being carved, Harry quickly recovered. He knew he had revealed himself, but he laughed it off.

As significant as the psychotic response is to a psychologist, it would not be understood or appreciated by a jury that would be charmed by Harry. When the hearing arrived, Harry was, in fact, so likeable that it was obvious the jury had been won over. The psychologist presented his test findings, which Harry, doing the cross-examination on behalf of himself, cut to shreds. He even had the jury laughing about the alleged significance of the one silly response to an inkblot, especially since the psychologist had to admit all of the other many responses were quite normal.

The jury did not release Harry, but only because the psychologist described with every gory detail how he had tortured and killed eight women. This was repeated annually for the next three years. Harry's writ was denied repeatedly because the jury was filled with revulsion when the murders were described. But Harry was not to be outdone. In putting in his fifth writ, he had already ascertained the psychologist would be out of the country and unable to appear. On that occasion, Harry charmed another jury and, with nothing to counteract the favorable impression, he was released.

Within 72 hours of his release, Harry killed again. This time, he decided he would dispose of the body in such a way as not to be detected. In the murdered woman's home, he began cutting up the body and putting it piece by piece in the garbage disposal. Not being a surgeon, Harry totally underestimated how long it would take to cut up a body, flesh and bone, in pieces small enough to be ground up in the garbage disposal. He had been at it for hours when the utility company meter reader walked past the side window and saw the blood-smeared kitchen. He called police and Harry was apprehended for his ninth murder.

This text describes a number of difficult cases and innovative ways to treat them. Unfortunately, psychotherapy has not acquired the sophistication to offset the risks to society of a serial killer, and the recommended approach to such patients is hospital commitment in a locked ward. There is currently a movement among some psychologists and psychiatrists to treat patients such as Harry in an outpatient setting so as to enhance their self-esteem toward eventually helping them overcome their drive to violence. A caveat here is important. A relapse in a serial killer is not as inconsequential as an alcoholic simply falling off the wagon. The consequences are literally deadly.

A psychotherapist's obligation is that any treatment attempted should be in a locked setting. The possibility of enhancing Harry's self-esteem cannot outweigh the probability of another victim.

LEGEND

Psychological Mechanism:	Denial, Attacking, Projection
Diagnosis:	Impulse Schizophrenia
Operational Diagnosis:	Writ of habeas corpus for release
Implicit Contract:	Testify I am sane
Personality Type:	Garlic
Homework:	Remain in hospital
Therapeutic Techniques:	None available other than continued locked hospitalization

Part III

SUICIDALITY

Patients are far more resilient than many therapists realize. The greatest consequences of incompetent therapy are that the patient abruptly quits the therapist or that the treatment process is unnecessarily protracted. Although these outcomes must not be taken lightly, they do not compare in magnitude with mistakes made in therapy with suicidal patients where treatment can be terminated abruptly by death. It is not surprising, therefore, that therapists tend to err on the side of too much caution, often inadvertently increasing suicidality and complicating recovery.

Skillful psychotherapists will differentiate their suicidal patients in terms of onion and garlic, and treat each accordingly. The silent, long-suffering patient (onion) depressive may commit suicide without even telegraphing the intent, while the loud, complaining, depressed patient with a borderline personality disorder (garlic) will learn quickly to use suicidal threats as a form of blackmail to obtain hospitalization when this suits his or her agenda. Overly cautious therapy may very well miss the lethality of the first example, while escalating the nonlethal suicidal activity of the latter. It is as important, therefore, to different onion and garlic suicidal patients as it is with all other categories of patients.

This is also true with regard to a patient's being analyzable versus nonanalyzable. Reactive depressions require skillful uncovering psychotherapy leading to the expulsion of the introject. Depressed borderline and other personality disorders require that uncovering be eschewed in favor of strengthening boundaries in the here and now.

As we have found in therapy with other categories of patients, most psychotherapists are more skillful with onion patients. But, in addition, the depressed garlic patient can present an overlay of suffering onion that will cause the psychotherapist to forget the requirement that garlic is always treated before onion. Therapists' offices are filled with garlic depressives who are exhorted in treatment to "speak-up," while their baffled family and friends are being flattened by the patient's verbal and physical hostility.

The differential treatment of onion and garlic depression is critical to effective and efficient treatment as the following case examples will demonstrate.

10

Treating Suicidal Patients

Suicide: Taking Responsibility for Another's Life

The suicide of a patient is a devastating experience for a psychotherapist, especially if the patient commits suicide at you. A psychiatrist sought treatment after a woman patient opened her purse in the middle of a session, took out a revolver, put the barrel in her mouth, pulled the trigger, and splattered the wall behind the therapy chair with blood and brains. He could no longer bring himself to see patients. He, of course, could not help but wonder what he had done and what he might have done differently. Many colleagues have been absolutely shattered and could not continue with their careers because of patient suicides.

Suicide follows families to the fourth generation. Even three generations later, people will whisper about Grandma or Grandpa or other family members killing themselves. The guilt and concern linger because all of us as human beings, some more and some less, have thought of suicide. A very common fantasy in childhood after being punished by Mom or Dad and sent to one's room is, "I'm dead. I'm sitting up here watching my own funeral and my parents are running around crying, Why weren't we nice to our child while still alive." Suicide scares us because there is no one who has not flashed on it. Thus, when confronted by depression in a patient, our first inclination is often to be overly kind.

The Suicidology Center at the National Institute of Mental Health (NIMH) studied suicide for over a 20-year period and sponsored hundreds of psychological autopsies on people who committed suicide. In studying these cases, one must come to the conclusion that most suicides are directed *at* somebody. This leads us to the axiom: Never, ever take responsibility for another person's life.

A psychiatric social worker was in an addiction group for his amphetamine addiction. The therapist announced to the group, "I won't be here next week. I'll be away, but we'll still get our requisite number of sessions. We'll just tack it on the end." I usually don't tell my patients why I'm away, because I'm interested in what their fantasies and transferences are. One woman in the group waited outside my office for several hours, convinced that I was seeing all of my patients but her. Finally, in the middle of the afternoon, she realized nobody was going in and out of my office, and that I really was away.

This social worker, however, had read in one of our professional newspapers that I was going to NIMH to receive an award. This angered him. He thought, "Nick's going away on this frivolity while I need him."

On the day that I was receiving the award, he went to the end of the pier at Aquatic Park just below the Golden Gate Bridge, wrote a 16-page suicide note in which my name was on every other line, took off his shoes, weighted the note down with his shoes, and then lowered himself from the end of the pier into the water. The water in San Francisco Bay, winter or summer, is around 50 degrees. As he's lowering himself in, he imagines the banner headlines in the San Francisco Chronicle, "PATIENT DROWNS SELF WHILE PSYCHOLOGIST RECEIVES AWARD." As he got up to his armpits in this ice cold water, he heard my voice say, "You dumb jackass."

He pulled himself out of the water, tore up the suicide note, threw it in the trashcan, put his shoes back on, and being too embarrassed to catch the bus home because he was soaking wet, walked home. It was in the middle of January. He came in to the next session with this terrible cold and said to us, "If I thought for one moment I could ruin Nick's career by killing myself, I would be dead now."

A psychotherapist must not take responsibility for another human life. In reality, you cannot; in practice, if you do, you set yourself up to stand for the significant person in the patient's life he/she wants to commit suicide at. This does not mean the therapist lacks empathy. However, misdirected empathy must not be allowed to encourage lethality. For the social worker, I stood for the father who was never there when he needed him. I had the audacity to be like his father when he was having a hard time staying clean. In his mind, I had the audacity to go to Washington, D.C., to get an undeserved award. The fury is disproportional to the event, but it was fueled by the years of fury at his own father.

Only the patient can make the decision to live. It is the therapist's responsibility to ignite in the patient the will to live. Without this, the therapist is really helpless. Hospitalization must at some point end, as must a nonsuicidal therapeutic contract (see the case of Linda in Chapter 3). The therapist, no matter how empathic and vigilant, cannot "police" the suicidal patient around the clock and into perpetuity. The significant number of suicides in psychiatric hospitals demonstrates our helplessness in the face of a determined patient. The therapist's responsibility, to reiterate, is to so hone his/her skills as to be able to help the patient's decision to live. This is often difficult, because our inclinations are to overly empathize and identify with someone suffering so much that he/she wishes to die. Successful interventions might require tough love, or what we term the spilling of some "psychic blood."

The threat of suicidality varies in seriousness and style according to diagnostic categories. Selected categories are discussed below, along with suicidality among adolescents and the elderly.

Suicide Among Hysterics

Hysteric patients very frequently, vocally, and histrionically threaten suicide. Hysterics are not of themselves lethal, but hysterics are the stumblebums of psychotherapy. They frequently miscalculate and kill themselves even when they don't intend to.

In one case, a man came in distraught because his wife had just committed suicide. They had been married for four years, and three or four times a year they would play the following game: They would argue. She would run to the bathroom, lock the door, and swallow a bottle of pills. He would break the door down, scoop her up, and drive her to the emergency room, where they would pump her stomach. Three or four times a year they would play this game. On this particular occasion, they were at a New Year's Eve party. They argued all the way home. They got home, and while he was putting the car in the garage, she ran into the house, locked herself in the bathroom, and swallowed a bottle of pills. He came into the house and passed out on the couch because he'd had too much to drink. When he came to, she was dead.

Even though hysterics are most likely to be gesturing, their threats must be taken seriously because they can and do miscalculate. But this does not mean that it should be taken so seriously that unnecessary hospitalization is seen as the answer. Expedient hospitalization can further exacerbate the suicidal risk. Hysterics will conclude, "My God, they really think I'm crazy," and in their hysteria be more prone to attempt to kill themselves.

Techniques that can be utilized in helping hysterics strengthen the part of them that is determined to live are illustrated in earlier case illustrations (Elaine, Linda). In both of these cases, misguided empathy would have been interpreted as pity and would have fueled the suicidality. Two caveats are indicated: The therapist must take the time to know and understand the patient, and the therapist must have honed his/her skills sufficiently so that the intervention is believable. This is why some of these interventions are not for the unskilled or the fainthearted (e.g., the case illustration of Lenore).

Suicide Among Borderline Personalities

Borderline personalities are less lethal than hysterics because they do not miscalculate. The borderlines are survivors. In one case in Orlando, a woman borderline demanded hospitalization, and her therapist appropriately refused. She called him at 11:00 that night and said, "I'm giving you your last chance to hospitalize me. If you don't,

I'm going to shoot myself." He refused, and the next thing he heard was "BAM!" He then heard the phone drop to the floor and a body fall. The therapist kept his cool, got to another line, left that line open, called 911, and the call was traced. The paramedics picked her up and took her to the hospital.

The therapist followed her into the hospital. The emergency room surgeon came out and said, "You know, she shot herself in the chest. But probably what you don't know is that this is the third time in two years she has shot herself in the chest and has never hit a vital organ. I as a surgeon knowing anatomy could not do that."

No one knows how they do it, but they do. In Phoenix, a borderline patient threatened the therapist when she was not hospitalized. She said, "I will leave here and kill myself by running my car into a telephone pole." She got in her car, hit the first telephone pole, knocked the telephone pole down, totaled her car, and didn't have a scratch on her. But 20,000 people in Phoenix were without power for several hours. Surviving their dysfunctional families must make everything else in life seem like a picnic to a borderline.

Borderlines will kill themselves in despair. When everyone has given up on them and they are locked on the back ward of a state hospital, they will kill themselves because they no longer can act out. As long as they can strut, can continue their projective identification, raise an uproar in the community, they stay alive. The acting out is the lifeblood of the borderline personality.

When one is working with borderline patients, maneuvers that will result in the flicker of a smile or the mischievous blink of an eye are effective. For example:

> One maneuver the senior author has used is to say, "You know, in 40 years of practice I've never had a successful suicide, and if you want to kill yourself, you could be Nick Cummings' first suicide. I have some feelings about this because I've had so many colleagues who have had patients who have suicided and I may retire very soon without ever experiencing how it feels to have a patient commit suicide. I'm going to ask you a favor. If you're going to be my one and only suicide in my entire career, make it worthy. Come up with a suicide that will at least make the headlines. Go home and think about it, come back next week and tell me what you've decided."

They may say, "Well, I've decided to jump off the Golden Gate bridge."

I would respond, "Jump off the Golden Gate bridge!? There's been over a thousand people who have done that. No big deal. Go on. Is that the best you can do? Kill yourself any way you want to, but you're not worthy of being my first suicide. The hell with you." You'll see that flicker of a smile.

If borderlines see that you're strong enough not to be conned, they love you. They start to think, "Maybe this is the person that will be able to stop me." Then they try you again, and every time you pass a test the respect goes up a thousand points. Until, finally, the testings grow further and further apart. But in the beginning they'll test you every five minutes. Your disaster comes when they write you off as a wimp. When they cannot feel secure that you're there for them, they will act out to punish you.

Paranoid Schizophrenics

Paranoid patients are lethal. Many successful suicides and notes have a paranoid flavor. You cannot make a suicide pact with a paranoid. It will have no effect because paranoids do not kill themselves. They go on to a higher plane of existence. A paranoid will kill his wife, children, and then shoot himself to keep his family intact. There is no divorce in Heaven, so they all go to Heaven where they live for eternity as a family. Paranoids believe that! Paranoids who are threatening suicide need to be in the hospital on antipsychotic medication. After they're stabilized, then psychotherapy is possible, but medication management must be a critical part of treatment. Paranoids are not only lethal to themselves but, because their defense mechanism is projection, they can be lethal to others as in the following (see also the case of Ernesto in Chapter 7).

This is a case the senior author encountered as chair of the APA Insurance Trust. One of our psychologists was sued for malpractice. The wife called in wanting to see this psychologist although he practiced some 100 miles away from their home.

Her father-in-law had done so well with him and had recommended the psychologist highly. She said that her husband was suicidal.

It was sometime between Christmas and New Year's, when all psychotherapists are busy up to their elbows, so the psychologist scheduled them as his last appointment. At 6:00 P.M., the psychologist went into the waiting room and saw a couple out of the 60s and 70s. He was in bell bottomed trousers with a 1970s hairdo. She had long, ironed out, perfectly flat hair and wore a flowing, busy little flowered peasant skirt. The therapist suspected they were on drugs but then determined that they were not. During the session the wife said that she had decided to leave him and her husband was threatening suicide. The therapist noticed that he kept attending to his tennis shoes and asked, "Why are you staring at your tennis shoes?"

The husband said, "Well, that's how they're conveying the messages."

"What messages?"

"Well, they're going to kill my wife."

After talking to them as a couple, the therapist saw the wife alone for an hour. The wife explained that she'd been trying to leave this man for several years, that she kept backing off because he threatened suicide, but that she was determined to leave this time. She wanted to get him into therapy because she was afraid he was suicidal. After finishing with the wife, the therapist spoke with the husband. Four times during the interview the husband said, "They're killing my wife in the waiting room." The therapist had to go outside the office, go downstairs to the waiting room, and show him that his wife was safe. Four times. At the end of this, he called them both back in and asked to see the husband the next day. The husband couldn't come in the next day or the day after, so they made an appointment three days later.

The couple left. By that time it was quite late at night. They drove the 100 miles home. Somewhere between 2:00 and 3:00 in the morning, the therapist was awakened by the emergency room in their town reporting, "We understand that these two people are your patients. He shot her, then shot himself, and miraculously they're both still alive." They recovered and they sued the psychologist.

The defense attorney took the position that a therapist can't know everything about a patient in one contact. The consultant said, "You'd better settle this one for what you can, because he should have known this." Because the defense mechanism in paranoia is projection, "They're going to kill her," means "I'm going to kill her." If they say, "They are going to kill me," it means, "I am going to kill me."

The Undetected Lethal Patient

The undetected lethal patient is the one who has been depressed over some time and does not respond to any therapeutic intervention. Just as you're getting very discouraged, the patient tells you, "Gee, doctor, I'm feeling better. Pressure's been lifted." Before you congratulate yourself, you must make sure that this patient's depression has not lifted because he or she has made the unverbalized determination to commit suicide and therefore no longer has to struggle.

If patients have made such a decision, they have decided when and how, and then have become amnesic to it. This is autohypnosis with a posthypnotic suggestion when and how to kill themselves, and the patients are no longer aware of the sequence. They go on autopilot because they do not have the courage to face the decision they have made, but even so they will always give the therapist a clue. Even after they have decided to kill themselves and are relieved that they will no longer have to struggle, the will to live in human beings is so strong that they will give the therapist one last chance to save them. But this last chance is most often missed by the therapist. Several examples follow.

A man was in treatment for depression, but there was no improvement for months. One day, the patient came in and said, "I'm feeling great. Thank you, you've finally helped me. My depression is lifted." During the course of the session, he said, "When I leave here, I'm going to the escrow office where I'm concluding the sale of our mountain cabin. I'm putting the money in a money market fund." The therapist knew that the man was an outdoorsman who loved hunting and fishing, and his wife was a city woman who hated the outdoors. She had been after him for years to sell that mountain cabin and invest it in a money market fund for retirement. He'd say, "No, I don't want to do that because when I retire I'm going to spend most of my time in that mountain cabin, hunting and fishing."

He is now going to sell the cabin because he's not going to be around to retire and use it. He left the therapist's office and bought 25 feet of garden hose on the way home. As he pulled into his driveway, his next door neighbor was trimming the hedge. He joked with his neighbor, opened up the trunk, pulled out the garden hose, and said, "You know, I don't know what the heck I bought this hose for. I must have 400 feet of garden hose around this place." He drove the car into the garage, closed the door, attached the new garden hose to the tail pipe, put the other end through the partially opened car window, sat in the front seat, and turned on the engine. When his wife came home, he was dead of carbon monoxide poisoning.

Another patient suffering from an illness that left him disabled and in a wheelchair was despairing that after three previous debilitating episodes, this time he would not have a remission. The therapist was not grappling with the issue successfully. After dropping out of therapy twice, the patient said in a session, "Last week I saw Dr. (name deleted). I thought he could help me because he was a student of (name deleted). This was my last hope. He referred me back to you." Yet in spite of his stating that the other therapist had been his "last hope," the patient is happy as a clam. He's no longer depressed about his condition. The therapist missed the significance. The patient went home. His wife said that in the next two days she had never seen her husband happier. He called up all his old friends and chatted with them. About 8:00 at night on the second day, he told his wife, "Well, it's finished. That was the last one." He wheeled himself into the bedroom, took the gun out of the bedside table, and killed himself. He was saying goodbye to all his friends. He had decided to kill himself and told the therapist, "Dr. (name deleted) was my last hope." The therapist had missed the incongruity between his affect and his statement.

A depressed woman was in treatment for weeks with nothing happening. She always talked about her wedding ring, which had belonged to her great-grandmother. It had been passed down through the generations when her grandmother, mother, and she were married. Her dream was to give the ring to her daughter, who at that time was 11 years old. One day, she came to therapy feeling much better and said during the session, "I gave my wedding ring to my daughter." She did this because she wasn't going to be around for the wedding. She wanted her daughter to have it now. The woman went home and poisoned herself.

The clue is there, but we are swept away by the sudden improvement. In the absence of any psychological reason for an elevation in mood, be suspicious. If you suspect that your patient is on automatic pilot, confront it in the most forceful way you know, "When and how did you decide to kill yourself?" You've got to get him or her out of automatic pilot. Two times out of three, you'll have a false positive. The patient will say, "Huh? I didn't decide to kill myself." Then you can apologize, "I picked up certain signs. I'd rather be safe than sorry. I'm sorry, I don't mean to alarm you." But that one time out of three, the patient will look at you and say, "Oh my God, it was day before yesterday when I was sitting in my office. I decided, and here's how I'm going to do it." The next hour must be spent going over and over the plan in every detail, over and over again, to make sure the patient comes out of automatic pilot and will not be able to go back in.

Suicide Among Adolescents

Jay Haley said, "Adolescence is not a time of life, it's a disease, that only age will cure" (Haley, 1976). In some ways, every adolescent is pathological, depressed, hysterical, acting out, and counterphobic. It is the time of major transition, of differentiating from our parents, and of establishing our own identities. The incidence of adolescent suicide has risen dramatically, however, because of drugs and cult rock music.

So many groups glorify suicide. The songs are constructed so adult ears do not hear it. The kids hear it. This does not mean ostensibly subliminal messages, but rather the cult rock music that blares out the naked glorification of suicide. They tell kids to kill themselves. If they are depressed and on drugs, suicide sounds like a great idea to adolescents. If a group is getting stoned and listening to cult music, one particularly disturbed adolescent can lead a mass suicide.

If therapists and parents are not inquiring about their adolescents' drug habits and their music habits, they are out of touch with the reality of the adolescent. If an adolescent tells you, the therapist, about a rock group that you know nothing about, say, "Bring me a tape," and listen to it until the words become understandable. If it is a cult and heavy metal kind of group that pushes suicide, forbid it. If they are also taking drugs, forbid this as a condition of treatment. If you don't, you're flirting with adolescent suicide. Because adolescents don't want to come in anyway, you might tell them, "It's up to you, but unless you come in here, your parents won't let you use the car. Your parents aren't going to trust you for this and that. Let's you and I work something out. In return for this, let's agree that we will see each other three times, for three weeks. Now you mean to tell me that you can't give up this damn music and these drugs for three weeks. You can't, can you? I can just see it in your face." This will often elicit the adolescent's oppositional compliance.

If it were not for cult rock music and drugs, the suicide rate among adolescents would probably be half what it is. There are other factors, but there always have been depressed adolescents. There have always been adolescents whose families are so achievement-oriented that if kids get a B+ instead of an A, they want to kill themselves. This is not what caused the epidemic. Drugs, depression, and cult music are a lethal combination.

Suicide Among The Elderly

An elderly man who has lost his sexual function, as often happens after prostate surgery, can get depressed to the point of being suicidal because male identity is so tied into sexuality, much more so than with women. This is the nature of the situation. A woman can fake interest in sex, but a man cannot. Many elderly men commit suicide because they would rather be dead than impotent.

The elderly person with a terminal illness who requests that he or she be taken off life support represents a special case. In such cases, it is important to have a bedside consultation with the person and make it very clear that it is not a philosophical issue that opposes suicide and that you are not there to reverse the patient's decision. One can appreciate how a person who has lived in dignity wants to die in dignity instead of in excruciating pain with triple the dosage of painkillers, and life support systems that allow for no quality of life. After the therapist has bonded, which can be accomplished in about an hour alone, by the bedside, then say to the person: "I have three questions I want to ask you: (1) Have you done everything that you need to do before you die? (2) Have you said everything to your loved ones that you want to say before you die? (3) If the answers to the first two are yes, would you be willing to have all of your family assembled by your bed? And I mean all, I don't care how far away they are. They should fly in to celebrate not your dying, but your life. Would you be willing to do that? I want you to think about these three things and I'll come back day after tomorrow and we'll talk some more."

Invariably the person will tell me, "No, I haven't done everything I need to do before I die. And I haven't said everything to my loved ones that l want to say before I die." My response is, "Well, let's get about it. And then we'll have the celebration of your life. And I want to be involved in that."

Every time this was done, the outcome was always the same. The person so reconnects with all of his or her loved ones and there's such an outpouring of love that the person comes alive and wants to hang on to the last few months of life to participate in this outpouring. The assembly of the family around the bedside, not to talk about death but to celebrate this person's life, is an incredible experience. The dying persons have told me this overshadowed everything— their wedding day, their graduation, the birth of their children. It was like all of this rolled up into one. It leaves them with such a glow that the last few weeks or months of life become not a drudgery, but a joy. Serendipitously when the person finally goes, he or she goes in a tremendous spirit of love and the family is left with a very joyous feeling. There's no unfinished business.

Finally, the recently widowed patient may be so depressed that he or she is determined to join the deceased (see the case of Arthur in Chapter 4). It is usually depression, not bereavement, that may trigger suicide in the surviving spouse. In the former, it is imperative to treat the introjection. In the latter, it is important to encourage mourning: crying, loneliness with yet the desire to be alone, giving in to missing the deceased.

APPENDIX

The Borderline Group Therapy Protocol

Although this volume has addressed individual psychotherapy, brief, intermittent therapy throughout the life cycle makes extensive use of group therapy. The group protocol developed for treatment of borderline personality disorders has been in great demand because this category of patients is among our most problematic. The group protocol is included here as an illustration of how focused, creative psychotherapy can be applied to group process.

It was developed by the senior author and his colleagues at Kaiser-Permanente, refined during the Hawaii Medicaid Project, and became a part of the Biodyne Training Manual (Cummings, 1985). Its development is summarized on pages 27 and 28 of this volume.

It would be useful to provide an example of these new group protocols, and that developed for borderline personalities has been selected. These patients are the product of dysfunctional families, and are thus proliferating exponentially. They can mimic any psychological condition, either to manipulate an advantage or ingratiate themselves to a therapist who is preoccupied by certain diagnoses. Most therapists would agree that the borderline personality is among the most difficult, problematic, demanding, and litigious of patients.

The suggestion that patients suffering from borderline personality disorder can be treated more effectively in group rather than individual therapy does, at first blush, sound onerous, indeed. Psychotherapists who have treated borderline patients know that one or two such patients in one's caseload is an exhausting and demanding experience. One borderline patient in the office often feels like a stampede. The image of six to eight such patients in the office at once is frightening to experienced therapists. Yet, our outcome research has demonstrated that such a group is not only more effective and efficient, but results in a great deal less wear and tear on the therapist than does the individual approach.

Review

This group protocol is based on several years of outcome research involving several false starts until the group method was attempted almost in exasperation at the failure of the individual approaches tested. In order to understand why the group protocol, it would be worthwhile to review very briefly the parameters of the borderline personality.

It cannot be overemphasized that the borderline personality is the product of dysfunctional families, and is thereby increasing exponentially. The parents manifested severe alcohol and drug dependency, and the child experienced neglect and physical/sexual abuse from birth. This interfered with successful bonding, rendering the child unable to successfully bond in adult relationships in later life. If bonding occurred before the parental alcohol/drug dependency became dysfunctional, the child is remanded to being a perfectionist, the obverse of the borderline. Named "adult children of alcoholics," these patients are destined to spend their entire lives attempting to recapture the *very early* acceptance experienced with the parent. The mechanism for doing this is by attempting to please the entire world.

The borderline patient is characterized by *projective identification* and *splitting*, which are both unconscious mechanisms and conscious, willful behaviors. Since they are deceitful, manipulative, and destructively hostile and rejecting, they project this "bad" self onto the object—in our case, the therapist—and hammer the poor therapist until he or she out of exhaustion does something that proves to the patient that the therapist is no better than the parents, lovers, author-

ity, society, and the world! They manage to split their entire environment (workplace, family, community, acquaintances), seducing some
while infuriating others. If you want to see who the borderline is on
a psychiatric ward, merely ask to see the patient whom half of the
staff feels so sorry for and is spending all resources to help, while the
other half despises that same patient and cannot wait until he/she is
discharged. This splitting is pervasive and unrelenting.

The psychotherapist, being a conscientious caregiver, is especially
vulnerable to the manipulativeness of the borderline, who is determined to prove the therapist is "no damn good" (like my parents) by
arousing anger in the therapist. The patients seldom, if ever, fail, for
they escalate acting out until the therapist's benevolence is exhausted.
The key to treating borderline patients is to never become angry.
The worst is to cover one's anger and deny this especially to oneself.
After all, as caregivers, we must be accepting, nonjudgmental, and
caring, we remind ourselves. Once we deny our anger by covering it
with more and more concern, caring, and acceptance, the borderline
identifies us as a phony toward whom the worst behavior is justified.

Our outcomes research indicates that the degree of demanding
acting out (nighttime phone calls, emergency room presentations,
suicidal behavior, hospitalizations, missed appointments) is directly
proportional to the therapist's attempt to prove there is no anger.
So, as the patient becomes more out of control and demanding, the
therapist attempts to meet all the demands. Eventually, the therapist
rejects the patient (called referring the patient on) and the patient
"wins," only to have lost because the process begins anew to prove
that the new therapist is no exception to the belief "everyone is no
damn good."

For these and other reasons, most authorities (E. Baker, Klineberg,
Masterson) believe that long-term individual therapy is the only approach, and finally succeeds after 15 to 20 years. Our experience and
research strongly contradict this view. Borderline patients so act out
as to make treatment impossible. Their behavior is intense and even
self-exhausting. Borderlines do slow down after age 40 and, especially,
after 45. Their degree of intensity cannot be maintained indefinitely,
at which point the long-term therapist erroneously attributes the
slowing down in acting out to the therapy. Seligman (1994) has consistently pointed to the large body of convincing research that shows

personality disorders are not altered by their being engaged in the reliving of their childhood traumas, a view that is in keeping with our own experience.

Our outcomes research indicates that the key to treating borderline patients is to show them how to manage themselves by first demonstrating they can be managed. The group method shifts the object of the acting out from the therapist to the peer group, and thereby relieves the therapist of the unrelenting barrage of demands that characterize the borderline. Whereas the therapist is never quite certain whether the current suicidal threat is the lethal one or just another manipulation in a long series of suicidal gestures, the fellow borderlines in the group are never fooled.

The Group

There are just as many male borderline personalities as there are female. Yet, most of the borderlines we see are women. This is because these men are usually remanded to the criminal justice system, while women borderlines invariably find themselves in the mental health system. Therefore, our groups almost exclusively involve women. We have had rare male groups when sufficient numbers presented themselves, but it is important not to assign the one or two males who appear to the women's group. In our research, we found that the flirtation, seductiveness, and grandstanding that occurs across genders will wreck the group. Overwhelmingly, the protocol is intended for women's groups, with either a male or female therapist equally effective.

The borderline group protocol implies all of the attributes of group process, and these will not be repeated here. What will be stressed are unique aspects and those that differ from usual group therapy procedure.

Early in the first session the therapist circulates a sheet of paper upon which each group member writes her name and telephone number. This is photocopied so that each group member receives a copy, with the instruction that when a personal crisis occurs the patient is to call the patient just below her own name. The person at the bottom calls the first name on the list. The patients do not call the therapist. Each patient is allowed one phone call to the therapist per week, which must take place during business hours and is subject to the majority of the group voting that the call to the therapist was justified. If the group votes that it was not justified, the patient forfeits her entitlement to call the therapist the following week. If the patient telephones the therapist more than once in a week's time, it is understood that the therapist will not return the call.

It is explained that the group is closed and time-limited to 20 sessions at one session per week. Once the group has begun no one else can join, but a group member can be expelled by majority vote of the group if that group member refuses to abide by the rules. Each group member signs an agreement which embodies all of these provisions.

It is further explained that each group member is entitled to one psychiatric emergency room visit during the 20 weeks, with the group voting at the next session whether or not this was necessary. If the group finds it was not, the patient forfeits two weeks worth of entitlements to call the therapist. More than one emergency room visit during the 20 weeks is considered a refusal to abide by the rules.

Each group member is entitled to one, and only one psychiatric hospitalization during the 20 weeks providing the majority of the group votes *in advance* that it is necessary, and the hospitalization does not result in the individual missing more than one group session. This is an interesting twist on the managed care concept of prior authorization. In this case, the authorization is rendered by one's peers, a decision that is quickly accepted and acknowledged by the borderline who is seeking hospitalization.

In all matters subject to vote, the therapist conducts the vote but does not vote. This is to consistently deflect the hostility from the therapist to the group. A tie vote goes in favor of the respective patient.

Attendance at all group sessions is mandatory. If a group member is ill or otherwise detained, at the next session the patient explains the reason and a vote is taken as to whether or not the absence was avoidable. If the majority of the group finds it was avoidable, it is recorded as an unauthorized absence. Two unauthorized absences require a vote to consider expulsion.

In the beginning, the patients tend to be lenient with each other, but soon they realize they have been had, and the therapist's task now becomes a matter of helping them to not be overly harsh.

Patients never cease to direct questions to the therapist. It is imperative that the therapist *never* get sucked in and that he or she always defer the question to the group. It often behooves the therapist to be a bit clever and redirect the question to a group member who has already caught on to that particular patient's brand of manipulativeness.

The patients are not allowed to dwell on their sordid pasts. Borderlines are enamored of retelling the abuse they suffered, embellishing the story with each successive retelling to the point of outright exaggeration and even fabrication. Even worse, dwelling on the past fosters a decompensation rather than a corrective emotional experience. When a patient falls into rehashing the past, the therapist calls this to the attention of the group and asks what should be done. The group will invariably curtail the behavior, if for no other reason than "If I can't, you can't." The therapist will usually get a hearty laugh from the group by suggesting that the group might want to vote on whether the patient should go on the Geraldo, Oprah, Sally Jesse Raphael, or Donahue TV shows.

The group is encouraged to look at today's work, school, social and other relationships, offering realistic ways of handling the problem or crisis without "flipping out." When the therapist is tempted to offer suggested solutions, she should bite her tongue. Remember, we are creating a peer system for patients who (1) are incapable of *really* bonding, and (2) would not tolerate therapist (parental) authority.

It is critical that the therapist never become angry (especially unconsciously) with the patient. One way of preventing this is to be straightforward (yet not punitive) when annoyed. To say to a patient, "You're usually hard to take, but today you are behaving downright obnoxiously. What's up?" may be the most assuring and therapeutic thing the therapist can do.

At the end of the 20 weeks, the group disbands as a group. Some, most, or, rarely, all of the patients will want to continue and another group is formed. It is part of the therapeutic plan that in each succeeding group there will be members who are in their second, third, or even fourth group. It will be noted that with each succeeding group the returning group member will increasingly identify with stability and avoidance of acting out. If a group member is expelled by the group, that patient may enter a subsequent group, but only after the group from which she was expelled has concluded the last of its 20 sessions.

Two procedures must be noted to avoid splitting of the therapist. Firstly, if there are two co-therapists conducting the group, extra care must be taken to be ever alert to the patients' unrelenting attempts to split the co-therapists. Secondly, these patients will demonstrate sheer genius in attempting to manipulate an individual contact with the therapist. This should be avoided as an example of splitting. If the patient makes it impossible to avoid, such as waiting for the therapist in the parking lot, the therapist should end the encounter and bring it up with the group at the next session. The group's reaction is the one that will effectively curtail any further such acting out.

Borderline patients delight in well-meaning games. So adept at game-playing are they that they are positively amused when the therapist suggests some poignant paradoxes, such as conferring the Yours-Is-the-Saddest-Story-I-Have-Ever-Heard Award. And, as is not unusual under this kind of peer process, if one group member becomes seemingly prudish, the Holier-Than-Thou Award may be in order. The therapist can always tell when the patient is positively engaged, even in the face of a negative tirade. There will be a momentary, split-second sparkle in the eyes or an involuntary, almost imperceptible grin just before the patient launches into her usual tirade. Though the therapeutic decisions are usually vigorously protested, the proof of effectiveness is the patient's change in behavior.

The repetition compulsion propels the patient to prove that no one (including the therapist) is better than her dysfunctional parents. When this is seemingly accomplished, she "wins" the game. But there exists the terror of a five-year-old, deep inside the patient, who says, "If I can manipulate everyone, who is strong enough to be there for me?" This part of the patient wants the therapist to "win," and is enraged when the therapist allows herself to be manipulated. In one patient's words, "The person who can be there for me has to be someone I can't deceive or manipulate".

This group protocol gives a therapist the tools to be that person. Even though borderlines are survivors and seldom kill themselves, the therapist is always faced with the dilemma that this suicide attempt may be the one in a thousand that is lethal. If it is, not to hospitalize may result in a suicide. If it is not, to hospitalize the patient is to be manipulated and thus, in the patient's eyes, be disqualified to be the strong, effective therapist. The therapist in such situations can rely on the group's accurate consensus. Remember, they are world class experts on manipulative behavior.

Therapists, even those with considerable experience, who have not conducted borderline groups will be skeptical. Why would not the patient just quit or get expelled by refusing to abide by the rules? Those who have conducted these groups are amazed that seldom does a patient quit or get expelled. The reason is twofold. First, the patient wants to stick around to defeat the therapist and the group; second, the terrified child within the patient is hoping that finally this will be the one person for her. One psychologist who was trained in the method and became exceptionally successful in conducting these groups put it this way: "I always wondered why Nick would say borderlines who do not succeed in manipulating the therapist will not quit, commit suicide, or get expelled from the group. It's because they want to see the end of the movie and if they get kicked out of the theater they'll never know how the movie ends. Part of them wants everyone dead, while the other part is hoping for a happy ending."

References

Bennett, M.J. (1994). Can competing psychotherapists be managed? *Managed Care Quarterly*, 2, 29–35.

Bloom, B. L. (1991). *Planned Short-Term Psychotherapy*. Boston: Allyn and Bacon.

Budman, S.H., & Gurman, A.S. (1988). *Theory and Practice of Brief Therapy*. New York: Guilford Press.

Cummings, N.A. (1969, September). *Exclusion Therapy: An Alternative to Going After the Drug-Cult Adolescent*. Paper presented at the annual meeting of American Psychological Association, Washington, D.C.

Cummings, N.A. (1970, September). Exclusion therapy II. Presented at the annual meeting of American Psychological Association, Miami, FL.

Cummings, N.A. (1977). Prolonged (ideal) versus short-term (realistic) psychotherapy. *Professional Psychology*, 8, 491–501.

Cummings, N.A. (1979). Turning bread into stones: Our modern antimiracle. *American Psychologist*, 34, 1119–1129.

Cummings, N. A. (1985). *The Biodyne Training Manual*. San Francisco: Foundation for Behavior Health.

Cummings, N.A. (1986). The dismantling of our health system: Strategies for the survival of psychological practice. *American Psychologist*, 41, 426–431.

Cummings, N.A. (1988a). Brief, intermittent psychotherapy throughout the life cycle. *News from EFPPA* [European Federation of Professional Psychologists Association], 2(3), 4–11.

Cummings, N.A. (1988b). Emergence of the mental health complex: Adaptive and maladaptive responses. *Professional Psychology: Research and Practice*, 19(3), 308–315.

Cummings, N.A. (1990). Brief intermittent psychotherapy throughout the life cycle. In Zeig, J.K. & Gilligan, S.G. (Eds.), *Brief Therapy: Myths, Methods and Metaphors*. New York: Brunner/Mazel, 169–184.

Cummings, N.A. (1991a). Arguments for the financial efficacy of psychological services in health care settings. In Sweet, J.J., Rozensky, R.G., & Tovian, S.M. (Eds.), *Handbook of clinical psychology in medical settings* (pp. 113–126) New York: Plenum Press.

Cummings, N.A. (1991b). Brief intermittent therapy throughout the life cycle. In

Austad, C.S., & Berman, W.H., *Psychotherapy in Managed Health Care* (pp. 35–45). Washington, D.C.: American Psychological Association.

Cummings, N.A. (1992). The future of psychotherapy: Society's charge to professional psychology. *The Independent Practitioner*, 12, 126–130.

Cummings, N.A. (1993). Psychotherapy with substance abusers. In Stricker, G., & Gold, J.R. (Eds.), *Comprehensive Handbook of Psychotherapy Integration* (pp. 337–352). New York: Plenum Press.

Cummings, N.A. (1994). The successful application of medical offset in program planning and clinical delivery. *Managed Care Quarterly*, 2, 1–6.

Cummings, N.A. (1995a). Behavioral health after managed care: The next golden opportunity for professional psychology. *Register Reports*.

Cummings, N.A. (1995b). Impact of managed care on employment and training: A primer for survival. *Professional Psychology: Research and Practice*,

Cummings, N.A., & Dörken, H. (1986). Corporations, networks, and economically sound models for practice. In Dörken, H., & Associates (Eds.), *Professional Psychology in Transition*, (pp. 165–174). San Francisco: Jossey-Bass.

Cummings, N.A., & Fernandez, L.E. (1985). Exciting future possibilities for psychologists in the marketplace. *Independent Practitioner*, 3, 38–42.

Cummings, N. A., & Follette, W. T. (1968). Psychiatric services and medical utilization in a prepaid health plan setting: Part 2. *Medical Care*, 6, 31–41.

Cummings, N. A., & Follette, W. T. (1976). Psychotherapy and medical utilization: An eight-year follow-up. In H. Dorken, (Ed.), *Professional Psychology Today* (pp. 176–197). San Francisco: Jossey-Bass.

Cummings, N. A., Kahn, B. I., & Sparkman, B. (1965). The effect of psychological intervention on medical utilization: A pilot project. Oakland, CA: Kaiser Foundation Reports.

Cummings, N. A., & VandenBos, G.R. (1979). The general practice of psychology. *Professional Psychology*, 10, 430–440.

Cummings, N.A., & VandenBos, G.R. (1981). The twenty-year Kaiser-Permanente experience with psychotherapy and medical utilization: Implications for national health policy and National Health Insurance. *Health Policy Quarterly*, 1(2), 159–175.

Dörken, H. (1974). Psychologist, is there a foundation in your future? *Journal of Community Psychology*, 2(2) 99–103.

Dörken, H., & Cummings, N. A. (1991). The potential effect on private practice of training in targeted focused mental health treatment for a specific population: A brief report. *Psychotherapy in Private Practice*, 9, 45–51.

Drager, D. (1974). *Modern Bujutsu and Budo*. Tokyo: John Weatherhill.

Follette, W. T., & Cummings, N. A. (1967). Psychiatric services and medical utilization in a prepaid health plan setting. *Medical Care*, 5, 25–35.

Fromm-Reichman, F. (1929). Transference problems in schizophrenia. *Psychoanalytic Quarterly*, 8, 406–422.

Fromm-Reichman, F. (1950). *Principles of Intensive Psychotherapy*. Chicago: University of Chicago Press.

Goldberg, I. D., Krantz, G., & Locke, B. Z. (1970). Effect of a short-term outpatient psychiatric therapy benefit on the utilization of medical services in a prepaid group practice medical program. *Medical Care*, 8, 419–428.

Haley, J. (1976). *Problem Solving Behavior*. San Francisco: Jossey-Bass.

Jones, K.R., & Vischi, T. R. (1979). Impact of alcohol, drug abuse and mental health treatment on medical care utilization: A review of the literature. *Medical Care*, 17 (suppl.), 1–82.

Kissin, B., Platz, A., & Su, W. H. (1970). Social and psychological factors in the treatment of chronic alcoholism. *Journal of Psychiatric Research*, 54, 708–713.

Malan, D.H. (1963). *A Study of Brief Psychotherapy*. New York: Plenum Press.

Malan, D.H. (1976). *The Frontiers of Brief Psychotherapy: An Example of the Convergence of Research and Clinical Practice*. New York: Plenum Press.

Miller, W. R., & Hester, R.K. (1987). The effectiveness of alcoholism treatment methods: What research reveals. In W. R. Miller & N. Heather (Eds.), *Treating Addictive Behaviors: Processes of Change* (pp. 102–114). New York: Plenum Press.

Mumford, E., Schlesinger, H.J., & Glass, G.V. (1978). A critical review and indexed bibliography of the literature up to 1978 on the effects of psychotherapy on medical utilization. NIMH: Report to NIMH under Contract No. 278-77-0049-M.H.

Neer, H.M. (1994, July). The future of occupational medicine. Address to the *National Workers' Compensation and Occupational Medicine Seminar*, Hyannis, MA.

Oss, M. (1993, June). Pro and con: A look at Harvard's new mental health and chemical dependency benefit plan. *Open Minds*, 7, 3–4.

Pallak, M.S., Cummings, N.A., Dörken, H., & Henke, C.J. (1993). Managed mental health, medicaid, and medical cost offset. *New Directions for Mental Health Services*, 59, (Fall), 27–40.

Rosen, J.C., & Wiens, A.N. (1979). Changes in medical problems and use of medical services following psychological intervention. *American Psychologist*, 34, 420–431.

Rosenhan, D.L., & Seligman, M.E.P. (1984). *Abnormal Psychology*. New York: W.W. Norton & Company.

Schafer, R. (1948). *The Clinical Application of Psychological Tests*. New York: International Universities Press.

Seligman, M.E.P. (1994). *What You Can Change and What You Can't*. New York: Alfred A. Knopf.

Sullivan, H.S. (1927). Affective experience in early schizophrenia. *American Journal of Psychiatry*, 6, 468–483.

Sullivan, H.S. (1940). Research in schizophrenia. *American Journal of Psychiatry*, 9, 222–248.

INDEX